Audiovisual Tourism Promotion

Diego Bonelli • Alfio Leotta
Editors

Audiovisual Tourism Promotion

A Critical Overview

Editors
Diego Bonelli
Victoria University of Wellington
Wellington, New Zealand

Alfio Leotta
Victoria University of Wellington
Wellington, New Zealand

ISBN 978-981-16-6409-0   ISBN 978-981-16-6410-6 (eBook)
https://doi.org/10.1007/978-981-16-6410-6

© The Editor(s) (if applicable) and The Author(s), under exclusive licence to Springer Nature Singapore Pte Ltd. 2021
This work is subject to copyright. All rights are solely and exclusively licensed by the Publisher, whether the whole or part of the material is concerned, specifically the rights of translation, reprinting, reuse of illustrations, recitation, broadcasting, reproduction on microfilms or in any other physical way, and transmission or information storage and retrieval, electronic adaptation, computer software, or by similar or dissimilar methodology now known or hereafter developed.
The use of general descriptive names, registered names, trademarks, service marks, etc. in this publication does not imply, even in the absence of a specific statement, that such names are exempt from the relevant protective laws and regulations and therefore free for general use.
The publisher, the authors and the editors are safe to assume that the advice and information in this book are believed to be true and accurate at the date of publication. Neither the publisher nor the authors or the editors give a warranty, expressed or implied, with respect to the material contained herein or for any errors or omissions that may have been made. The publisher remains neutral with regard to jurisdictional claims in published maps and institutional affiliations.

Cover illustration: Matteo Colombo, GettyImages

This Palgrave Macmillan imprint is published by the registered company Springer Nature Singapore Pte Ltd.
The registered company address is: 152 Beach Road, #21-01/04 Gateway East, Singapore 189721, Singapore

Acknowledgements

This book would have not been possible without the invaluable support provided by Joshua Pitt and MD Saif at Palgrave Macmillan.

We would like to thank those colleagues and friends who volunteered their time and knowledge to this project. We are particularly grateful to Paige Macintosh and Nirmal Kumar Gnanaprakasam (for assisting with the editing and proofreading process) and the anonymous reviewers for their insightful suggestions.

We are indebted to Thierry Jutel, Miriam Ross, and Missy Molloy for providing sage advice and encouragement at various stages of the project.

We would also like to thank Victoria University of Wellington for the research grant that allowed us to complete the volume.

Our gratitude also goes to our families and friends for their unconditional support throughout this project.

Contents

1 Introduction   1
Diego Bonelli and Alfio Leotta

Part I   Media Forms   11

2 Australian Tourism Film 1926–1975: Promoting Australia in the Age of Government-Led Film Production   13
Diego Bonelli

3 More than Just Safety: A Critical History of In-flight Safety Briefing Videos   37
Rowan Light

4 The Promotion of Tourism on Radio Waves   63
Luís Bonixe and Gorete Dinis

5 Digital Content Creation and Storytelling at the Time of COVID-19: Tourism Ireland's Online Film *I Will Return*   87
Alessandra De Marco

Contents

6	Virtual Tourism in the Age of COVID-19: A Case Study of the Faroe Islands' 'Remote Tourism' Campaign *Alfio Leotta*	107

Part II	Recent Developments in Screen-Induced Tourism	127
7	Fabulous Locations: Tourism and Fantasy Films in Italy *Giulia Lavarone*	129
8	How Do Video Games Induce Us to Travel?: Exploring the Drivers, Mechanisms, and Limits of Video Game-Induced Tourism *Jiahui (Yolanda) Dong, Louis-Etienne Dubois, Marion Joppe, and Lianne Foti*	153
9	Screen Tourism on the Smartphone: A Typology and Critical Evaluation of the First Decade of Smart Screen Tourism *Cathrin Bengesser and Anne Marit Waade*	173

Part III	Tourist Gaze, Identity, and Race	197
10	Wonderland of the South Pacific: Romantic and Realist Tendencies in Amateur Tourist Films *Rosina Hickman*	199
11	A 'White' Country for 'White' People: Poland in Tourism Promotional Videos of Regions and Metropolitan Cities *Piotr Dzik and Anna Adamus-Matuszyńska*	221

12 **Colourful Scenery, Colourful Language: Representing White Australia in the 'Where the Bloody Hell are you?' Australian Tourism Campaign** 247
Panizza Allmark

Index 269

Notes on Contributors

Anna Adamus-Matuszyńska is a sociology and public relations specialist, and a professor at the University of Economics in Katowice, Poland. Her research interests focus on public relations as the scientific discipline and visual identification of places. She lectures in sociology, conflict management, and public relations. She is the author and co-author of around 140 articles and 8 books.

Panizza Allmark is the Associate Dean of Arts, and an associate professor in the School of Arts and Humanities at Edith Cowan University, Perth, Australia. She leads the Media and Cultural Studies programme. Allmark is also the chief editor of the international journal *Continuum: Journal of Media and Cultural Studies*.

Cathrin Bengesser is Assistant Professor of Digital Media Industries at Aarhus University, Denmark. She researched screen tourism, transnational audiences, and European Creative Industries policies during her Post-Doc in the Horizon 2020 project DETECt (2018–2021). She received her PhD from Birkbeck, University of London.

Diego Bonelli holds a PhD in Film from Victoria University of Wellington, New Zealand, and an MA in History from the University of Parma, Italy. His academic work deploys archival research and his primary research interests focus on tourism film, documentary film, the relationship between media and tourism, and Italian cinema. Bonelli's work has been published in *Studies in Australasian Cinema*, *The Journal of New Zealand Studies*, *The Journal of New Zealand and Pacific Studies*, *Journal of Tourism History*, *NEKE—The New Zealand Journal of Translation Studies*, and the *Journal of Italian Cinema and Media Studies*.

Luís Bonixe holds a PhD in Communication Sciences, with a specialisation in journalism from Faculty of Social and Human Sciences (FCSH)—Universidade Nova de Lisboa, Portugal. He is the author and co-author of four books. He has written several chapters and articles in national and international academic journals on radio, journalism, local journalism, online journalism, and media and tourism. He is Professor of Journalism at the Polytechnic Institute of Portalegre, Portugal, and a researcher at Instituto de Comuniçácao da Nova (ICNOVA).

Alessandra De Marco is SEO Webwriting and Localisation Specialist at Arkys Digital Marketing. Former Lecturer in Language and Linguistics, she carries out independent scholarly research in digital marketing, tourism, and advertising. Among her latest publications is *Destination Brand New Zealand. A Social Semiotic Multimodal Analysis* (2017).

Gorete Dinis holds a PhD in Tourism; an MSc in Innovation, Planning, and Development Policies; and a BSc in Tourism Management and Planning from the University of Aveiro, Portugal. She is coordinator and professor of the BSc in Tourism at the School of Education and Social Sciences of the Polytechnic Institute of Portalegre, Portugal, and member of the Research Unit 'Governance, Competitiveness and Public Policies' and of the 'CITUR Algarve.'

Jiahui (Yolanda) Dong holds an MSc in Tourism and Hospitality Management from Gordon S. Lang School of Business and Economics, Canada. During her graduate and undergraduate study, Dong participated in several research projects in the organisational behaviour domain. She is interested in tourism studies with particular emphasis on media-induced tourism.

Louis-Etienne Dubois is Associate Professor of Creative Industries Management at Ryerson University's School of Creative Industries,

Canada. He is the director of the Future of Live Entertainment lab, a research partnership with Cirque du Soleil Entertainment Group. Dubois holds a PhD from HEC Montréal and from MINES ParisTech.

Piotr Dzik is a sociologist and political scientist, consultant and practitioner, and lecturer at the Academy of Fine Arts in Katowice, Poland. He conducts research in the field of visual identification systems of local government units, and he is the author and co-author of over 20 peer-reviewed papers in this field. He is also the co-author of the book (with Anna Adamus-Matuszyńska) *Visual Identity of Polish Provinces, Cities and Counties. Identification, Presentation, Meaning*.

Lianne Foti is an associate professor in the School of Hospitality, Food and Tourism Management at the University of Guelph, Canada. She received an MBA from EDHEC Business School, France, and a Doctorate from the University of Bradford, UK. Prior to her academic career, she worked in both the food and energy industries. Foti's body of research largely focuses on consumer behaviour, ethical decision-making, and online marketing.

Rosina Hickman is an experimental filmmaker, film historian, and educational video producer based in New Zealand. Her research explores the history of home movies and their archival afterlife in the public sphere. She holds a PhD in Film from Victoria University of Wellington.

Marion Joppe is a professor in the School of Hospitality, Food and Tourism Management at University of Guelph, Canada. She specialises in destination planning, development and marketing, and the experiences upon which destinations build. She has extensive private and public sector experience, having worked for financial institutions, tour operators, consulting groups, and government, prior to joining academia.

Giulia Lavarone is Research Fellow in Film Studies at the University of Padova, Italy. She has authored several scholarly articles and chapters in edited books, as well as the book *Cinema, media e turismo* (PUP, 2016). Her research interests mainly concern the relationships between cinema and other arts, cinema and the city, film landscapes, and film-induced tourism.

Alfio Leotta is Senior Lecturer in Film at Victoria University of Wellington, New Zealand. His primary research interests focus on the relation between film and tourism, national cinema, the globalisation of film production, and fantasy cinema. His first book *Touring the Screen: Tourism and New Zealand Film Geographies* (2011) examines film-induced tourism in New Zealand. Leotta is also the author of *The Bloomsbury Companion to Peter Jackson* (2016) and *The Cinema of John Milius* (2018).

Rowan Light is Lecturer in History at the University of Auckland, New Zealand. His research focuses on histories of remembrance and representation shaped by cultures of nationalism in transnational and comparative contexts.

Anne Marit Waade is Professor of Global Media Industries at Aarhus University, Denmark. Her research interests include location studies, Nordic noir, transnational television series, and screen tourism. Her recent publications include 'Screening the West Coast: Developing *New Nordic Noir* Tourism in Denmark' (2020), *Locating Nordic Noir* (2017), *Wallanderland* (2013), and 'When Public Service Drama Travels' (2016).

List of Figures

Fig. 9.1	Typology of smartphone and technology use in screen tourism. (Developed from Waade and Bengesser 2020)	188
Fig. 10.1	Publicity poster designed by Marcus King, c.1955. Reproduced courtesy of Tourism New Zealand	200
Fig. 10.2	*Romantic New Zealand: The Land of the Long White Cloud* (1934). Public Domain	204
Fig. 10.3	*Maori Village: A Concert Rehearsal Near Rotorua* (1945) and *Meet New Zealand: The People* (1949). Collection of Archives New Zealand (CC BY 3.0)	209
Fig. 10.4	Women at Whakarewarewa recorded by Bernadine Bailey, 1956. Reproduced courtesy of Indiana University Libraries Moving Image Archive	215

List of Tables

Table 4.1	Criteria and parameters used for the analyses of radio programmes	74
Table 4.2	Characterization of the corpus	76
Table 8.1	Game descriptions	155
Table 11.1	Number of promotional videos analysed—*voivodesips*	230
Table 11.2	Number of promotional videos analysed—cities, capitals of the regions	230
Table 11.3	'Others' in Polish promotional videos	235

1

Introduction

Diego Bonelli and Alfio Leotta

Media play a key role in both shaping discourses about travel and tourism and constructing tourist experiences (Lester and Scarles 2013, 255). Dean MacCannell argues that mass media boost the appeal of tourism destinations by influencing the way in which they are represented and perceived (1999). Similarly, John Urry claims that tourism practices are intrinsically associated with visual consumption, particularly with the commodification of images produced by movies and television (2002). Although the relationship between media and tourism has been receiving increasing academic attention over the last two decades (Urry 2002; Crouch et al. 2005; Beeton 2016; Beeton et al. 2000), the way in which tourism destinations and activities are promoted in audiovisual media remains severely under-researched. For example, despite the fact that a number of scholars argue that advertising is crucial to the survival of the tourism industry (Morgan and Pritchard 1998; Urry 2002; Govers et al. 2007; McCabe 2010), relatively little attention has been devoted to the

---

D. Bonelli (✉) • A. Leotta
Victoria University of Wellington, Wellington, New Zealand
e-mail: alfio.leotta@vuw.ac.nz

analysis of both the aesthetic characteristics of tourism TV commercials (TVCs) and the contexts of their production and circulation (Pan et al. 2011, 2017; Pan and Hanusch 2011; Gong and Tung 2017; White 2018). Even fewer studies have attempted to investigate what media objects as diverse as movies, TV travel series, and Virtual Reality (VR) share with TVCs in terms of their promotional potential.

Drawing upon our previous work (Bonelli 2018; Bonelli et al. 2019; Leotta 2020), this volume deploys the concept of 'audiovisual tourism promotion' to account for the shared promotional functions performed by a vast array of diverse media texts including tourism films, feature films, promotional videos conceived for online circulation, video games, and TV commercials. From this point of view, this book aims to fill a major gap in the literature by providing the first comprehensive critical overview of audiovisual tourism promotion as a distinct media field.

Audiovisual Tourism Promotion

Tourism promotion has often been conceived as an element of destination image formation (Beerli and Martín 2004; Govers et al. 2007). Gartner (1994), for example, suggests that tourism depends on 'image formation agents' to construct appealing destination images for prospective tourists. Similarly, Urry claims that advertising plays a key role in the tourist decision-making process:

> Overtime via advertising and the media, the images generated of different tourist gazes come to constitute a closed self-perpetuating system of illusions which provide the tourist with the basis for selecting and evaluating potential places to visit. (2002, 7)

However, despite recognising the importance of advertising, the existing scholarship on tourism promotion lacks a shared theoretical framework and terminology to account for the multiplicity of its media forms. Scott McCabe (2010), for example, acknowledges the wide range of tourism advertising channels, but does not engage in a discussion of their specificities. Pan et al. (2011), Pan and Hanusch (2011), and Pan (2011) focus on the examination of tourism TVCs, while Shani et al. (2010) and Leung et al. (2017) discuss promotional videos conceived for online distribution which they define as Destination Promotion Videos (DPVs). Neither Shani et al. (2010) nor Leung et al. (2017), however, attempt to explore the differences and similarities between tourism TVCs and DPVs. Similarly, Gong and Tung (2017) define certain types of online promotional videos as 'mini-movies,' while Fullerton and Kendrick (2011) refer to similar videos as simply 'tourism advertising.' Finally, in his pioneering work in this field, Bonelli used the concept of 'tourism film' as an umbrella term that encompasses a number of different media objects including TVCs, DPVs, and actual films. His theorisation of the tourism film, however, did not account for technologies such as VR and AR or user-generated videos. None of the terms mentioned above—TVC, DPV, or tourism film—manages to cover effectively the variety of tourism audio-visual promotion media forms which include texts as diverse as tourism and travel films (both short and feature length), travel TV shows, safety videos produced by airlines to promote their countries as tourism destinations, user-generated content (such as amateur footage circulated by tourists on social media), and so on.

Drawing upon the work of Leotta (2020), in this volume we will use the concept of 'audiovisual tourism promotion' to refer to a variety of media technologies, aesthetic forms, and platforms for distribution. Despite their significant formal, thematic, and production differences, media texts such as the ones discussed in this edited collection share a certain commitment to both place and the shaping of the viewer's tourist gaze. One of the challenges associated with the field of audiovisual tourism promotion relates to the fact that not all these texts are originally designed to have a primary promotional purpose. By contrast, some audiovisual texts that are explicitly conceived as destination promotional tools often serve other functions, such as the promotion of civic pride and the forging of national identity (Hillyer 1997; Peterson 2006; Fullerton and Kendrick 2011; Pan et al. 2017).

Audiences' decoding processes play a crucial role in determining the way in which texts featuring tourism destinations are read. From this point of view, it is the audience that ultimately filters the way in which a media text contributes to their perception of a given destination. The 'mediated places' featured in audiovisual tourism promotional texts are structurally anchored to meaning by a 'discursive framework' (Leotta 2020). French philosopher Michel Foucault (1969) defined discourse as a way of organising knowledge that structures the constitution of social relations through the collective acceptance of the discourse as a social fact. According to Foucault, discourse produces 'practices that systematically form the objects of which they speak' (Foucault 1969, 135). In turn, the discursive framework, namely the way in which place and space are understood in audiovisual tourism promotional texts, is informed by textual and contextual factors (Leotta 2020).

Textual factors include aesthetic conventions, enunciative strategies, and narrative structures that have the potential of appealing to the so-called tourist imagination of the viewer. Crouch et al. (2005, 1) articulated the concept of tourist imagination to account for the sense of global physical and virtual mobility engendered by the daily consumption of digital media. At the aesthetic level certain generic conventions of tourism films and TVCs (e.g. bird-eye views of spectacular natural landscapes) may generate certain visceral responses in the viewer, possibly influencing their desire to visit the locations depicted on screen. Similarly, as argued in the chapter by Dong et al., the immersive potential of media such as video games can play a crucial role in shaping prospective tourists' attitudes towards a given destination.

Narrative structures may also stimulate the viewer's 'tourist imagination' by developing a certain construction of space in the story. For example, a series of textual factors such as the foregrounding of landscape as spectacle, the production of space as an active character, and the focus on the journey as the main narrative drive might explain the tourist spin-off of a film franchise such as *The Lord of the Rings* (2001–2003) (Leotta 2015). Enunciative strategies refer to the way in which the intended receiver of the text is inscribed in it. For example, many tourism TVCs address viewers as prospective tourists by featuring images of travellers enjoying the interaction with the landscape. These TVCs often encourage the identification with these characters while suggesting potential ways of relating to place and space. Enunciative strategies often affect the construction of certain narrative structures. For example, the foregrounding of the tourists as onscreen simulacra of the viewers in tourism TVCs often implies a narrative which revolves around notions of travel and exploration. Faroe Islands' Remote Tourism, the case study analysed in Leotta's chapter, pushes this logic to the extreme by encouraging prospective tourists to control a local guide in an attempt to enhance the authenticity of the virtual tourist experience.

The contextual factors are the different ways in which the promotional texts are circulated and received. These factors comprise platforms and modes of distribution, the space and time of exhibition, media discourses surrounding the circulation of the texts, and audiences' backgrounds and expectations (Leotta 2020, 208). The context of circulation and reception of these texts plays a crucial role in determining their performative function. For example, the screening of a tourism TVC about Dublin for an audience of Dubliners might foster a sense of civic pride rather than stimulating tourism growth. By contrast, the screening of a feature film such as *Harry Potter and the Philosopher's Stone* (2001) within the context of a tourism trade event might be considered as a promotional tool, potentially contributing to an increased interest in visiting Britain. In their respective chapters on screen-induced tourism, Lavarone, and Bengesser and Waade discuss how the way in which certain screen locations are mediated and promoted might lead to radically different outcomes in terms of their success in attracting tourists.

As Morgan and Pritchard (1998) point out, the production and circulation of audiovisual promotional texts about tourism both express and reproduce dominant power relations. Many of the chapters featured in this collection highlight how the discursive framework, namely the textual and contextual factors that inform the reading of audiovisual promotional texts, is influenced by power dynamics. Usually, these texts are produced by institutions or companies endowed with significant economic and political power; therefore, the way in which place is represented reproduces certain economic and political interests. Similarly, the way in which audiovisual promotional texts are distributed, exhibited, and discussed is also often framed by such economic and political interests. For example, in order to produce and distribute a TVC, a Destination Management Organisation (DMO) needs to have access to significant financial resources. DMOs that possess more financial or political resources than others can therefore guarantee a more widespread and effective media coverage of certain destinations. Similarly, the strategic decisions of a DMO, which in turn might affect the representation of the destination itself, are also informed by internal power dynamics such as different national stakeholders competing for hegemony. In turn, this might potentially result in the over-representation of certain places or activities (Leotta 2020).

Due to the heterogeneity of its specific manifestations, we argue that the analysis of multiple case studies is the best approach to illustrate the dynamic character and scope of audiovisual tourism promotion. This edited collection includes 11 interdisciplinary contributions that deploy various theoretical and historical perspectives to examine case studies located in geographical areas such as Australasia, Europe, and North America. The chapters will be divided into three parts. Part I, 'Media Forms', examines the role that media as diverse as tourism films (Bonelli), digital commercials (De Marco), in-flight safety videos (Light), radio networks (Dinis and Bonixe), and virtual interactive media (Leotta) play in tourism marketing. Some of these contributions, particularly the chapters by De Marco and Leotta, also analyse the impact of the COVID-19 global pandemic on digital destination marketing and audiovisual tourism promotion. Part II, 'Recent Developments in Screen-Induced Tourism', examines emerging phenomena like fantasy film-induced tourism in Italy (Lavarone), film location phone apps (Bengesser and Waade), and video game-induced tourism (Dong et al.) as new tendencies within the broader field of screen-induced tourism. Finally, Part III, 'Tourist Gaze, Identity, and Race', analyses the role played by both amateur holiday films (Hickman) and tourism marketing campaigns (Allmark, and Dzik and Adamus-Matuszyńska) in shaping, conveying, and promoting cultural, racial, and gender identities. The themes treated in the three parts often intertwine—for instance, the tourist gaze which informs the making of amateur holiday films (as discussed by Hickman in Part III) often reflects the governing vision conveyed by tourism films produced by government-led production companies (a topic explored by Bonelli in Part I). Similarly, the study of the deployment of new digital mobile media to promote film locations as tourism destinations (Bengesser and Waade) intersects with some of the debates analysed in Part I of the book ('Media Forms'). It is our hope that by focusing on the analysis of a number of different media platforms and case studies, the chapters featured in this volume demonstrate how audiovisual tourism promotion is a discursive framework which is constantly renegotiated by technological innovations, power dynamics, economic imperatives, and historical contingencies.

Works Cited

Beerli, Asunciòn, and Josefa D. Martín. 2004. Factors Influencing Destination Image. *Annals of Tourism Research* 31 (3): 657–681. https://doi.org/10.1016/j.annals.2004.01.010.

Beeton, Sue. 2016. *Film-Induced Tourism*. 2nd ed. Buffalo: Channel View Publications.

Beeton, Sue, Glen Croy, and Warwick Frost. 2000. Introduction: Tourism and Media into the 21st Century. *Tourism Culture & Communication* 6: 157–159.

Bonelli, Diego. 2018. *This Is Wellington: The Representation of Wellington in New Zealand Tourism Film from 1912 to 2017*. PhD Thesis, Victoria University of Wellington, NZ.

Bonelli, Diego, Thierry Jutel, and Alfio Leotta. 2019. 'Selling the Creative City': Wellington Tourism Film in the Neoliberal Era. *Studies in Australasian Cinema* 13 (2–3): 32–50. https://doi.org/10.1080/17503175.2019.1693149.

Crouch, David, Rhona Jackosn, and Felix Thompson. 2005. *The Media and the Tourist Imagination*. London: Routledge.

Foucault, Michel. 1972 [1969]. *The Archeology of Knowledge and the Discourse on Language*. Trans. Sheridan Smith. Reprint, New York: Pantheon Books.

Fullerton, Jami A., and Alice Kendrick. 2011. Australia Tourism Advertising: A Test of the Bleed-Over Effect Among US Travelers. *Place Branding and Public Diplomacy* 7 (4): 244–256. https://doi.org/10.1057/pb.2011.17.

Gartner, William C. 1994. Image Formation Process. *Journal of Travel & Tourism Marketing* 2: 191–216. https://doi.org/10.1300/J073v02n02_12.

Gong, Tianyi, and Vincent Wing Sun Tung. 2017. The Impact of Tourism Mini-Movies on Destination Image: The Influence of Travel Motivation and Advertising Disclosure. *Journal of Travel & Tourism Marketing* 34 (3): 416–428. https://doi.org/10.1080/10548408.2016.1182458.

Govers, Robert, Frank M. Go, and Kuldeep Kumar. 2007. Promoting Tourism Destination Image. *Journal of Travel Research* 46 (1): 15–23. https://doi.org/10.1177/0047287507302374.

Hillyer, Minette. 1997. *We Calmly and Adventurously Go Travelling: New Zealand Film, 1925–35*. MA Thesis, University of Auckland, NZ.

Leotta, Alfio. 2015. *Peter Jackson*. London: Bloomsbury.

———. 2020. 'This Isn't A Movie... It's a Tourism Ad for Australia': The Dundee Campaign and the Semiotics of Audiovisual Tourism Promotion. *Tourist Studies* 20 (2): 203–221. https://doi.org/10.1177/1468797619894462.

Lester, Jo-Anne, and Caroline Scarles. 2013. *Mediating the Tourist Experience*. London: Routledge.

Leung, Daniel, Astrid Dickinger, and Lyndon Nixon. 2017. Impact of Destination Promotion Videos on Perceived Destination Image and Booking Intention Change. *Information and Communication Technologies in Tourism 2017*: 361–375. New York: Springer.

MacCannell, Dean. 1999. *The Tourist: A New Theory of the Leisure Class*. Berkeley: University of California Press.

McCabe, Scott. 2010. *Marketing Communications in Tourism and Hospitality*. London: Routledge.

Morgan, Nigel, and Annette Pritchard. 1998. *Tourism Promotion and Power: Creating Images, Creating Identities*. Hoboken, NJ: Wiley.

Pan, Steve. 2011. The Role of TV Commercial Visuals in Forming Memorable and Impressive Destination Images. *Journal of Travel Research* 50 (2): 171–185. https://doi.org/10.1177/0047287509355325.

Pan, Steve, and Folker Hanusch. 2011. Tourism TV Commercials: A Delicate Balance Between Aural and Visual Information Load. *Journal of Travel & Tourism Marketing* 28 (5): 465–480. https://doi.org/10.1080/10548408.2011.587750.

Pan, Steve, Henry Tsai, and Jin-Soo Lee. 2011. Framing New Zealand: Understanding Tourism TV Commercials. *Tourism Management* 32 (3): 596–603. https://doi.org/10.1016/j.tourman.2010.05.009.

Pan, Steve, Carla Santos, and Seongseop Kim. 2017. Promoting Tourism, Projecting Power: The Role of Television Commercials. *Journal of Travel & Tourism Marketing* 34 (2): 192–208. https://doi.org/10.1080/10548408.2016.1156610.

Peterson, Jennifer Lynn. 2006. 'The Nation's First Playground': Travel Films and the American West, 1895–1920. In *Virtual Voyages: Cinema and Travel*, ed. J. Ruoff, 79–98. London: Duke University Press.

Shani, Amir, Po-Ju Chen, Youcheng Wang, and Nan Hua. 2010. Testing the Impact of a Promotional Video on Destination Image Change: Application of China as a Tourism Destination. *International Journal of Tourism Research* 12 (2): 116–133. https://doi.org/10.1002/jtr.738.

Urry, John. 2002. *The Tourist Gaze*. London: Sage.

White, Leanne. 2018. Qantas Still Calls Australia Home: The Spirit of Australia and the Flying Kangaroo. *Tourist Studies* 18 (3): 261–274. https://doi.org/10.1177/1468797618785617.

Part I

Media Forms

2

Australian Tourism Film 1926–1975: Promoting Australia in the Age of Government-Led Film Production

Diego Bonelli

Introduction

Over the last 25 years, academic research in Commonwealth countries such as Britain, New Zealand, Canada, and Australia has been drawing increasing attention to understudied aspects of film history such as institutional, utilitarian, educational, and ephemeral films, as shown in works by Hillyer (1997), Leotta (2011), Anthony (2012), Weckbecker (2015), Bonelli (2018), and Williams (1995, 2008), amongst others. Such studies emphasised how government-led film production was often informed by the attempt to foster a sense of nationhood in former British colonies. More specifically, some of them examined the role settler culture played in shaping early travelogues and tourism films (Leotta 2011; Hillyer 1997; Bonelli 2018, 2020).

Studies in institutional filmmaking generally identify the early 1930s as a turning point in government-led film production in most settler countries. In 1932, Stephen Tallents, secretary of the Empire Marketing

D. Bonelli (✉)
Victoria University of Wellington, Wellington, New Zealand

© The Author(s), under exclusive license to Springer Nature Singapore Pte Ltd. 2021
D. Bonelli, A. Leotta (eds.), *Audiovisual Tourism Promotion*,
https://doi.org/10.1007/978-981-16-6410-6_2

Board between 1926 and 1933, claimed that "no civilised country can today afford either to neglect the projection of its national personality or to resign its projection to others" (1932, 11). In fact, Britain's government-led film production in the pre-WWII era was informed by what Anthony defined as Tallents's "educational and patriotic conception of public relations" (2012, 29). Tallents's emphasis on national visibility and on the manufacturing of a specific, easily recognisable, and well-marketable national character—as well as his efforts towards the production of educational, promotional, and propaganda films—characterised government-led film companies not only in Britain but also in British dominions and colonies. Films released by government agencies such as the New Zealand National Film Unit, the Australian Commonwealth Film Unit, and Canada's National Film Board, besides showing a very similar ideological approach to filmmaking, shared patterns of circulation and distribution. They targeted domestic as well as international audiences, and besides being screened in movie theatres (and, from the mid-1960s onwards, broadcast by TV networks), they were circulated in a variety of contexts such as schools, churches, men's clubs, women's organisations, exhibitions, educational associations, international film festivals, embassies, trade legations, travel clubs, and travel agencies (Anthony 2012; Rice 2019; Bonelli 2020).

British documentarist and film theorist John Grierson visited Canada, New Zealand, and Australia from 1938 to 1940, representing the Imperial Relations Trust, which employed him to provide assistance and advice to various national film boards and to supervise and assess their work. In Canada, the government Motion Picture Bureau was established in 1917; its "mandate was to publicize and promote Canadian products abroad as well as to support the tourist and other industries at home" (Rodger 1989, 260). It was replaced in 1939 by the National Film Board, whose establishment was encouraged and inspired by John Grierson. Similarly, in New Zealand, the government-driven National Film Unit—established in 1941 following Grierson's visit to New Zealand—was characterised by the production of didactic documentaries as well as promotional and tourism films (Bonelli 2018, 2020).

Within such a cultural and creative climate, Australia was no exception. Grierson's visit to the country in 1940—as well as the subsequent importation and proliferation of Grierson's disciples who developed new directions in Australian film production—was considered fundamental for the establishment, in 1945, of the Australian National Film Board (NFB), which was modelled on the British and Canadian Film Boards (Williams 1995; Ansara and Milner 1999; Greenhill and Tyo 1949; Shirley and Adams 1989). According to McKenzie and Rossiter (2018), throughout the 1940s the Australian government started to be increasingly involved in filmmaking. Grace (1982) highlights how, after Grierson's visit to Australia, Australian government-led film production gradually moved from entertainment to national publicity and to an open and systematic promotion of Australia's national character mainly aimed at foreign audiences. John Grierson's influence on Australia's government-sponsored filmmaking is similarly stressed by Williams (1995), who highlights how the Commonwealth Film Unit (CFU)—which replaced the NFB from 1956—was headed by Stanley Howes, a committed Griersonian. The role government-led filmmaking played in the process of Australia's nation building is widely acknowledged (Moran 1988); in this regard, Foster highlighted how academic literature in Australian cinema "naturally recognizes and even critically assesses the place of government film in promoting an Australian national identity" (2001, 64). However, as Bertrand (1997) and Williams (2008) noted, institutional film production dates back much further than Grierson's visit, starting, in fact, at the dawn of the twentieth century with the establishment of the Limelight Department of the Salvation Army in 1901.

The majority of the films produced and released by government-led film production companies in the Commonwealth, besides sharing similar platforms of circulation and distribution, was characterised by a strong promotional goal. While documentaries, didactic, and educational films constitute the majority of Commonwealth government-sponsored films, a relevant percentage of institutional films focuses on the tourism promotion of specific locations. In this regard, Bonelli (2018, 2020) and Bryson (2002) came to similar conclusions. According to the former, a considerable number of institutional films produced during the golden age of New Zealand government-led film production companies can be categorised as tourism marketing tools; similarly, the latter argued that the films produced by the CFU, established in Australia in 1956 as the natural continuation of the NFB, "were totalising representations of Australia in a form which could easily be compared to tourist brochures" (7). Such films display a promotional purpose and are an integral part of an overall tourism marketing and place-branding strategy, thus falling under the definition of tourism film provided by Bonelli. According to him, tourism film is a media form that has an explicit or implicit promotional goal as the result of cross-institutional collaborations. The tourism film can have different purposes and is framed by a socially organised way to look at the land, shaped around certain pre-existing representations and expectations about the landscape (2018, 49).

Through the textual analysis of 28 case studies, 26 produced and released by Australian government-driven film production companies and 2 early films from unidentified producers, this chapter aims to identify and analyse Australian tourism film's narrative and stylistic trajectories between 1926 and 1975. The choice of this time frame was determined by the earliest and latest production years of Australian tourism films currently available in the online archives of the National Film and Sound Archive of Australia. This chapter will first examine Australian tourism promotion's recurring emphasis on specific geographic and cultural spaces such as the beach, suburbia, and urban centres. It will then describe tourism films' narrative and stylistic patterns, identifying in their formal hybridity and in their multiple purposes their most relevant characteristics.

The Beach: Australia's Favourite Tourist Playground

From a thematic point of view, the textual analysis of tourism films produced in Australia in the 1926–1975 time period displays a prevailing focus on urban and seaside tourism. Until the 1970s, wilderness tourism still played a minor role in Australia's tourism marketing compared to geographically and culturally proximate countries such as New Zealand, where, on the contrary, the representation of the extra-urban space had traditionally taken the lion's share in tourism promotion (Bonelli 2018; Leotta 2011). While extra-urban locations such as the outback, mountains, and tropical forests are only occasionally present, Australia's tourism marketing is characterised by a constant visual and narrative emphasis on the beach as Australians' leisure space and tourist destination *par excellence*. Academic discourse has focused extensively on Australia's beach-going and on the Australian suburban beach as the privileged, egalitarian, and democratised meeting point for the urban masses. The beach, in fact, besides being a cornerstone of national publicity and tourism marketing, has been playing a fundamental role in shaping the country's cultural identity.

Fiske et al. (1987, 54) describe the Australian beach as a mythical place and an integral part of modern Australian identity. According to Dutton (1985) the beach in Australia is an equaliser, a place able to harmoniously encompass multiple ethnicities, shapes, sizes, and genders, while Metusela and Waitt noted how during the twentieth century, "the beach became naturalised and bounded as an idyllic leisure place for British Australians" (2012, xix). In his seminal work on Australian beach culture, Booth similarly recognises the foundational role the beach plays in Australian culture. In his words, "Australians are surrounded by beaches. But this enclosure is more than a geographical fact for the inhabitants of an island continent; the beach is an integral part of the cultural envelope" (2001, 1).

The representation of the Australian beach, far from just being the mere celebration of scenic coastal landscapes, goes hand in hand with the promotion of a specific lifestyle. Tourism films' narratives about the Australian beach mostly revolve around its celebration as a reassuring, family friendly, and commodified space, and a playground for sports and outdoor activities. This is evident from the dawn of Australian tourism film. In the pre-NFB era, the black and white, silent *Beautiful Bondi* (1926)'s intertitles describe Sydney's most famous beach as a mecca for 'care-free worshippers of the glorious sunshine,' showcasing the surrounding tourist facilities and celebrating the efficiency and reliability of local lifeguards. This film relies on a large number of panning extreme-long shots able to capture the vastness of Bondi's coastal landscape. On the contrary, beach life and beach-goers are mostly depicted through panning long and medium shots. *The Sunny South-West* (1936) revolves around the celebration of 'pure white sand' and 'golden sand' beaches depicted through a succession of long and medium shots. *Call of the Surf* (1935) describes Australia as "a land of incomparable beauty, a surfer's paradise (...)" adding that "Australia possesses innumerable sandy beaches (...) directly facing the open ocean." Stylistically, like in *Beautiful Bondi*, in this film coastal landscapes are mainly portrayed through panning extreme-long shots, while the dynamism of beach life is often framed through high-angle, tracking or panning long shots

A few years later, during the NFB's era, new narratives unfolded. the most recurring of which focused on the beach as Australians' preferred meeting place and family playground. In *Souvenir of Sydney* (1954), the voice-over narrator, after claiming that "there is no other city in the world that has so many beaches, so many places in which to play," comments on shots of crowded beaches stating that "everybody goes to the beach in Sydney, some to swim, some to watch, some just to stand around doing nothing," thus highlighting the multiple leisure opportunities available for kids and families. In *Souvenir of Sydney*, Sydney's beaches and coastal landscapes are mainly framed through high-angle, panning extreme-long shots. The 1948 film *Famous Beach is Popular Summer Playground* relies on a very similar camera style, revolving around the depiction of Manly Beach, another popular and commodified Sydney suburban beach. In 1955, *Gold Coast is Attraction for Sun Worshippers* depicts the Gold Coast as a perfectly functioning tourist system, in which an efficient network of tourist facilities is available to all holidaymakers. In 1956s *A Day at the Beach* an unusually female voice-over narrates the fictional Mitchell family's day at the beach, stating that they "come to the beach nearly every Saturday during summer."

The films produced in the CFU era (1956–1972) are similarly characterised by family centred narrative and thematic patterns, often relying on fictional plots in which actors play the Australian Everyman. *Australian Weekend* (1960) emphasises the centrality of the beach and beach-related activities in Australian leisure; *Queensland Playground* (1957) places emphasis on the outdoors and beach life, depicting children playing on the beach. The beach is not only portrayed as a holiday and leisure space, but also as an integral part of Australians' everyday life. *Another Sunny Day in Western Australia* (1961) describes a day in the life of local children starting their day at one of Perth's beaches, before heading to their suburban house and having breakfast with their parents. In *Life in Australia: Cairns* (1964), family man Tony starts his day at the beach, fishing and providing food for his family. Similarly, in *Life in Australia: Sydney* (1966), static and panning long and extreme long shots taken from both high and low angles emphasise the size and dynamism of urban beaches, mainly focusing on Sydney's main tourist hotspot, Bondi Beach. By utilising a common narrative trope in Australian tourism films, this film depicts the life of a family holidaying on the beach. The omniscient narrator introduces the protagonists: "The Donalds, like every other family in Sydney, look forward to the summer. Spring comes in September and October and the Pacific Ocean is warm and welcoming again." A family man—embodying the quintessential Australian adult male—sets the beach umbrella after emptying the car boot, while his kids rush to the sea with their surfboards. As extensively shown in this film, the beach is the ideal leisure space for children, who engage in all kinds of water games, especially surfing and sailing.

Similarly, *Life in Australia: Brisbane* (1964) opens with a high-angle long shot of the beach portrayed, as usual, as the ideal family playground; by adopting a docu-drama approach reminiscent of *Life in Australia: Sydney*, it then depicts a young couple having a picnic on the sand. Towards the end of the film, a high-angle extreme-long shot frames the vastness of Brisbane's coastal surroundings. *Surf Beach* (1965) provides an overview of Australia's beach lifestyle, mainly focusing on the widespread and efficient national surf life-saving system. According to the voice-over, "over the past 10 years, board riding has become a major surf sport in Australia." Moreover, the voice-over narrator stresses how "surf life-saving developed on metropolitan beaches, [and] today there are more than 230 of these clubs in Australia alone." After emphasising the safety of beach-related activities, the voice-over narrator highlights how "visiting the beach has become a family custom, a national tradition." In its finale, which portrays families happily returning home after a day at the beach, this tourism film showcases the usual emphasis on family tourism and leisure. The 1964 film *Life in Australia: Mount Gambier* is similarly characterised by a narrative focus on family life, portraying a typical Australian family whose day starts and ends on the local beach.

The early 1970s marked a turning point in global tourism that was increasingly characterised by the spread of long-haul flights, by growing tourist flows to Australasian destinations, and by a new focus on the diversification of tourist options, as pointed out by Pearce et al. (1998). According to these scholars, "in tourism the recognition of market segmentation came (...) in the 1970s and 1980s. Today most tourism marketers regard market segmentation as a prerequisite for effective market" (55). According to the global changing nature of tourism, a whole range of new activities began to be promoted in Australia. In fact, from the early 1970s and throughout the late CFU and early Film Australia (FA) period, Australia's tourism marketing and tourism film showed a shift from family based narrative to an unprecedented focus on youth tourism. CFU's *The Big Island* (1970), for instance, while providing the audience with an overview of the country, places particular visual emphasis on groups of tourists in their twenties while engaged in beach-related activities. The crucial role still played by Australian beaches as tourist magnets is apparent in the film's structure, characterised by an opening scene specifically focused on young people surfing, and ending with an aerial shot of a young couple running on a large and unusually deserted beach. 1975 FA's *Travellin' Round*, a fiction film made for the Australian Tourism Commission whose narrative structure and stylistic features closely recall road movies, follows the adventures of a group of young friends travelling by campervan across Australia and features a number of recent trends in tourism such as camping, snorkelling, kayaking, as well as an unprecedented focus on the outback as an appealing tourist destination. *Travellin' Round* marks a turning point in the representation of the Australian beach. This 30-minute film barely depicts coastal areas and when it does, it portrays rocky, unspoilt landscapes. Common visual and stylistic tropes such as high-angle, extreme-long panning shots, bird's-eye views, or aerial shots are dismissed and suburban beaches are not portrayed. Such new tendencies represent an exception in the representation of Australia's coastal areas during the time frame considered in this chapter, and openly contrast with previous depictions of the beach as a highly commodified, well-organised, and safe suburban fringe provided with tourist facilities, a proper playground for city dwellers, and an essential complement to the city itself.

As noted above, until the early 1970s the beach was portrayed in Australian tourism marketing as a natural complement to the city. Within this framework, Australia's urban and suburban areas also assume an essential role in the country's tourist representation and promotion.

Lush Suburban Gardens and Summer All Year Long: Suburbia in Australian Tourism Films

Interestingly, along with the celebration of urban and suburban beaches and beach life, the majority of Australian tourism films regularly feature depictions of city suburbs as an integral part of tourism promotion. Such cinematic representations are often characterised by slow tracking shots of detached suburban houses and their lush private gardens. These recurring portrayals of the suburban 'quarter acre paradise' convey a wealthy, attractive, and reassuring image of suburbia. In this ideal world, suburbanites are often portrayed while gardening, relaxing in the sun, or returning home after a day spent at the beach.

According to Brown (2008) "there is no denying that Australia *is* a suburban country." Bunker identifies in the 1945–1975 time frame "the suburban long boom" (1985, 83), a phenomenon that has lasted up to the present day, as shown by the recent and apparently unstoppable expansion of Australian cities (McGuirk and Argent 2011). Due to Australian cities' striking suburban sprawl—and the high percentage of people living in suburbia—the suburban space has assumed a major cultural importance, becoming an integral part of the Australian way of life (Hogan 2003; Rowse 1978). From this perspective, the suburban world—or 'suburbia'—is a specific cultural space that can be considered, in Silverstone's (1996) words, "as the embodiment of the same ideal as well as the same practical solution, imperfectly realized in both cases, and arguably unrealizable: the attempt to marry town and country and to create for middle class middle cultures in middle spaces in middle America or Britain or Australia" (3). The main aesthetic feature of Australia's suburban development is its lateral rather than vertical structure: indeed, single, detached dwellings rather than high buildings are the predominant housing units of the commuter suburbs that surround every major Australian city. Such urban structure reflects the national aspiration of owning a home of one's own. Sociologists and urbanists have focused on the aesthetic features and urban characteristics of Australia's main urban centres, with particular attention to their impressive, distinctive suburban expansion. According to Kilmartin and Thorns (1978) the lateral structure of national suburban development and the predominant housing units of the commuter suburbs reflect a capitalistic, individualistic ethic. They noted how residential building densities have dominated Australia's urban areas; a rapid growth of this suburban form occurred in the 1950s and 1960s as a result of migration (both internal and from overseas) and the baby boom. The suburban world was characterised by single-family, one-storey houses, typically the three-bedroom bungalow, each on its own 'quarter acre section.' Over time the size of the section has decreased, so that subdivisions are now more likely to be one-fifth of an acre (around 600 square metres). The ownership of a small piece of land, according to Perkins and Thorns (2001), influenced suburban habits: "the presence of sections around most houses has resulted in gardening—both for production and leisure—being a significant part of many people's experience" (37). Suburbs are, once again, a liminal space where landscape and the city merge and integrate, and suburbia is still a geographic and cultural space *in limine*, on the threshold, on the fringe of nature and civilisation (Bonelli 2018; Hogan 2003).

In tourism film, Australia's suburban sprawl is constantly celebrated alongside the country's best-known attractions. In NFB's *North to the Sun* (1951), the voice-over of a tourist describes Cairns as a quintessential Australian city, characterised by warm climate, broad streets, and a sprawl of suburban houses with large verandas and lush private gardens where all sorts of tropical plants, flowers, and fruits grow spontaneously. A panning extreme-long shot taken from a high-standing point portrays Cairn's suburban expansion. In NFB's *Brisbane City in the Sun* (1954), the narrator emphasises how in Queensland's capital city tourists enjoy both the warm climate and the many facilities and a more general "sense of well-being." These cities are advanced, besides being warm, friendly, and well-organised; they have industries, hospitals, and schools and in suburban gardens "all types of fruits grow here," as a close up of blooming flowers in a lush suburban garden intends to show.

The celebration of Australian suburbia as a national attraction becomes even clearer from the 1960s onwards. *Life in Australia: Cairns* focuses on Cairns as the favourite choice of tourists who "seek the warm climate all year long," and points out how the locals are fortunate enough to always wear summer clothes. Local suburbanites are described in this film as people who "take life at an easy pace," in love with their relaxed lifestyle, their detached houses, their private gardens, and driveways. This film utilises a common narrative trope in Australian tourism film: that is, to describe life in the suburbs by following a day in the life of an Australian fictional family. Such narratives reflect a traditional family culture where the family man provides for the family by going to work in the morning while his wife—who is normally a mother-of-two—deals with household chores. Overall, life in the suburbs is depicted as idyllic. According to the voice-over narration, "the Taylors enjoy their life in Queensland, they wouldn't live anywhere else but in the tropical far North of Queensland." *Life in Australia: Sydney*, after providing bird's-eye views of the city suburbs, focuses on the city's commuter culture through the idyllic depiction of a fictional, patriarchal family characterised by a working family man and a stay-at-home wife and mum. According to the voice-over, Sydney's suburbs are efficiently linked to the city centre through a network of electric trains. The suburban family is shown spending a weekend at the beach after which they return to their thriving suburb where "everywhere houses are going up". A similar plot is repeated in *Life in Australia: Melbourne*, that similarly portrays families in their suburban quarter-acre paradise, and in *Life in Australia: Brisbane*, that revolves around a family based suburban narrative. *A Place to Live* (1972) describes life in lush suburbia as one of Australians' main ambitions. While depicting suburban streets through a succession of tracking shots, the voice-over states that "most prefer to be away from the city centre with a surrounding block of land where a variety of fruits and vegetables may be grown."

In the *Life in Australia* series, produced by the CFU between 1964 and 1966, the coexistence and intertwining of tourism promotion and colonial agenda become apparent. These films were made for the Department of Immigration to attract English-speaking immigrants from Europe; they were used as a marketing tool and Australia was presented as an ideal destination where everyone led happy lives (Gonzalez n.d.). Australia is depicted—through the images spread by tourism films—as a land where prosperity is directly linked to suburban lifestyle; according to this self-congratulatory narrative, Australia is celebrated as the land where Australians themselves can legitimately aspire to the suburban 'quarter acre paradise.' The emphasis on Australia as an egalitarian society appears to be linked to attempts to enhance national pride and reinforce national identity. The recurring focus on suburbia and suburban life also stresses the possibility of belonging to a new country and forging a sense of identity which arises out of the experience of a new land. The emphasis on the suburban sprawl seems to fully embody the identification with a newly settled land and their projection towards the future. Such cultural and ideological perception of suburbia is reflected in Australian tourism films from the NFB and the CFU's eras. While a partial turning point in the choice of themes and displayed locations is apparent only starting from the early 1970s, the variety of Australian tourism film's stylistic and narrative trajectories, and the duplicity of its goals and purposes, traverses the entire historical period analysed in this chapter.

Stylistic and Narrative Trajectories in Australian Tourism Film

From the Tropics to the Snow, a 1964 CFU film, perfectly embodies the dialectical tensions underpinning Australia's national publicity, tourism marketing, and tourism film production during the 1960s. This 25-minute fictional film (that the opening credits describe as "a film about a film about Australia") portrays a script meeting between CFU's Producer-in-Chief, a scriptwriter, and a director. While discussing the production of a new tourism film about Australia, the director endorses a conventional approach that recalls well-established government tourism films' narrative and stylistic tropes. According to the director, this new film's plot should revolve around a family of American tourists arriving in Sydney on a cruise ship, enjoying Australia's typical outdoor activities and gradually discovering the beauty and diversity of the country. The film's main focus would be Australian tourist icons such as Sydney's Harbour Bridge, the Gold Coast, the endemic wildlife, as well as Australia's quintessential beach-related and outdoor sports activities. Strongly disappointed by the banality of such family based and reassuring narratives, the scriptwriter would like to do "something different, something creative," and declares that the film should instead be "fresh, and show the off-beat side of the country, the sort of things you can't find anywhere else in the world, examine 'em with new eyes, reveal their hidden beauty." In his point of view, rather than focusing on worn-out ideas and narratives, the film should be based on off-beat characters such as a solitary painter on a lush remote island in the Great Barrier Reef, or a crocodile hunter in the wild far North. Instead of indulging in the reassuring and commodified representations of Australian nature, it would showcase the pristine and untouched environment of the outback or the Far North's lush and untamed beaches. Even though the fictional protagonists of *From the Tropics to the Snow* do not seem to get to any clear and final agreement, this film's self-reflexive and ironic take on national tourism marketing perfectly succeeds in pointing out the thematic, narrative, and stylistic clichés that characterised Australian tourism film production in the previous decades, as well as the naivety of most of the innovators.

From the spread of the talkies in the early 1930s until the mid-1960s, the vast majority of government-sponsored Australian tourism films shared a number of narrative and stylistic similarities. According to Aveyard et al. (2017) and Moran (1987) one of the recurring characteristics in this period was the use of a particular type of expository voice-over, known as 'Voice of God.' In Aveyard et al.'s words, such a voice was "always confident and authoritative" (70). Moreover, it is described as "invariably male, neither obviously young, old, nor ethnic and apparently classless in accent. In other words, as a means of affirming and maintaining its authority, this voice is impersonal, objective, acting on behalf of the general interest" (70). Wolfe, similarly, describes this narrative style, common in documentaries from the 1940s, 1950s, and 1960s, as "disembodied (…), fundamentally unpresentable in human form, connoting a position of absolute mastery and power outside the spatial and temporal boundaries of the social world the film depicts" (1997, 149). The 'Voice of God,' along with the careful selection of represented themes and the use of specific cinematic techniques, shows the extent to which government-sponsored filmmaking was the expression of strategically planned governing visions of national publicity, tourism promotion, and tourism marketing. However, during the 1960s, in Wolfe's words, such narrative devices started to be "rejected as authoritarian, didactic or reductive" (1997, 149). In fact, over the 1960s, within Australia's government-sponsored films different stylistic tendencies emerged. According to Moran:

> Whilst the classic documentary style is the dominant style of documentary produced, other styles were adopted in a significant body of films. If the classic documentary style typically uses an off screen, voice-over exposition of a problem and has the visual images acting as both illustrations and anchor for commentary, these other styles might utilise dramatic fictional codes and tend toward a lyrical and observational (rather than rhetorical) treatment of their subject matter. (1988, 57)

Fitzsimons et al. pointed out how "the Commonwealth Film Unit between the mid-1960s and mid-1970s included attempts to create zones of independence inside the bureaucratic structure" (2011, 65).

Such attempts to pursue a more original narrative style (albeit within well-defined parameters) and to break away from well-established formal and stylistic patterns are also apparent in the gradual change of tourism films' narrative structure. In fact, while the majority of NFB and CFU tourism films released until the late 1950s rely on the 'Voice of God,' a number of CFU films released throughout the 1960s and early 1970s such as *Australian Weekend* (1960); *Life in Australia: Perth* (1965); *Life in Australia: Hobart* (1966); *Life in Australia: Melbourne* (1966); *Life in Australia: Launceston* (1966); and *At The Beach* (1971)—although visually and thematically very similar to other contemporary Australian tourism films—no longer utilise an omniscient voice-over narrator. Instead, to convey a sense of place, they exclusively rely on the dynamic intertwining of images and instrumental soundtracks.

While tourism films released in the pre-WWII era were characterised by the juxtaposition of postcard-like images and intertitles or, from the early 1930s, Voice-of-God narration, throughout the 1950s and 1960s resorting to fictional narratives became a common practice in tourism film production. In order to provide foreign audiences with a portrait of the Australian lifestyle, a large percentage of government-sponsored films relied on fictional family narratives. In many of these films, the Voice of God tells the story of a day in the life of a white middle-class, English-speaking, traditional family of four. *Life in Australia: Cairns* provides an overview of the town, its attractions, and facilities while following the Taylor family in their daily tasks—the father and son while going to town to work, the daughter while biking to school, and the housewife and mother-of-two while engaged in her daily household chores. *Life in Australia: Sydney* portrays a day in the life of the Donalds, a similarly suburban family. *A Day at the Beach* follows the Mitchell family while enjoying their outdoor weekend leisure. *Life in Australia: Melbourne* and *Life in Australia: Brisbane* are equally characterised by suburban, family based narratives. In 1953s *The Melbourne Wedding Belle* narrates the adventures of a group of relatives all heading to a wedding in Melbourne; their trip is used as an original narrative device to display the city's main attractions and best scenic views. However, Australian tourism films do not exclusively rely on family based narratives. For instance, in order to showcase Tasmania's capital city's best locations, *Life in Australia: Hobart* exclusively relies on the visual narration of a day in the life of a local postman. In *North to the Sun* (1951) it is the enthusiastic voice-over of a tourist that enumerates Queensland's attractions and qualities; in *Travellin' Round* there is no voice-over, and the story of a tourist trip through Australia is narrated by the very protagonists of the film, a group of friends in their twenties.

Alongside the above-mentioned shifts and turning points in narrative devices and thematic tendencies, tourism films' aesthetics also embody the conflation between tourism and the settler gaze. As Gibbons noted, through the lens of the colonial gaze, images depicting colonial landscapes became "as important as words" (2002, 9). Such images were characterised, according to Pratt (1992), by a multilayered complexity and a density of meaning. Australian tourism films' cinematography, and more specifically the tendency to frame coastal areas' landscapes through the use of high-angle, panning, extreme-long shot, and suburbs through bird's-eye views and aerial shots, closely embodies what Byrnes defined as "the colonial utilitarian attitude towards land" (2002, 8), reflected in the strong visual focus on the land's "commercial potential and value" (2002, 41)—an attitude previously displayed in a number of nineteenth-century paintings characterised by landscape views taken from high standpoints, a colonial pictorial *leitmotiv* that encouraged viewers and potential settlers to take possession of the land.

Tourism Promotion and Colonial Agenda: A Tight Intertwining

Throughout the period considered in this chapter, images of Australia's cities, beaches, and suburbs were employed in local tourism marketing and local tourism film production as a means to convey to the audience a set of specific, multilayered meanings. In fact, settler culture and the related settler gaze have always been a persistent ideological factor able to adapt to different socio-economic conditions and to regularly inform the representation of Australia in government-sponsored tourism films. The persistence of settler culture traversed like an unbreakable thread the representation of Australia's tourist spots to the extent that, because of the duplicity and tight intertwining of their purposes and objectives, the boundaries between tourism promotion and colonial agenda in these films are often blurred. In fact, the intention of addressing and attracting not only tourists, but also potential settlers from overseas and especially from English-speaking Europe, is apparent in the majority of case studies analysed here.

In *North to the Sun*, the voice-over narrator of a tourist, after highlighting "the very enjoyable time" he had in Queensland "cruising on the Barrier Reef, fishing, sailing and water-skiing," enthusiastically describes the North-eastern Australian state. In his words: "I was very impressed with what I saw in the North. They seem to have everything up there (…). The only thing they are really short of, is people (…). But now people are moving in all the time. They can make a good life for themselves in the North." In *Life in Australia: Wagga Wagga*, the Voice of God, after praising the well-organised and efficient tourist bureau and the town's tourist facilities, states that "there's plenty of space around it." Along with the celebration of Wagga Wagga as a tourist destination, this emphasis on the abundance of land clearly seems to address an audience of potential settlers. A similar coexistence of different purposes is shown in *Brisbane City in the Sun*. In this tourism film the Voice of God, while focusing on the city's tourist attractions and leisure options, emphasises Queensland's "huge territory," the warmth of its climate, and the abundance of tropical fruits that grow everywhere, even in private suburban gardens. It concludes by stating that Brisbane gives you "a sense of well-being." Similarly, in *Life in Australia: Cairns*, the voice-over, after promoting the town's tourist attractions and facilities, claims that the fictional protagonists of the film, the Taylor family, "wouldn't live anywhere else but in the tropical far north of Queensland." The underpinning role of the settler gaze and settler promotion that have been playing in Australian tourism films is even more evident in the above-mentioned *From the Tropics to the Snow*. During his meeting with the producer-in-chief, the scriptwriter wishes to include in his representation of the country shots of Australian steelworkers in a blast furnace. When the producer-in-chief objects, "What are steel workers in a factory doing in a tourist film," the scriptwriter replies, "We are building you the image of a nation on the go." This dialogue from CFU's film makes explicitly clear the multifaceted nature of Australia's government tourism films, as well as the constant duplicity of their goals.

Conclusions

This chapter, through the analysis of 30 case studies released by Australian government-led film production companies from 1926 to 1975, highlighted Australian tourism film's three most relevant aspects: their substantial thematic consistency, their stylistic variety within defined parameters, and the explicit duplicity of their goals.

Thematically, the celebration of the beach as the favourite, commodified, suburban space for urban masses traverses the whole period analysed, with only few exceptions. Similarly, the depiction and promotion of Australia's suburban areas have constantly played a crucial role in the promotion and marketing of Australia to foreign audiences. By contrast, in the 1926–1975 time period, natural extra-urban areas unsuitable for settlement (i.e. the Outback, deserts, forests, and untamed beaches) are rarely portrayed. Similarly, there is no reference to Australia's indigenous culture. Such thematic silence suggests a carefully planned suppression of themes and narratives considered at the time unsuitable to an audience of white-European potential tourists and settlers.

Stylistically, the variety of solutions adopted in the analysed time frame makes Australian tourism film a hybrid, opportunistic, and overall hardly definable media form. While in the representation of urban and suburban landscapes these films largely rely on high-angle, extreme-long shots, bird's-eye views and aerial shots; in terms of narratives they show a gradual shift from conventional documentary tropes such as the use of the omniscient 'Voice of God' narrator to the adoption of more experimental devices such as the total disappearance of the voice-over narrator or the use of fictional plots and narratives and professional actors.

Finally, tourism films' multilayered nature and diversity of goals emerge from the examination of chosen themes, stylistic features, and narrative choices. The representation of Australia as a commodified, advanced, and well-organised urban and suburban playground addressed an audience of both potential tourists and settlers. Similarly, recurring narratives revolving around the depiction of middle-class typical Australian families aimed to convey the reassuring image of a country whose 'safe' appeal potentially suited family tourism and, at the same time, represented the promise of a new beginning for a white, European audience of potential settlers.

Works Cited

Ansara, Martha, and Lisa Milner. 1999. The Waterside Workers Federation Film Unit: The Forgotten Frontier of the Fifties. *Metro Magazine: Media & Education Magazine* 119: 28–39. https://search.informit.com.au/documentSummary;dn=713685158069215;res=IELAPA.

Anthony, Scott. 2012. *Public Relations and the Making of Modern Britain: Stephen Tallents and the Birth of a Progressive Media Profession*. Manchester: Manchester University Press.

Aveyard, Karina, Albert Moran, and Errol Vieth. 2017. *Historical Dictionary of Australian and New Zealand Cinema*. Lanham: Rowman & Littlefield.

Bertrand, Ina. 1997. Stanley Hawes and the Commonwealth Film Unit. *Australian Journal of Communication* 24 (3): 85–97. https://search.informit.com.au/documentSummary;dn=980807728;res=IELAPA.

Bonelli, Diego. 2018. *This Is Wellington. The Representation of New Zealand Tourism Film from 1912 to 2017*. PhD diss., Victoria University of Wellington. https://researcharchive.vuw.ac.nz/xmlui/handle/10063/7045.

———. 2020. 'A Wonderful Advertisement for Our Country'. New Zealand Tourism Film's Dynamics of Circulation 1923–1989. *Journal of Tourism History* 12 (2): 116–138. https://doi.org/10.1080/1755182X.2020.1740338.

Booth, Douglas. 2001. *Australian Beach Cultures: The History of Sun, Sand and Surf.* Hove: Psychology Press.

Brown, Sarah. 2008. *Imagining 'Environment' in Australian Suburbia: An Environmental History of Suburban Landscapes of Canberra and Perth, 1946–1996.* PhD diss., University of Western Australia. https://research-repository.uwa.edu.au/en/publications/imagining-environment-in-australian-suburbia-an-environmental-his.

Bryson, Ian. 2002. *Bringing to Light: A History of Ethnographic Filmmaking at the Australian Institute of Aboriginal and Torres Strait Studies.* Canberra: Aboriginal Studies Press.

Bunker, Raymond. 1985. Urban Consolidation and Australian Cities Built Environment. *Urban Australia: Issues and Policies* 11 (2): 83–96.

Byrnes, Giselle. 2002. *Boundary Makers: Land Surveying and the Colonisation of New Zealand.* Wellington: Bridget Williams Books.

Dutton, Geoffrey. 1985. *Sun, Sea, Surf, and Sand: The Myth of the Beach.* Melbourne and New York: Oxford University Press.

Fiske, John, Bob Hodge, and Graeme Turner. 1987. *Myths of Oz: Reading Australian Popular Culture.* Crows Nest: Australia.

Fitzsimons, Trish, Dugald Laughren, and Pat Williamson. 2011. *Australian Documentary: History, Practices and Genres.* Cambridge: Cambridge University Press.

Foster, Robert, J. 2001. Five Unvarnished Truths. Maslyn Williams and Australian Government Film in Papua and New Guinea. In *Colonial New Guinea: Anthropological Perspectives*, ed. Naomi McPherson, 64–81. Pittsburgh PA: University of Pittsburgh Press.

Gibbons, Peter. 2002. Cultural Colonization and National Identity. *New Zealand Journal of History* 36 (1): 5–17.

Gonzalez, Miguel. n.d. An Idyllic Vision of the 1960s. *National Film and Sound Archive of Australia.* https://www.nfsa.gov.au/latest/life-australia. Accessed 20 May 2021.

Grace, Helen. 1982. 'The Public Wants Features!': The (Creative?) Underdevelopment of Australian Independent Film Since the 1960s. *Filmnews* 12 (Nov–Dec): 6–8.

Greenhill, Leslie, and John Tyo. 1949. *Instructional Film Production, Utilization, and Research in Great Britain, Canada, and Australia*. Port Washington: Office of Naval Research, Special Devices Center.

Hillyer, Minette. 1997. We Calmly and Adventurously Go Travelling – New Zealand Film 1925–1935. MA diss., University of Auckland.

Hogan, Trevor. 2003. 'Nature Strip': Australian Suburbia and the Enculturation of Nature. *Thesis Eleven* 74 (1): 54–75. https://doi.org/10.1177/07255136030741005.

Kilmartin, Leslie, and David Thorns. 1978. *Cities Unlimited: The Sociology of Urban Development in Australia and New Zealand*. Sydney: Allen and Unwin.

Leotta, Alfio. 2011. *Touring the Screen*. Bristol: Intellect.

McGuirk, Pauline, and Neil Argent. 2011. Population Growth and Change: Implications for Australia's Cities and Regions. *Geographical Research* 49 (3): 317–335. https://doi.org/10.1111/j.1745-5871.2011.00695.

McKenzie, Jordi, and Craig Rossiter. 2018. Film Funding in Australia: Recent History and Empirical Analysis. In *Handbook of State Aid for Film*, ed. Mathias Karmasin, Paul Clemens Murschetz, and Roland Teichmann, 227–249. London: Springer Nature.

Metusela, Christine, and Gordon Waitt. 2012. *Tourism and Australian Beach Cultures: Revealing Bodies*. Bristol: Channel View Publications Ltd.

Moran, Albert. 1987. Australian Film in the 1950s. *Continuum: The Australian Journal of Media & Culture* 1 (1): 57–79.

———. 1988. Nation Building: The Post-War Documentary in Australia (1945–1953). *Continuum* 1 (1): 57–79. https://doi.org/10.1080/10304318809359319.

NFSA Films. *A Day at the Beach*. 1956. Directed by Malcolm Otton. Produced by The National Film Board. https://www.youtube.com/watch?v=Aa0AcXYlZWI.

NFSA Films. *A Place to Live*. 1972. Directed by Stuart Glover. Produced by The Commonwealth Film Unit. https://www.youtube.com/watch?v=W0Epqc3q15Y.

NFSA Films. *Another Sunny Day in Western Australia*. 1961. Directed by Ian Dunlop. Produced by The Commonwealth Film Unit. https://www.youtube.com/watch?v=9TcC83wEOcM.

NFSA Films. *At The Beach*. 1971. Directed by Wayne LaClos. Produced by The Commonwealth Film Unit. https://www.youtube.com/watch?v=j77S5hQPYBg.

NFSA Films. *Australian Weekend*. 1960. Directed by Rhonda Small. Produced by The Commonwealth Film Unit. https://www.youtube.com/watch?v=K2Q6T7__BKY.

NFSA Films. *Beautiful Bondi*. 1926. Unknown director. Unknown production company. https://www.youtube.com/watch?v=0lU0EeUo6LY&t=24s.

2 Australian Tourism Film 1926–1975: Promoting Australia… 33

NFSA Films. *Brisbane City in the Sun*. 1954. Directed by Hugh McInness. Produced by The National Film Board. https://www.youtube.com/watch?v=Wgy-EGJovhw&t=5s.

NFSA Films. *Call of the Surf*. 1935. Directed by Jack Fletcher. Unknown production company. https://www.youtube.com/watch?v=rD8D9-v9_Yc&t=20s.

NFSA Films. *Famous Beach Is Popular Summer Playground*. 1948. Unknown director. Produced by The National Film Board. https://www.youtube.com/watch?v=WhcfRHqKNDg&t=10s.

NFSA Films. *From the Tropics to the Snow*. 1964. Directed by Richard Mason and Jack Lee. Produced by The Commonwealth Film Unit. https://www.youtube.com/watch?v=62v2k6kiUwQ.

NFSA Films. *Gold Coast Is Attraction for Sun Worshippers*. 1955. Directed by Jack Allan. Produced by The National Film Board. https://www.youtube.com/watch?v=7KFhX0x_sU0&t=14s.

NFSA Films. *Life in Australia: Brisbane*. 1964. Directed by Robert Parker. Produced by The Commonwealth Film Unit. https://www.youtube.com/watch?v=KbukeJZftOs&t=1104s.

NFSA Films. *Life in Australia: Cairns*. 1964. Directed by Bruce Hillyard. Produced by The Commonwealth Film Unit. https://www.youtube.com/watch?v=4sXtjcqV_IA.

NFSA Films. *Life in Australia: Hobart*. 1966. Directed by Donald Anderson. Produced by The Commonwealth Film Unit. https://www.youtube.com/watch?v=b69NkdZHM-U&t=952s.

NFSA Films. *Life in Australia: Launceston*. 1966. Directed by Peter Young. Produced by The Commonwealth Film Unit. https://www.youtube.com/watch?v=mlklnP25_2A&t=186s.

NFSA Films. *Life in Australia: Melbourne*. 1966. Directed by Douglas White. Produced by The Commonwealth Film Unit. https://www.youtube.com/watch?v=TC7D5T_m_-k&t=816s.

NFSA Films. *Life in Australia: Mount Gambier*. 1964. Directed by Cristopher McCullough. Produced by The Commonwealth Film Unit. https://www.youtube.com/watch?v=KMdPliYFcGk&t=38s.

NFSA Films. *Life in Australia: Perth*. 1965. Directed by Henry Lewes. Produced by The Commonwealth Film Unit. https://www.youtube.com/results?search_query=life+in+australia+perth.

NFSA Films. *Life in Australia: Sydney*. 1966. Directed by Joe Scully. Produced by The Commonwealth Film Unit. https://www.youtube.com/watch?v=DUdeLgfWgUM.

NFSA Films. *North to the Sun*. 1951. Directed by John Martin Jones. Produced by The National Film Board. https://www.youtube.com/watch?v=m9kIe5NmQaA&t=8s.

NFSA Films. *Queensland Playground*. 1957. Directed by Richard Mason. Produced by The Commonwealth Film Unit. https://www.youtube.com/watch?v=No6DicYORJE.

NFSA Films. *Souvenir of Sydney*. 1954. Directed by Angelo Revello. Produced by The National Film Board. https://www.youtube.com/watch?v=yFyTcXNq8Ko&t=29s.

NFSA Films. *Surf Beach*. 1965. Directed by Bern Gandy. Produced by The Commonwealth Film Unit. https://www.youtube.com/watch?v=sr5UYKt8gAc&t=7s.

NFSA Films. *The Big Island*. 1970. Directed by Keith Gow and Don McAlpine. Produced by The Commonwealth Film Unit. https://www.youtube.com/watch?v=lHkyAzIcyoA.

NFSA Films. *The Melbourne Wedding Belle*. 1953. Directed by Colin Dean. Produced by The National Film Board. https://www.youtube.com/watch?v=xJVMoemz_zY&t=46s.

NFSA Films. *The Sunny South-West*. 1936. Unknown director. Produced by The Cinema Branch of the Department of Agriculture. https://www.youtube.com/watch?v=IStbjtDmK1s&t=1s.

NFSA Films. *Travellin' Round*. 1975. Directed by Brian Hannant. Produced by The Commonwealth Film Unit. https://www.youtube.com/watch?v=Cj9YRRAQzWQ.

Pearce, Philip, Alastair Morrison, and Joy Rutledge. 1998. *The Backpacker Phenomenon: Preliminary Answers to Basic Questions*. New York: McGraw Hill.

Perkins, Harvey, and David Thorns. 2001. Houses, Homes and New Zealanders Everyday Lives. In *The Sociology of Everyday Life in New Zealand*, ed. Claudia Bell. Palmerston North: Dunmore Press.

Pratt, Mary Louise. 1992. *Imperial Eyes: Travel Writing and Transculturation*. London: Routledge.

Rice, Tom. 2019. *Film for the Colonies: Cinema and the Preservation of the British Empire*. Oakland: University of California Press.

Rodger, Andrew. 1989. Some Factors Contributing to the Formation of the National Film Board of Canada. *Historical Journal of Film, Radio and Television* 9 (3): 259–268.

Rowse, Tim. 1978. Heaven and a Hills Hoist: Australian Critics on Suburbia. *Meanjin* 37 (1): 3–13. https://search.informit.com.au/documentSummary;dn=601870272415273;res=IELLCC.

Shirley, Graham, and Brian Adams. 1989. *Australian Cinema: The First Eighty Years*. Redfern: Currency Press.
Silverstone, Roger. 1996. *Visions of Suburbia*. London: Routledge.
Tallents, Stephen. 1932. *The Projection of England*. London: Faber & Faber.
Weckbecker, Lars. 2015. *Governing Visions of the Real. The New Zealand National Film Unit and Griersonian Documentary Film in Aotearoa New Zealand*. Bristol: Intellect.
Williams, Deane. 1995. The Commonwealth Film Unit: Precursors and Predecessors. *Metro* 104: 52–57.
———. 2008. *Australian Post-War Documentary Film: An Arc of Mirrors*. Bristol: Intellect Ltd.
Wolfe, Charles. 1997. Historicising the 'Voice of God': The Place of Vocal Narration in Classical Documentary. *Film History* 9 (2): 149–167. https://www.jstor.org/stable/3815172.

3

More than Just Safety: A Critical History of In-flight Safety Briefing Videos

Rowan Light

Introduction

Ladies and gentlemen, I'd like to direct your attention to your monitor—even if you fly with us often.

Variations of these words open one of the seminal scripts of global modernity, the in-flight safety briefing video. In the synonymy between globalisation and air travel, safety videos are a ubiquitous part of global aviation and its homogeneity, while also reflecting its "dynamic mobility"—the experience of flying as unsettling, disruptive, and threatening—as suggested by the common addendum, "even if you fly with us often". This chapter explores the in-flight safety video as a cinematic "demonstration" that, accompanied by flight attendants and borrowing from the aesthetics of tourism film, paradoxically performs safe airspace even as it calls attention to this displacement and transformation. Stephen Groening (2013)

R. Light (✉)
University of Auckland, Auckland, New Zealand
e-mail: rowan.light@auckland.ac.nz

points to in-flight cinema as a form of filtering; both part of the affectation of flying as "carefree" (285) and part of the architecture of aerial practices that allow passengers to simultaneously focus and look away, "from each other, from the risk and uncertainty of air travel (and modernity itself); from their own fears and anxieties and boredom" (295). In his seminal work *Cinema Beyond Territory*, Groening (2014) outlines how in this "atmosphere" of globalisation, in-flight cinema sits at the heart of a techno-fantasy: a universal, immaterial, and invisible network of constant communication. The airplane itself becomes a "harbinger and symbol of globalisation":

> Airline passengers are instructed in the protocols of globalisation inside the plane: the inflight magazine is full of travel articles, tips on negotiating a business deal, advertisements for language-learning software, not to mention the maps of airline route networks and floor plans for airports of different nations, and of course, inflight entertainment menus of movies, television shows, museums and talk shows. (22)

This chapter extends Groening's framework around cinematic airspace to focus on in-flight safety videos as a central product and practice within aviation marketing. In-flight safety videos are crucial to the rendering of airspace as usable, manageable, and consumable. Indeed, in mediating airspace as safe, in-flight cinema—from its earliest history—reinforced the connection between aviation and tourism, promoting the world as "accessible through technology and available for European exploration and inspection" (Groening 2013, 288). The "jet age" history of these texts shows how the intersection of Anglo-American cultural authority, new screen technologies, changing roles of flight attendants as safety experts, and political economies of air travel were extended and heightened with the advent of in-flight safety videos. Post-9/11 air travel gave new impetus for affecting safe airspace, and a new nostalgia for a lost world where flying was sexy and carefree.

A second boom in commercial flying—a 50% growth since the 1990s (Boeing 2018)—has produced a convergence of aviation safety and marketing through the in-flight safety briefing video. Whereas historically airlines did not use safety in advertising, at best discussing maintenance

3 More than Just Safety: A Critical History of In-flight Safety...

without directly referring to its implications for safe flying, the introduction of the in-flight safety video brought the issue of safety to the fore of airline marketing. In-flight cinema would inform, reassure, and distract passengers from their fear of flying. Conversely, as if to underscore this latent advertising, research suggests in-flight safety videos are less useful for imparting actual safety information as passengers "switch off" from the now familiar practice (Hood 2009). As safety has become a consumer product, briefing videos of increasingly high production value have become central texts in marketing campaigns to differentiate airlines from their competitors. Humour, sex, and celebrity have been deployed to "sell safety" (Molesworth et al. 2016). American airline Delta Airways successfully branded itself as a cool, retro airline with its linking of safety demonstrations with its marque personality 'Deltalina' (Brown 2008). More recently, Qantas, Australia's national carrier, produced a legacy video to mark '100 years of safety'; the 8-minute video now looking like something of a swansong after the collapse of global aviation during the COVID-19 pandemic (Qantas 2019).

The chapter then presents an analysis of in-flight safety videos through a case study of marketing campaigns by Air New Zealand, New Zealand's national carrier, since 2007, with a special focus on the convergence of marketing, tourism, and Peter Jackson's Middle-earth film franchise. Air New Zealand offers a rich example of in-flight safety video marketing for several reasons. As tourism film, Air New Zealand's safety campaigns offer an important example of "an audiovisual media form that features one or more geographical locations", which is often the result of "cross-institutional collaborations" with both implicit and explicit promotional purposes, "inviting viewers to visually or physically experience the location depicted" (Bonelli et al. 2019, 33). Air New Zealand is also a relatively minor aviation player willing to risk experimentation. Furthermore, New Zealand's relative geographic isolation in the South Pacific has made it crucial for the national carrier to perform narrations of the country as an otherworldly fantasy (and thus desirable) but also accessible through safe technology. This has been particularly critical during the contemporary period when global aviation has been critically cast as both an accessory to terrorism and a contributing factor to climate change. Finally, Air New Zealand has taken advantage of the advent of social media, especially YouTube, which constituted the single most important technological change in aviation marketing since the development of in-flight screens (Sahin and Sengün 2015; Avraham and Ketter 2012). These components of the Air New Zealand safety marketing reflect the interdependence of commercialism and national identity (Jutel and Leotta 2014).

Through this dynamic of distraction and attention, the regimentation of passenger behaviour and responses—to the experience of flying, to crew and to each other, and to their destination—points to the way that the shared global scripts of in-flight safety videos condition the mobility and representations of captive audiences. Certainly, what is at stake is more than simply the conveying of safety information. The fusion of Air New Zealand as a carrier of national consumer products and identity, and of filmic imaginaries, relies less on the experience of flying *per se* and more on the global ubiquity, homogeneity, *and* transience of this modern narration. If international flying is "to experience and participate in the financial, informational, and ecological customs that constitute globalisation" (Groening 2014), then in-flight safety videos are a key script.

> Now we request your full attention as the flight attendants demonstrate the safety features of this aircraft.

Part 1: In-flight Safety Briefing Videos—A Historical Overview

Pre-flight or in-flight safety video demonstrations evolved from the convergence of regulation, personnel, and technology in commercial aviation flying from the 1930s to the 1970s. This was shaped by a simple, underlying imperative: as more and more people began to travel on increasingly reliable aircraft, there was an increasing need to reassure flying was safe and secure. In-flight safety demonstrations were part of the set of practices and procedures that attempted to make manageable what Peter Pigott (2016) refers to as the "tight coupling of interacting systems" (2) that leads to aviation catastrophe. The interaction between private firms and the power politics of states competing for control over emerging airspace added complexity to the standardisation of aviation safety practices. Airlines supported by national governments or 'flag carriers' very much blurred the division between national and private, local and global.

The first vector of the changing world of aviation was the early regulation of global commercial aerial navigation across British and North American authorities. Freight and then passenger air travel became increasingly dependable and profitable in the late 1920s. Industry leaders, such as Pan American Airways, Western Airways, and Imperial Airways, launched commercial passenger services that would dominate trans-Atlantic and Pacific air travel for the better part of the twentieth century. A burgeoning aviation industry demanded increased regulation and standardisation of aircraft and aviation infrastructures to ensure sustainable and safe air travel and commerce. Air traffic control centres were established across the continental United States by airlines, for example, under the encouragement of a newly minted Bureau of Air Commerce, established in 1926. This was a patchwork of commercial, state, and federal authorities; a new "juridical regime" of airspace (Groening 2014). It was not until after the Second World War, in which much of the aviation infrastructure was co-opted for strategic and defence purposes, that the operation of airport towers became a permanent part of state responsibility.

The 1944 Chicago Convention on International Civil Aviation established the International Civil Aviation Organization under the auspices of the United Nations. Article 29 required signatory states to regulate airlines through certificates of registration, airworthiness, and crew training, although this was weighted towards mechanics and ground crews preparing aircraft for transit (Convention 1944). The Convention, above all, asserted the continued control over airspace by the nation state, coupled with "the liberalisation of airspace via the creation of an international network of air pathways for civil aviation" (Groening 2014).

The Federal Aviation Authority was established in 1958 under federal law to ensure American interests in international air travel. The FAA, as well as encompassing Air Traffic Control as part of an emerging architecture of air travel, provided grants for airport construction, as well as producing the Federal Aviation Regulations (FAR). The FAR regulated many aspects of aviation, including airport safety, issuing compliance for aircraft design and build—part of the tacit control the FAA wielded over international aviation. The law also attended to regulating aircraft spaces: it was now a crime to interfere with an active flight crew or carry weapons onboard an aircraft.

FAA interventions reflected the advent of mass commercial flying. The British Overseas Aircraft Corporation introduced its first commercial jet service in 1952. By the 1950s, a range of jet airlines was being flown along international routes, many designed by US companies. The expansion of the Federal Aviation Administration under the Department of Transportation in 1967 marked the apogee of American aviation power. These "foundations of modern commercial safety regulations" (FAA 2019)—relating to the design of aircraft and on-board safety features—remained dominant up until 1973.

This broader context of shifting state authority had a profound impact on international aviation safety. FAA prescriptions around safety procedures emerged from American attempts to dominate airspace. Requiring a complex set of safety requirements to be signed off by the Federal Aviation Authority placed the United States in the centre of an international network of commercial aviation, crucial to the standardisation of aviation safety. In-flight safety demonstrations emerged as part of the practices of safety, alongside increased standardisation, that ensured "the freedom of the air" was, in fact, tightly regulated—state sovereignty remained intact in airspace by controlling this movement of people (Budd 2009).

The traditional method of the in-flight cabin safety demonstration, dating from the 1950s, involved a flight attendant silently showing the proper method to fasten a seatbelt, how to wear an oxygen mask, and miming the location of the exits. Meanwhile, another attendant verbally instructed passengers over the public address system of the airplane. The split between the image and sound portions of the demonstration was mainly a practical solution to the problem of cabin noise. The early form and context of safety demonstration pointed to the second vector in the scripts and practices of global air travel: the changing role of cabin crew. Growing technological innovation and passenger numbers in the 1960s normalised aviation as part of global travel, which gave new attention to the experience of flying. During the inter-war period, when American and British airlines were established as commercial ventures, flight attendants, most famously the 'first stewardess' Ellen Church, were hired from the ranks of trained nurses to provide care and reassurance for male passengers (Nolan 2010).

As flying became increasingly mainstream in the post-war period, 'the art of flying' was repackaged with a new emphasis on glamour, rather than safety, as evidenced in the changing perception of flight attendants themselves. Flight attendants evolved from 'flying nurses' with a broad range of skills, to a service-oriented role which would make flying more pleasant and carefree for commercial passengers. "No longer a flying nurse or mother figure in a utilitarian uniform and sensible shoes bringing comfort to queasy passengers", Drew Whitelegg argues, "she was now pimped out to be a *Playboy* bunny in the sky" (2007, 81). Flight attendants increasingly 'auditioned' for their roles as cabin crew, rather than interview for what was an 'informationally dense safety role'; they were entertainers, rather than safety professionals (Whitelegg 2007).

Conversely, in the face of this objectification of cabin crew the safety demonstration provided a way to secure their place in a fluid labour force. Safety was strategic: "a labour force composed of experienced permanent safety experts, rather than transient co-eds" (Whitelegg 2007, 102). Crucially, the image of the flight attendant became the central pillar in aviation advertising. By embedding themselves in the safety demonstration, flight attendants were able to assert their roles or 'space out' as professional safety experts in a burgeoning commercial industry that sought to sexualise them.

Adding to this mix of regulation and practice of air safety was the changing technological context of in-flight aviation screens, through in-flight cinema projectors to embedded display screens, and, later, to the emergence of personal devices and social media beyond the space of the cabin. In-flight entertainment first appeared on Trans World Airways (TWA) flights across the Atlantic in August 1961. The promise of flying now offered access to cinema. This innovation provoked challenges similar to the demands for aerial architectures of safety and control. As TWA increased its share of trans-Atlantic passengers, European airlines complained that TWA was violating fare regulations; passengers were, in effect, paying for a double service—flying and cinematic—and so needed to pay for a more premium ticket (Groening 2014, 70). Attempts to ban in-flight films by the International Aviation Transport Authority, however, were struck down by the federal government which saw this as a threat to the American film industry's ability to sell its products (Groening 2014, 71).

The Transwestern Airlines incident pointed to a convergence in the experience of flying and cinema, and set an important international precedent. By 1965, for example, Philippines and Pakistan airlines had followed suit. Groening (2014) rightly notes how the innovation marked the end of the 'imperial era' of aviation, and signalled a new epoch of globalisation in which air travel was increasingly de-territorialised. With this came new juridical regimes of airspace, now encompassing the screen fantasies of passengers. The World Airline Entertainment Association (WAEA) was established in 1979 to bring together disparate groups, including airlines, aircraft manufacturers, content producers, and distributors, to regulate, standardise, and create greater coherence in the development of in-flight entertainment.

Airline executives cited fear of flying as the reason for the introduction of in-flight video entertainment. In a 1972 interview, United Airlines former vice-president of external affairs, Robert F. Johnson, noted that while airlines were never going to make money from the provision of movies, entertainment was necessary to overcoming the "monotony" of long-distance flying and giving people "something to do"; moreover, this entertainment would "distract them if they're nervous" (Friedlander 1972, 29). There was a clear subtext here: idleness breeds anxiety, and passengers needed assistance to diminish their fear of flying.

Adding to the challenge of groups like the World Airline Entertainment Association was the fact that different in-flight systems were needed to accommodate the diversity of aircraft types and capabilities. This was met with rapid technological change over the late twentieth century: 16 mm projection, 8 mm cassettes, videotape, and closed-circuit television systems, all came and went until DVD technology came to dominance in the 1990s, which, crucially, coincided with the introduction of user interfaces and interactions (Norman White 2009, 4–5). This created a period of continuity into the 2000s after two decades of rapid technological change which, as we will see, allowed for an embedding of safety video practices and corporate marketing strategies.

Underpinning these three contexts—emerging national and international regulations, the "spacing out" of flight attendants, and the rise of in-flight cinema—were the demands of an increasingly globalised commercial aviation. Flying needed to be marketed as safe and consumable: excitingly cosmopolitan, but also a passive form of travel. The tension between FAA as regulator and promoter; the significant use of flight attendants to sell flying, in which 'auditioning' for the role and *performance* of safety professionalism became increasingly important; finally, cinematic technology in commercial aviation was treated as a crucial way to pacify, entertain, and reassure passengers during the experience of flying. In this way, aviation safety was as much a marketing performance as it was prudential; aviation safety helped modulate airspace, not least the cabin itself, as a human environment.

This convergence of entertainment and the need for passive passengers were underscored by a Boeing-sponsored survey in 1980 that suggested one in three American adults was anxious or afraid to fly. The aviation industry's response to the problems in cultural attitudes to flying was technological development. "The distraction of the audio-visual on the screen gives the passengers the opportunity to imagine themselves somewhere else" (Groening 2014, 8); at the same time, airlines were required by international regulations to inform passengers of procedures and protocols in case of an accident, hence the in-flight safety demonstration. The year 1984 proved to be a seminal year in this marketing of aviation safety. On 9 October 1984, advisory circular FAA 135-12 was released to the aviation industry informing airline companies that pre-flight safety demonstrations were now approved for video. As if to underscore the logic of the 135-12 circular, a 1985 National Transportation and Safety Board found the majority of passengers viewed less than half of the safety presentation. "In an airplane environment", the survey stated, "passengers are passive participants who, for the most part, are unaware of 'why' the safety information they are given is important" (NTSB 1985). The circular also introduced the underlying assumption that the video screen would be more absorbing than the flight attendants miming the safety procedures and practices.

This led to experiments around video programmes by some airlines to increase attentiveness. Animated videos could be mass produced by specialist production companies. Nine airlines used an animated safety briefing video produced by Windmill Lane Pictures, an Irish video and film production company over the early 1990s (Flight Safety Digest 2000). By purchasing this global product, airlines saved expenses which would have otherwise been spent on using actors and aircraft for a briefing video. Importantly, this international production also meant the briefing video script became more standardised.

Aviation marketing and safety concerns were increasingly entwined. This reflected burgeoning commercial passengers; some 480 million people flew in the United States alone in 1991, for example (US Department of Transportation 1994). Alongside this growth, passenger surveys increasingly pointed to the perception of an airline's safety record as a factor in consumer choice. A National Business Travel survey found that over 85% of passengers surveyed would be willing to pay more for increased safety procedures on flights, while also identifying in-flight features that made them feel safer (Becker 1992).

A circular issued by the FAA in 1999 encouraged airlines to make the safety briefing 'interesting' and 'meaningful', as well as informative (FAA 1999). The FAA reiterated that "every airline passenger should be motivated to focus on the safety information in the passenger briefing", while adding that "motivating people, even when their own personal safety is involved, is not easy". One way to increase passenger motivation is to make the safety information briefings and cards "as interesting and attractive as possible". This reflected the FAA's dual role as promoter, as well as regulator, of air travel (Flight Safety Digest 2000).

The impact of 9/11 and "the war on terror" underscored the role of video on flights as a form of pacification. A *Wall Street Journal* article quoted WAEA spokesperson Robert Brookler saying that he believed, following 9/11, "in-flight entertainment increased its importance because jittery passengers needed soothing and entertaining" (McCartney 2001). Newly introduced headphones acted as a way to block out engine noise, further disconnecting image and sound (Groening 2014). Nostalgic imagery of flight attendants accompanied this growth of safety marketing. If flight attendants performed airspace as healthy and safe as "flying nurses" and, in the 1960s, as glamorous entertainers, their performance has been a key text by which this post-9/11 transformation has played out. Just as safety was a strategy for securing professional status in an emerging jet-age consumerism, flight attendant professionalism was re-ordered, as safety is increasingly simulated and projected through choreography on screen. This calls for careful attention to generic styles and conventions deployed by safety films.

A burgeoning suite of *pre*-safety videos, to frame the safety briefing, emerged as one strategy at the turn of the century. In 2001, Northwest Airways introduced a monthly "safety open": a high-production preface to signal passengers the need to pay attention to the safety briefing. Described by Northwest as pulling passengers "away from what [they] are doing to the screen, that is what gets everybody started" (Flight Safety Australia 2001). The content of the safety video opens ranged from a story about the family members employed by the airline to a music video featuring American blues guitarist and singer B. B. King. These productions were explicitly identified as a way to market the airline to a captive audience. Northwest's manager of on-board communications Kellie Schechinger stated how "our videos are a critical part of a communication with passengers. We change our video safety briefing every couple of years to have a different look and feel. Each time, we think through the need to capture and keep passenger's attention" (Flight Safety Foundation 2000). Rather than simply a technical script, the Northwest "safety open" was meant to entertain passengers in order to hold their attention; to distract from other distractions, in order to regiment their responses to emergency situations.

This "captive audience" became a common refrain in tourism safety marketing. Julie Martin, senior air safety auditor for cabin safety at CASA, in an interview in *Flight Safety* (2001), stressed how difficult it was "for cabin crews to maintain interest and contentiousness in regard to attracting passengers", because of the briefing's repetitive nature, as well as commercial pressures to ensure an efficient departure. Martin added that:

> Not enough emphasis is put on the importance of the pre-flight safety briefing during initial and recurrent training. Training often emphasises the passenger briefings required during a prepared emergency, but not so much the everyday pre-flight safety briefings.

Martin's comments, and the experimentation by Northwest Airline, pointed to the growing production values of safety briefings and investment by airline marketing teams—especially as surveys continued to indicate that fewer passengers listened to or watched the safety briefing.

The mix of cabin crew instruction, screen technology, and cinematic production offered a paradoxical emphasis on "distracted attention". In the growing diversity of technological platforms, airlines competed for passengers' attention—reflected in the use of a range of strategies, such as emitting a signal which, Pavlov-like, aims to signal to passengers the need to pay attention to the safety briefing, or conveying the safety narrative over the public address system, rather than through the individual headsets—to overcome the possibility of passengers using their own listening devices. The safety video *audio*, at least, becomes inescapable.

The introduction of new faster, interactive display screens in the 2000s, as well as the license provided by a FAA 2003 circular, saw increasing experimentation around the safety briefing video. Flight attendants occupied an uncertain place here. The strategic response to expanding commercial flying over the 1960s and 1970s by flight attendants, as identified by Whitelegg, was increasingly brought into question by the mid-2000s. Flight attendants' desire to present themselves as safety workers was undermined by both passengers "who do not take them seriously" and the tacit downplaying of their importance by airlines themselves (Whitelegg 2007). A marketing campaign by Independence Air, for example, removed the airline staff from the briefing video entirely. Instead, comedian Darren Miller narrated the requisite safety information, a marketing gimmick that CEO Kerry Skeen defended by claiming that his airline had "come up with an approach that's not only innovative and fun, but will create more awareness of the safety information from being presented" (quoted in Groening 2014). Conversely, in the mid-2000s, a new period of official corporate strategies aligned with new safety concerns after 9/11, the burgeoning media platform provided through YouTube (launched in 2005), and the increasing ubiquity of smartphones.

This intersection was exemplified by Delta Airways, which launched a series of marketing campaigns over 2006 and 2007. Later lauded as "turning a page" in airline marketing strategies, the Delta campaigns centred on crafting a celebrity persona around model flight attendants, most famously, Katherine Lee (Martin 2014). In 2006, Lee modelled new Delta Airways' flight attendant uniforms while giving a live safety briefing on a 2007 episode of *The Ellen DeGeneres Show*, when the entire show took place aboard a Delta flight. 'Deltalina' offered a nostalgic image of aviation safety following the purchase of Delta by United States Airways, as part of a wider attempt to restore the national airline industry post-9/11 (Economist 2006). This was a re-assertion of familiar tropes of aviation history: the alignment of American power with its airline industry, embodied in a "sassy and sexy" flight attendant as *Forbes* magazine put it ('a lesser known Angelina Jolie, serving you a drink at 35,000 feet'); while connected to marketing air travel, ostensibly through safety (Martin 2014). As scholar Ian Bogost noted in his book *How to Do Things With Videogames* (2011), Delta's marketing had very little do with actual safety instructions, and more with the "minor celebrity" of Lee; a "weird historical inversion", as Bogost put it, in which the red-haired Deltalina "very much *is* your father's Pan Am" (143). In this "safety theatre", airlines *perform* the appearance of safety, "to comply with regulations while imposing the lowest cognitive and emotional burden possible on the passenger so as to suppress fear and agitation" (Bogost 2011, 144).

Bogost reiterates the "techno-fantasy" of safety videos as forms of gaming, engaging passengers' interest in order to regiment and drill responses. This 'gamification' of air safety was underscored by Virgin Airways' release of its 2007 marketing campaign 'What's Wrong with this picture?', based on a comedic animated version of the safety announcement. The video begins by asking passengers to check out the safety card in the seat pocket in front of them—'Not only does it have pretty pictures, but it has important information'. Flying fish, matadors, and a multitasking nun were part of the 'game' played by passengers to identify what was atypical. By subverting passengers' expectations, Virgin Airways were pointing to what was otherwise shared and assumed in the script of safety briefing videos.

Although "Deltalina" offered something of a strategy for flight attendants in a new period of aviation labour and capital, the loss of professional respect for flight attendants, as Whitelegg (2007) warns, "is the first step towards removing [the profession's] sense of permanence". Cabin crew became perceived as complicit in trivialising the safety purposes of the in-flight briefing video. This was underscored in an 'honest safety video', produced by tourism consultant Doug Lanksy, premised on telling passengers what "Airlines Are Afraid to Show You" (YouTube 2020). "There's some stuff we should know about airline safety", Lansky writes on the video's description, "but they're not telling us"—*they* being airlines. Lansky posits, in the video, that the in-flight safety video—which he ironically notes "cost the airline millions of dollars to produce by marketing team"—is a broken product. There is a need for "a more truthful telling" of the safety briefing, in which the survivability of passengers is expressed in statistical data. Instead of a flight attendant, it is the pilot who delivers "the real safety demonstration" over the intercom—a repudiation of the fantasy of the briefing as regimented by civil and corporate authorities, performed by safety specialists, and projected through in-flight cinema.

Part 2: Destination Middle-Earth—Air New Zealand Safety Marketing

The in-flight safety video has developed into a form of tourism marketing, enmeshed in the logic of tourism film and shaped by safety rooted in regulation, flight attendant professionalism, and technology. Air New Zealand provides a useful case study to explore the ways in-flight safety videos borrow from the aesthetic of tourism commercials. Because of its marginal economic and geographic position, Air New Zealand needs to resort to 'unconventional publicity tools', such as in-flight safety videos, which are circulated extensively on social media to promote both the airline and the country. Ongoing tensions between safety as a professional standard and a source of marketing can be seen with the role of flight attendants as "actors" in in-flight safety videos, increasingly tied to multimedia marketing campaigns.

Air New Zealand's development as a national carrier reflects some of the global history of aviation safety. The New Zealand Civil Aviation Authority was established in the 1990s to protect the country's stake in the international circulation of global aviation. Similarly, Air New Zealand was nationalised under the Clark Labour Government to secure consistent air travel to New Zealand, as tourism became increasingly vital to the national economy. The airline thus constituted the 'flagship' of a new national branding heading into the new century, positioning New Zealand culture as a global consumer product and becoming increasingly central to marketing strategies by the New Zealand government and a cooperative private sector to shape the country's tourism images.

Air New Zealand's marketing is, therefore, as much about non-flying audiences as "captive audiences" in its aircrafts. The airline has drawn international attention since 2009 (New Zealand Herald 2009) with a reputation for experimenting with the in-flight safety video as a form of tourism marketing. For example, Air New Zealand's first major safety video production, *Bare Essentials of Safety* (2009), was the centre of a wider marketing campaign rolled out on television, airport billboards, and the airline's own website. The premise of the video—to capture the attention of passengers by having cabin and ground crew perform the safety briefing naked, with Air New Zealand "uniforms" displayed with body-paint—was intended to convey the airline's low airfares and transparency as New Zealand's national carrier, as well as "capturing" passengers' attention. "Even if you fly with us often", the central narrator Flight Attendant Michaela says with a coy smile, "we'd appreciate it if you'd take … a second look".

Subsequent media campaigns have extended much of these elements, focusing on New Zealand travel destinations and the use of celebrities. *Bear Essentials of Safety* (2013) was centred on UK television personality and celebrity survivalist Bear Grylls who narrated the safety briefing—part of an international boom in the use of celebrities to market safety (Molesworth et al. 2016, 989), linked to increased audience engagement (Molesworth 2014). The narration given by Grylls directly addresses the intention to capture the audiences' attention: "even if you've been flying for years, it'd pay to watch carefully, as I've learnt some things in the wild you might not have seen before". Although Grylls provides the majority of the comedic narration, there is a strategic use of Air New Zealand Flight Attendant Marina Roodt, who delivers the actual safety information. The voice of Roodt, the safety expert, rather than the comical celebrity of Grylls, pulls the audience back into the reality of the cabin space. The range of styles produced in Air New Zealand's safety videos point to common themes: the cinematic experience of the safety videos are premised on removing audiences from the cabin space, and placing them in a techno-fantasy simulation performed and embedded in the New Zealand landscape. Air New Zealand imagery coalesces around flight attendants as stylish and carefree entertainers, rather than professionals or safety experts.

Air New Zealand's in-flight safety video productions would become central to the airline's most significant marketing campaign, *The Most Epic Safety Video Ever Made* (2014). The campaign was tied to the wider pivot of New Zealand tourism around the Middle-earth films. Following the success of the *Lord of the Rings* trilogy, the marketing strategy around the *Hobbit* 'prequels' was expanded with an increase in government and private sector investment. Whereas during the earlier films, Air New Zealand was a junior partner in the marketing strategy, the airline took a more central role in the Hobbit campaign. "Just as Peter Jackson is able to transport audiences to the magical world of Middle-earth", one Air New Zealand spokesperson stated when the *Hobbit* films went into production, "Air New Zealand brings people to the breath-taking landscape that has been home to these epic productions" (YouTube 2014). To underscore this partnership, the official start of filming began at an Air New Zealand hangar, with film cast and crew welcomed to the backdrop of an Air New Zealand 777. If New Zealand was to become Middle-earth, then Air New Zealand would bring "the magic to life for travellers" (ibid.). This was to be a multifaceted marketing campaign, centred on the in-flight safety video which formed the basis of viral online marketing. The "most Epic safety video ever made" was released to coincide with the final instalment of the *Hobbit* trilogy in 2014, *The Battle of the Five Armies*, and was a key foundation for the entire three-year campaign, reflecting the global history of the safety briefing as one of the central practices of aviation culture. The briefing video provided the necessary anchor for this multifaceted campaign, precisely because it is a consistent and legally necessary practice of aviation safety.

This was, in fact, the second hobbit-themed safety video produced by Air New Zealand. The comparatively modest "An Unexpected Briefing" safety briefing video, first screened in 2012, featured mostly passengers and cabin crew in Middle-earth garb, with a celebrity cameo from Jackson inside an Air New Zealand jet. Whereas this earlier video featured mostly crew and passengers in an Air New Zealand aircraft cabin, the 2014 instalment was a four-and-a-half-minute affair, directed by New Zealand director Taika Waititi and produced on a big budget. The changes between the first and final safety briefing video reflected not only the greater role of Air New Zealand in the wider publicity of the films and the greater state and corporate investment in the marketing, but ultimately in the abstraction of the flying experience—through safety—from its potential for catastrophe. The safety video was a literal and figurative rendering of the flying experience.

"The Most Epic Safety Video", in this way, built on the success of earlier safety campaigns. The video itself revolved around the story of two movie fans who, flying with Air New Zealand, are magically transported to Middle-earth. The safety briefing was performed in various spectacular locations throughout New Zealand. Cabin seating and parts of the fuselage were embedded in the landscape, while characters both mythical and real engaged in various adventure activities—bungee jumping and whitewater rafting—pointing to the imagined destination of New Zealand-as-Middle-earth. In the globalised air space, full of possibilities of departures and arrivals, Air New Zealand—"The official airline of Middle-earth"— transported its passengers across time and space in their journey to the techno-fantasy of Middle-earth; at once timeless, magical, and storied with myth, but also rendered by the CGI and cinematic experiences of the safety briefing video itself. At the end of the briefing, Peter Jackson signs off, saying "I hope you've enjoyed the journey"—referring simultaneously to the Air New Zealand flight the passengers were embarking on, physically or virtually, and also the production of the films themselves which, with the final film, brought a close to the Middle-earth film franchise under Jackson's direction.

The aesthetic of the video was also distinctly cinematic, in part due to the partnership between Air New Zealand and Weta, the special effects company, which created high-quality costumes, set designs, and CGI graphics. Basic tenets of air safety, such as the storing of luggage and electronic devices, life jackets, and oxygen masks, are incorporated into the video's narrative and landscape. Visually stunning, the video incorporated the epic panning shots of the landscape from helicopters which were the signatures of the Jackson films, to recreate a cinematic velocity and pictorialism. This connection between the aviation video and the epic spectacle of this fantasy was reinforced by the airplane seats and fuselage being physically embedded in the various locations. In this sense, the video was a clear marketing of the plummeting, sweeping experience of air travel wrapped around the safety of the cabin space, what Claudia Bell and John Lyall call "accelerated sublime", in which individual consumption and self-expression occur not through pictorial capture but through embodied motion and immersion. The safety demonstration, by drawing on the operations of the film, immersed passengers in the tourism marketing, rather than making them passive viewers of it. The high-production values were reflected in an international design award and the video's 60 million views on YouTube (Air New Zealand 2014).

The video was wrapped around two broader marketing components. The first consisted of Air New Zealand working with Weta to turn two of its planes into "flying billboards". A Boeing 777-300 and 777-200 were painted with film characters to coincide with the film premieres and the release of the viral safety video. These "flying billboards" provided exclusive content for American audiences, being, for example, the first glimpse of the mythical dragon Smaug made available to the public. The experience of flying with Air New Zealand would be linked to the experience of the films and, by extension, a participation in the magical world of Middle-earth/New Zealand. This was capped off by the creation of a "real" Smaug in Wellington Airport—a prosthetic dragon head whose eyes glowed as passengers walk out of the terminal—the city itself modelled as the "creative capital" of this innovative fantasyland (Bonelli et al. 2019).

The aesthetics of the tourism film was reinforced by the second component of the campaign, made up of fan events, competitions, and special online media content. These included opportunities to attend the film premieres and meet the stars of the movies, all tied closely with the safety marketing campaign. *The Hobbit Fan Fellowship*, for example, was an international competition in which 75 winners (selected from 140,000 entries) were given a 6-day trip around New Zealand, visiting some of the locations associated with the films. *Middle-earth, Is Closer than you Think* was a promotional competition run by Air New Zealand which gave

3 More than Just Safety: A Critical History of In-flight Safety...

three Hobbit movie fans from around the world the opportunity to attend the world premiere screening of *The Hobbit: An Unexpected Journey* (Air New Zealand 2017). The by-line, 'closer than you think', was tied to a series of videos, such as 'Just Another Day in Middle-earth', which could be consumed by a broader viewership (YouTube 2017). The video was released with the description, "here in Middle-earth, everyday tasks can reveal out of this world surprises and before you know it everything can turn a bit Hobbit-shaped" (ibid.). It depicted a "typical" operating day for Air New Zealand staff and crew, undertaking various safety procedures and checks, "with a cheeky film-inspired twist" (Air New Zealand 2017). As the video progressed, Air New Zealand crew were magically transformed into dwarves, hobbits, and elves, and New Zealand place names were converted into Middle-earth locations.

In these journeys to New Zealand, passengers were transported symbolically to an imagined landscape populated with magical creatures. The *Just another Day in Middle-earth* video aimed, according to the Air New Zealand YouTube channel, "to inspire travellers from around the world to take their own unexpected journey"—with the key message at the end of the video: "You know, a lot of people believe that what we see at the cinema is just a load of fanciful imaginings, but I'll have you know that Middle Earth is closer than you think", narrated by the voice of Sylvester McCoy, the *Hobbit* trilogy's Radagast the Brown (YouTube 2017). The video, which received over two million views in two weeks of being released online, plays on airspace as dynamic and changing. The space of the airline becomes a kind of 'portal' to Middle-earth which—being *closer than you think*—threatens to burst into reality. In the flying experience, the fuselage, the filmic imaginary of the safety briefing videos, and the destination of Middle-earth meld into one. The conceptual space of flying as a transformative "portal" is repeated in the airline's sponsorship of New Zealand's national rugby team, the All Blacks. This video shows passengers 'becoming' All Blacks as they pass through the security gate to board an Air New Zealand jet (Air New Zealand Facebook 2017).

Cabin crew were deployed as part of this aesthetic: By having Air New Zealand crew become the mythical races by dressing as elves, hobbits, and dwarves with prosthetics and CGI enhancements, the video deliberately blurred the spaces of the cabin and destination. Cabin staff were themselves branded as "middle-earth", as their identity became a vacant category equating literally and figuratively the selling of services. As in historical patterns of air cabin personnel, cabin crew embodied the airline's brand—cool, innovative, and playful. The role of film stars was a recurrent feature of the broader publicity videos and experiences of the *Hobbit* publicity campaign. Actors appeared *as their character* or at least with the distinction between real and imaginary intentionally blurred. Interviews with cast and crew imbued the Air New Zealand campaign with a perception of authenticity, rather than pre-scripted marketing slogans, while constructing the central tourism image: New Zealand as an ancient, timeless landscape to be read and consumed through the epic story of the films.

This positioned host and tourist in the narrative of epic spectacle, centring on the European-American audience, and the transformative space of the airline. These American 'voices' of the campaign were intended to attract American audiences, even as they constructed the national brand identity for New Zealand. Media scholar Alfio Leotta notes how tourists see "this fantastic universe of Middle-earth through the eyes of characters who have [also] never seen these places before", so that viewers are able to identify with them as they travel and collaborate in the imaginative transformation of the land (Wilderness Magazine 2016).

The logic of tourism film in the safety campaign was taken to its fullest extent in the final major Tourism New Zealand/Air New Zealand collaboration before the release of the final *Hobbit* film in 2014. A publicity event featuring the stars of the film was held in Los Angeles for media and exclusive VIP guests titled "the Book of New Zealand" (Tourism NZ 2014). The premise of the event was a 'pop-up book', in which the sets from the film were rebuilt to the backdrop of scenes of the New Zealand landscape. Guests were invited to pose for photos with actors and immerse themselves in the magical world of Middle-earth/New Zealand; experiencing, as MC Nancy Jay put it, "a unique merging of the fantasy of Middle Earth and the reality that is a slice of heaven, New Zealand" (ibid.). The phrase "slice of heaven" invoked the song of the same name by David Dobbyn, one of New Zealand's iconic musicians, used as the soundtrack of the New Zealand *100% Pure* campaign (Dobbyn 1986). "The Book of New Zealand" launch entailed a specific representation of space embedded in the safety demonstration.

Kevin Bowler, Tourism New Zealand chief executive, described the objective of the "Book of New Zealand" as supporting the international story of the country as a fun, must-see destination, an innovative and creative nation, with a viable film industry. "All our campaign work", Bowler said, "aims to connect the fantasy, movie landscapes of Middle-earth with the actual experiences of New Zealand and demonstrate how easy it is for people to come to New Zealand, see Middle-earth first-hand and experience all the country has to offer" (Scoop 2014). The ease of travel was enmeshed in the safety practices of the airline: Air New Zealand staff moved throughout the crowds, also posing for photos with guests and film stars—providing the visual connection between 'the Book of New Zealand' and the wider airline campaign, and rendering actors, film creators, and airline cabin crew as part of the same (safe) continuum of film experience. The 'Book of New Zealand' was linked to an online version of 'the book' on Tourism New Zealand's primary website, which aimed to show how visitors can 'experience key film locations amongst some of New Zealand's most spectacular landscapes', divided into different tour packages (ranging from the one-week 'Halfling's Ramble' to the three-weeks 'Great Wizards tour'), which, as the book stressed, "ensure [tourists] get to experience the very best of what this mythical community has to offer" (Tourism New Zealand 2016).

In 2014, Air New Zealand signed a Memorandum of Understanding with the New Zealand Government according to which the two partners would collaborate to develop the country's tourism marketing into the future. As a kind of victory lap, Air New Zealand sponsored a celebratory exhibition, *Air New Zealand 75 Years: Our Nation. The World. Connected*, to mark the 75th anniversary of Tasman Empire Airways, the airline's predecessor established in the imperial age of aviation travel. As part of the roadshow, the exhibition displayed the "future of safety"; a VR-headset-based safety video into which passengers are immersed in a total fantasy. Released in 2018 as a prototype, the premise of the VR was the transportation of passengers "to a magical world where they witness a giant kauri tree grow, meet a grumpy Hobbit, get splashed by a breaching whale, and have a bird's eye view of a helicopter bungee jump"—stemming from the idea of families and friends coming together to play a board game when travelling (Ideolog 2018). This new phase of Air New Zealand safety marketing to three-dimensional gaming points to the future of "safety distraction", an immersion through a cinema of safety tourism especially evident in the Middle-earth marketing campaign.

Conclusion

In his review of *The Spectacle of Flight: Aviation and the Western Imagination, 1920–1950* by Robert Wohl, novelist J. G. Ballard satirised safety briefings in this way:

> Before take-off the cabin crew perform a strange folkloric rite that involves synchronised arm movements and warnings of fire and our possible immersion in water, all presumably part of an appeasement ritual whose origins lie back in the prehistory of the propeller age. The ceremony … has no meaning for us but is kept alive by the airlines to foster a sense of tradition. (Ballard 2005)

Ballard's playful invocation of a "sense of tradition" points to the qualities of in-flight safety demonstrations and videos as a shared script which regulates relationships and responses. Like any moral story, in-flight safety offers a double-inscription. It is organic, unseen, part of the cultural rhythms of life. Conversely, and paradoxically, the very experience of global aviation throws into doubt any permanence of order. Regimented responses create a sense of airspace as a human environment, even as it calls this 'state' into question.

This chapter brought to the fore this history of in-flight safety videos as a practice and genre firmly embedded in global air travel. There is nothing essential to these videos for the purposes of air travel, yet their development sits at different intersections of aviation history. The tensions between aviation authorities as both regulators and promoters, for example, point to the way safety demonstrations are required to fulfil essential safety checks and also be "innovative" and entertaining to keep passengers interested—even as the videos form part of the "weary ennui of contemporary air travel" (Bogost 2011, 142).

Air New Zealand, as a case study, also points to the value of historical perspectives in analysing the advent of safety marketing in aviation. As a national carrier bringing global passengers to the "edge" of a global network of aviation travel, we see the connection between safety and the ongoing commercial viability of safe air travel. In Air New Zealand's safety tourism, cabin crew have inserted themselves into the safety demonstration in new ways, especially in the era of social media in which authenticity is marked by access to "real" people. Moreover, the safety video continues to be shaped by new technology in which the "screen" is now located outside of the fuselage of the aircraft. The generic elements of the tourism film are, in this way, amplified in the context of social media marketing. In *The Most Epic Safety Briefing Video* campaign, social media shape passengers as active participants in the safety demonstration, which is subsumed into a cinematic experience of aerial sublime. In one of modern aviation's many, ongoing paradoxes; the success of this dynamic marketing belies the fact that it is conveyed through a safety procedure premised on conformity, regulation, and repetition.

Works Cited

Air New Zealand. 2014. *The Hobbit Fan Fellowship Arrives in Middle-Earth*. Press Release, November 2.

———. 2014. *The Most Epic Safety Video Ever Made*. YouTube. https://www.youtube.com/watch?v=qOw44VFNk8Y. Accessed 20 June 2021.

———. 2017. *Air New Zealand*. Facebook. https://www.facebook.com/AirNewZealand/videos/10153101913205777/. Accessed 20 June 2021.

———. 2017. *Just Another Day in Middle-Earth*. YouTube. https://www.youtube.com/watch?v=C7q7WFMuxsg. Accessed 20 June 2021.

———. 2017. *Middle-Earth – Closer than You Think*. Air New Zealand. http://www.airnewzealand.co.nz/press-release-2013-middle-earth-closer-than-you-think. Accessed 16 May 2017.

Avraham, Eli, and Erian Ketter. 2012. The Social Revolution of Place Marketing: The Growing Power of Uses in Social Media Campaigns. *Place Branding and Public Diplomacy* 8 (4): 285–294. https://doi.org/10.1362/146934715X14441363377999.

Ballard, James Graham. 2005. Book Review of Robert Wohl, The Spectacle of Flight: Aviation and the Western Imagination, 1920–1950. *Guardian Weekly*.

Becker, Tim A. 1992. Passenger Perceptions of Airline Safety: Marketing Safety Records. *Flight Safety Digest*.

Boeing. 2018. Statistical Summary of Commercial Jet Airplane Accidents- Boeing Commercial Airplanes, 1959–2018. https://www.boeing.com/resources/boeingdotcom/company/about_bca/pdf/statsum.pdf.

Bogost, Ian. 2011. *How to Do Things with Videogames*. Minneapolis: University of Minnesota Press.

Bonelli, Diego, Thierry Jutel, and Alfio Leotta. 2019. "Selling the Creative City": Wellington Tourism Film in the Neoliberal Era. *Studies in Australasian Cinema* 13 (2–3): 32–50. https://doi.org/10.1080/17503175.2019.1693149.

Brown, Joe. 2008. Delta's New Sexy Safety Starlet. *Wired*. https://www.wired.com/2008/03/deltas-new-safe/.

Budd, Lucy. 2009. Inflight Magazines: Their History and Future. *Airliner World*: 70–73.

Dobbyn, Dave. 1986. *Slice of Heaven [Sound Recording]*. Auckland: Magpie Records.

Economist. 2006. America's Airlines: The Elephants Learn to Dance. https://www.economist.com/business/2006/11/16/the-elephants-learn-to-dance.

FAA. 1999. Advisory Circular 121-24B: Passenger Safety Information Briefing and Briefing Cards. https://www.faa.gov/documentlibrary/media/advisory_circular/ac121-24c.pdf.

———. 2019. Safety: The Foundation of Everything We Do. https://www.faa.gov/about/safety_efficiency/.

Flight Safety Australia. 2001. Listen Up: Creative Methods May Be the Answer to Improving Passenger's Attention to Safety Briefings Before Take-off.

Flight Safety Digest. 2000. Passenger-Mortality Risk Estimates Provide Perspectives About Airline Safety. https://flightsafety.org/wpcontent/uploads/2017/03/fsd_apr00.pdf.

Friedlander, Paul J.C. 1972. 43 Years of Commercial Aviation. *New York Times*.

Groening, Stephen. 2013. Aerial Screens. *History and Technology* 29 (3): 281–303. https://doi.org/10.1080/07341512.2013.858523.

———. 2014. *Cinema Beyond Territory: Inflight Entertainment and Atmospheres of Globalisation*. New York: Houndmills.

Hood, Ralph. 2009. The Passenger Experience. *Airport Business* 23 (4): 14.

ICAO. 1944. Convention on International Civil Aviation Done at Chicago on the 7th Day of December 1944. https://www.icao.int/publications/Documents/7300_orig.pdf.

Ideolog. 2018. Air New Zealand Releases Its Latest Piece of Tech: A Spatial Computing Travel Experience for Magic Leap One. https://idealog.co.nz/tech/2018/10/air-new-zealand-releases-its-latest-piece-tech-spatial-computing-travel-experience-magic-leap-one.

Jutel, Theirry, and Alfio Leotta. 2014. *Goodbye Middle Earth*. Victoria University of Wellington. https://www.victoria.ac.nz/news/2014/goodbye-middle-earth. Accessed 20 June 2021.

Martin, Grant. 2014. United's New Safety Video Helps Turn a Page in Airline Marketing Strategy. *Forbes*. https://www.forbes.com/sites/grantmartin/2014/08/04/uniteds-new-safety-video-helps-turn-a-page-in-airline-marketing-strategy/.

McCartney, Scott. 2001. In-Flight Movies Are Big Business as Airlines Compete for Travelers. *Wall Street Journal*. https://www.wsj.com/articles/SB1023193255429454040.

Milne, Rebecca. 2009. Cheeky Safety Video Takes Off in Popularity. *New Zealand Herald*. https://www.nzherald.co.nz/nz/cheeky-safety-video-takes-off-in-popularity/ZBILMSTVLONDEFYZCNP7WGXYLU/.

Molesworth, B.R.C. 2014. Examining the Effectiveness of Preflight Cabin Safety Announcements in Commercial Aviation. *International Journal of Aviation Psychology* 24 (4): 300–314. https://doi.org/10.1080/10508414.2014.949511.

Molesworth, Brett, Seneviratne Dimuth, and Marion Burgess. 2016. Selling Safety: The Use of Celebrities in Improving Awareness of Safety in Commercial Aviation. *Ergonomics* 59 (7): 989–994. https://doi.org/10.1080/00140139.2015.1109712.

Nolan, Shane. 2010. United Airlines Celebrates 80 Years of the Flight Attendant Profession. *AV Stop*. http://avstop.com/news_april_2010/united_airlines_celebrates_80_years_of_the_flight_attendant_profession.htm.

Norman White, Ian. 2009. A History Inflight Entertainment. *Experience Association*. http://c.ymcdn.com/sites/connect.apex.aero/resource/resmgr/IFE-Resources_docs/History_of_IFE_version_2_JNW.pdf.

Pigott, Peter. 2016. *Brace for Impact: Air Crashes and Aviation Safety*. Toronto: Dundurn.

Qantas. 2019. 100 Years of the Spirit of Australia. https://www.qantas.com/nz/en/promotions/brand/100-years-of-the-spirit-of-australia.html.

ReThinking Tourism. 2020. *The Honest Pre-flight Safety Demonstration Video that Airlines Are Afraid to Show You.* YouTube. https://www.youtube.com/watch?v=SZB4_-tiRt0&ab_channel=ReThinkingTourism.

Sahin, G., and Gunce Sengün. 2015. The Effects of Social Media on Tourism Marketing: A Study. *Management and Administrative Sciences Review* 4 (5): 772–786. https://doi.org/10.1177/1468797619873107.

Tourism New Zealand. 2014. The Book of New Zealand Open to View in Los Angeles. *Scoop.* http://www.scoop.co.nz/stories/BU1312/S00004/the-book-of-new-zealand-open-to-view-in-los-angeles.htm. Accessed 21 June 2021.

———. 2016. Celebrating 15 Years of Middle-Earth. https://www.newzealand.com/nieuw-zeeland/feature/new-zealand-15-years-middle-earth/. Accessed 19 June 2021.

U.S. National Transportation and Safety Board. 1985. *Safety Study – Airline Passenger Safety Education: A Review of Methods Used to Present Safety Information.* NTSG/SS-85/90.

United States Department of Transportation. 1994. *Transportation Statistics Annual Report 1994.* https://www.bts.gov/sites/bts.dot.gov/files/legacy/publications/transportation_statistics_annual_report/1994/pdf/report.pdf.

Walker, Megan. 2016. Identity Crisis. *Wilderness Magazine.* https://www.wildernessmag.co.nz/identity-crisis/. Accessed 21 June 2021.

Whitelegg, Drew. 2007. *Working the Skies the Fast-Paced, Disorienting World of the Flight Attendant.* New York: New York University Press.

4

The Promotion of Tourism on Radio Waves

Luís Bonixe and Gorete Dinis

Introduction

Due to its unique industrial characteristics and peculiarities, the tourism sector is strongly dependent on information. Tourism stakeholders therefore need up-to-date and credible information so that they can justify their decision-making in a timely manner. There are various sources of information that they can use, and their choice depends on several different elements: for example, the type of information they need and the characteristics and interests of each stakeholder. Among these, the

---

L. Bonixe (✉)
Polytechnic Institute of Portalegre, Portalegre, Portugal

Instituto de Comuniçãcao da Nova (ICNOVA), Lisbon, Portugal
e-mail: luisbonixe@ipportalegre.pt

G. Dinis
Polytechnic Institute of Portalegre, Portalegre, Portugal

Governance, Competitiveness and Public Policies (GOVCOPP),
Aveiro, Portugal
e-mail: gdinis@ipportalegre.pt

© The Author(s), under exclusive license to Springer Nature Singapore Pte Ltd. 2021
D. Bonelli, A. Leotta (eds.), *Audiovisual Tourism Promotion*,
https://doi.org/10.1007/978-981-16-6410-6_4

traditional media and the so-called new media stand out as important vehicles for information; this contributes to the construction of citizens' desires and aspirations and to the early formation of an image of the destination or tourist service.

In information or advertising channels, the media has the great advantage of reaching a large number of citizens or targeted groups of people who may be located in different places. Thus, the organizations responsible for communicating and promoting a tourist destination or service face a great challenge, which consists of choosing the communication channel which is best suited to the strategy or action they intend to carry out.

However, consumer behaviour in tourism has changed over the years and consumers currently consider the information circulating in the media—disseminated by journalists or by other consumers who use these means to share their tourist experiences—as being more credible compared to the information disclosed in the form of advertising. As Tasci and Gartner (2007) maintain, high credibility and ease of access gives the media the power to influence the formation of the image of the tourist destination and is thus fundamental for tourism organizations to understand how and why consumers make decisions (Heitmann 2011).

The role of the media in helping consumers make travel decisions is also changing, making it essential to understand how the media—as well as autonomous information sources—have considered the theme of tourism. Radio has certain characteristics that distinguish it from other media. Knowing such characteristics is the only way to understand the potential of this channel to convey tourist information; however, studies that link the area of tourism with journalism and radio programming are still incipient.

The purpose of this chapter is to ascertain what information tourism content radio stations are disseminating and how this channel has been used by organizations to promote destinations and tourist resources.

This study is structured in four parts. The first part focuses on the literature review on the intertwining nature of tourism, promotion, and media; the second part deals with the description of the methodology; and the third part with the presentation and discussion of the results. Finally, the conclusions are presented, along with the limitations of the study and suggestions for further research.

Tourism, Promotion, and Media

Over the past six decades, tourism has become one of the largest and fastest-growing economic sectors in the world. The sustainable growth of this sector contributes to the socio-economic progress of many destinations through the creation of jobs and enterprises, export revenues, and infrastructure development (UNWTO 2017).

In Portugal, tourism is fundamental to the development of the economy, with around 7% of the Portuguese population employed in this sector, and international tourism revenues contributing 8.7% of the gross domestic product (TP 2020a). It is a major category of international trade in services (UNWTO 2017) and is the leading sector in the Portuguese export market (representing 18.6% of the total). In the last three years, Portugal has been awarded several accolades—including best tourist destination by the World Travel Awards—which has contributed to the sector's development and international recognition.

However, the evolution of tourism at an international and national level is strongly affected by the spread of the global pandemic COVID-19, which is causing stagnation or breaks in the sector: prospects for 2020 point to a 58% to 78% decline in tourist international arrivals (UNWTO 2020).

The impact of this crisis in the tourism sector will vary between different countries, destinations, and segments of the sector. However, the effects of the crisis are expected to have a permanent impact on consumer behaviour (OECD 2020) and on the criteria for selecting destinations. This conjunctural reality can also be seen as an opportunity to rethink the tourism system (OECD 2020) and to establish a new development model for the sector that should be based on three pillars: (i) portfolio of products and services; (ii) human resources; and (iii) marketing and communication (Costa 2020). To face and respond to the crisis, a growing number of countries, including Portugal, have applied measures to restart the sector, particularly safety protocols, in order to promote the country as a safe destination, with domestic tourism as a priority (OECD 2020).

Communication was already an indispensable function in the face of the increased competition in tourist destinations (Arino 1999); however, in this context, communication and marketing are essential areas for the sector to recover and achieve the desired performance levels.

By tourist communication, Baldissera means "all communication that takes place within the scope of tourism relations, in its different processes, supports and contexts" (Baldissera 2010a, 68). Communication thus consists of updating or materializing meanings related to tourism ideas and practices, which can be at a formal (official) or informal (unofficial) level. This comprises features such as (i) promoting and disseminating ideas; (ii) persuading and seducing in order to consume a product/service; (iii) informing different stakeholders (e.g. the press, the government, the private sector, visitors, and the community); (iv) training through communication actions that aim at the development and qualification of human resources to work in the tourism area; (v) qualifying relationships and being predisposed to collaborative actions; (vi) aiming at people's commitment; (vii) sensitizing and raising awareness of tourism and the need to preserve or conserve natural and historical and cultural heritage (Baldissera 2010b).

According to Ruschmann, communication will be effective when "the communicator (sender) is able to detect the tastes and preferences of people (recipients), creating images that favorably influence them, encouraging them to travel to a specific destination" (2006, 43). On the one hand, he adds that the success of communication depends on how "messages are communicated, using the most influential channels and the most effective means of communication in the market" (2006, 43).

On the other hand, "tourist promotion" means the communication process between the agents of the destination (or their intermediaries in the communication channels) and the potential consumers (Mill and Morrison 1985 in Fakeye and Crompton 1991). In recent years, tourism communication has evolved rapidly alongside developments in wider media practices influenced by social, economic, and political forces and advances in technology (Pace 1997 in Park 2015).

There are different types of media: (i) media that includes communication channels through which news, entertainment, education, data, or promotional messages are disseminated; (ii) media that includes every broadcasting medium such as newspapers, magazines, TV, radio, billboards, direct mail, telephone, fax, and internet; (iii) the internet and social media.

Technological advances and the development of the internet have contributed to potential consumers having access to varied information about a certain tourist destination in an easier and instantaneous way; it has become the most effective means of communication with regard to the dissemination and exchange of tourist information worldwide (Marujo 2008). The internet has allowed potential consumers to control the amount of information and the moment at which they intend to view it, as well as consumer-to-consumer information exchanges (Francesconi 2014).

The consumer currently assumes a decisive role in online communication, as it is "his interest in a particular subject that activates communication and not the company's interest in making him know about his product" (Brandão 2001, 3). The search for information from other consumers is now an increasingly commonplace occurrence, with the proliferation and popularization of social networks. In the opinion of Curtichs et al. (2011) in Bernardo (2012), social media works as a source of information because, at their core, these sites are constructed from stories, stories that can be shared, known, praised, and memorized. The content of the message transmitted thus assumes a role that is as decisive and significant as the form in which it is presented to consumers (Brandão 2001).

Communication has become global, informal, and democratic (Francesconi 2014), so in order to inform, convince, or capture the attention of potential consumers, the organizations responsible for promoting and communicating the tourist destination must adapt their speech to what consumers find interesting, relevant, and accessible (Okaka 2007).

Defining a media communication strategy therefore involves taking into consideration decisions such as (i) knowledge of the audience's familiarity with and exposure to different media; (ii) characteristics of the target public; (iii) effectiveness of different media; (iv) opinion leaders that can be engaged in the project. In relation to this subject, Hubley (1980) in Okaka (2007) states that there should be a deliberate effort to understand the communication environment, including target groups, appropriate media platforms, messages, and forms of interaction.

The relationship between tourism and media is vital and complex, and tourism is highly dependent on the media. The characteristics and particularities of products, services, and tourist destinations—especially their intangibility and inseparability—reinforce the needs and the role of information in tourism. When starting the process of selection and planning of the trip, tourism consumers look for tourist information that helps their decision-making. There are several sources of tourist information on which consumers can base their choices; how and where the traveller searches for information depends on personal, situational, and product-related factors (Fodness and Murray 1999).

Since potential consumers cannot visit the destination before their tourist experience, the promotional discourse seeks to anticipate the experience with the potential consumer, portraying as faithfully as possible what the visitor will find at the destination; however, visitors must "know how to transform any trip into something that above all reflects the universe, the tastes and aspirations of those who want to travel" (Conceição 1998). This promotional information recommended to the potential consumer remains in his memory, helping him to idealize and create a preconceived image of the destination, reinforcing his relationship with the site (Trauer and Ryan 2005). The primary objective in a promotional speech is to project an image of the destination that corresponds to the interests of the potential consumer and that arouses in him a need and desire to travel and an interest in that destination (Fakeye and Crompton 1991; Reisinger and Turner 2004).

Although the factors that interact with information and affect the formation of tourism destination images in the minds of travellers are diverse, "*the media is a primary source of destination images*" (Daye 2005, 14). When the image that potential consumers hold of destinations is formed through messages that come from "non-tourist" sources, these are called organic images and are deemed to be more influential and credible than induced images formed based on tourism advertising, promotions, and campaigns (Daye 2005).

The information conveyed through the media contributes to informing, influencing, and encouraging tourism consumers. The media elaborate on and transmit information about different places through images, sounds, and words, helping the potential traveller to build an image of the destination. In fact, the narratives conveyed by the media are fundamental for the target audience's imaginary (Gotardo and Ferreira Freitas 2017). However, because of its capacity to reach potential consumers on a large scale and in a short period of time, and given their geographical reach and high credibility, the media can exert influence on changing individuals' perceptions of a destination in a positive or negative fashion. The effect of bad news or a developing crisis on a tourist destination can be devastating, and relations with the media must be carefully managed in order to avoid potential undesirable impacts (Jihwan 2015) because "The way the image of a place is conveyed by the media can be fundamental to the tourist decision process when visiting a country or region" (Marujo and Cravidão 2012, 282).

As mentioned earlier, in the last few years we have witnessed the spread of the internet as a source of information and a communication channel; however, the traditional communication channels (television, radio, press) continue to be relevant for certain market segments, such as baby boomers, who still prefer to receive information about destinations through these channels. In a study carried out annually from 2007 to 2012, Xiang et al. (2015) concluded that some traditional media have become even more important in recent years, which means that travellers consciously seek a variety of information in order to form a more comprehensive and less biased opinion about tourist destinations and products.

The developments that have occurred in the media industry over the past few years have increased the quality and variety of programmes, from commercial, entertainment, educational, and infotainment formats, meaning that a "variety of media contents (e.g. podcasts, voices, texts, pictures) can be digitally retained, retransmitted and transported, enabling an interaction by the user, exactly at the moment that is convenient to the user" (Emilija 1999 in Okaka 2007).

World tourism is facing changes and experiencing a period of some uncertainty; Yeoman (2008) points out the search for new experiences, luxury, culture, and authenticity as tourist trends. In his opinion, interests in culture, food, and sport are increasingly shaping the way people approach their choice of holiday, and tourist consumers want to sample the ethnicity of the destination. The pandemic crisis brought new implications for tourist destinations, making factors such as hygiene and health important considerations in travel decisions (Chebli and Said 2020). The author recommended that tourism managers focus on a media strategy, cultivate positive images, and stimulate tourism during and after the crisis, namely in low season by presenting the advantages of such travel and destination resources (attractions, activities, services, etc.). This also constitutes an opportunity to build customer loyalty.

Radio and Tourism

The radio sector in Portugal consists of national, regional, and local radio stations. With the possibilities that the internet offers, there are also web radio stations. Despite competition with other media and new media, on the one hand, the radio continues to have a stable audience in Portugal. According to data referring to the first half of 2020, "78.3% of residents in the Continent aged 15 and over listened to the radio at least once a week and 50.7% did it the day before" (Marktest 2020). On the other hand, internet radio listening is growing in Portugal, which gives radio a degree of importance in the daily lives of the Portuguese.

In fact, radio is an important way to get to know the world, not only through hard news but also through the diversity of information it conveys about places, communities, and heritage.

The characteristics of mobility, proximity, and immediacy give it some advantages for listeners who choose it when they commute from home to work, for example. Its capacity to adapt to a context marked by the new media has also allowed verbal communication to continue to be a valuable option in this new era of media consumption.

In fact, in spite of other potentialities, it is the specificity of its sound-based language that gives radio a unique and even innovative character, both in terms of the production of content and formats, such as podcasts. The language of radio is composed of four sound elements: word, ambient sounds, music, and silence (Balsebre 2004), and it is through their use that the radio message is constructed. Since it has no image, radio combines these expressive elements, creating mental images in the mind of its listeners.

For this reason, radio has the ability to create its own space generated by the sounds that make up the object of the message. This sound narrative—in conjunction with the listeners' repertoire—is seductive and appealing, calling audiences to a sonosphere that characterizes the radio message.

Arnheim (1986) recalls that the world is mainly represented through images and that only two forms of communication do not do this: music and radio. Without image or written word, radio establishes a communicative link with its listeners based on the codes and icons of reality that the different sounds build when emitted. Through radio, it is possible to build an image of events using the sounds that compose them, combining the expressiveness of radio (word, music, ambient sounds, and silence) to build the message that will be received by the listeners.

Soengas (2003) identifies three functions of sounds in radio journalistic discourse: (i) informative, as they help to understand the content of the information, facilitating its decoding; (ii) referential, since they establish a connection between the listeners and the reported geographical space; and (iii) expressive, because it is through the sounds that listeners receive sensations that help them to assimilate connotative aspects of messages. For this process to occur, the same author emphasizes, it is necessary to consider two distinct spaces: the real and the audience. It means that the radio subtracts the sounds that compose it from the real, manipulating them, conjugating them, and creating a sound narrative. The real space is where the facts take place. The audience space is multiple since it depends on the referents of the real space that the listeners have. The role of radio journalists is to transmit significant sounds from the real space so that they are apprehended and understood by the audiences.

This can be done by describing the space, using the word for it, or through sounds captured at the place of events. In this case, the sounds emitted must be known to the receiver, or the message will be lost. As Schafer recalls, the sounds we capture result from our own experience and the environments around us:

> For instance, we found that at first when men were scarce and lived a pastoral existence the sounds of nature seemed to predominate: winds, water, birds, animals, thunder. Men used their ears to read the sound-omens of nature. Later on in the townscape men's voices, their laughter and the sound of their handicraft industries seemed to take over the foreground. Later still, after, the Industrial Revolution, mechanical sounds drowned out both human and natural sounds with their ubiquitous buzz and whirr. (Schafer 1969, 6)

Radio is, therefore, the result of the work of capturing and editing sounds on the spot, listening to testimonies, silences, and music with meaning that are introduced in the narrative and that together reconstruct the events, places, and people. The sound of waves on a beach is intended to mean exactly waves on a beach. In this sense, the sound effects accentuate the impression of reality (Balsebre 2004) in the radio message. The combination with other constituent elements of the radio language creates a positive redundancy that helps to assimilate the meaning of the message.

The sequence of sound segments in a radio space is often ensured by sound effects. When this is the case, they are performing a narrative function. It means that they aim to complement the radio message. The transposition from one space to another is transmitted to the listener by a sound effect:

> (…) we can say that sounds, whether in the world or on the radio, are generally indexical. We could of course say that recorded sound on the radio is iconic in the elementary sense that it is an icon or image of the original sound or that a sound in a radio play is an icon of a sound in the real world (…). (Crisell 1994, 44)

The expressive potentials of radio—combined with the relevance it still has in the lives of individuals—make this medium an important platform for promoting tourism. Radio emerges as an important communication and advertising channel for tourism organizations, especially if the objective is to reach local audiences, constituting an obvious choice when it comes to publicizing events. Its advantages over advertising media when compared to other media are (i) it is relatively cheap; (ii) the message can be repeated many times; (iii) audiences can be targeted geographically; (iv) production costs are low; and (v) voice and sound can be used.

A study conducted by Alhmedat (2013) in Al-khasawneh (2018) concluded that radio programmes can explain the services and facilities available in tourist destinations, and also influence the behaviour of people during the practice of tourism activities, increasing the demand to visit some tourist attractions.

Methodology

The objective of the study is to ascertain how Portuguese radio represents and promotes tourism in Portugal. To this end, nine programmes that focus on tourism broadcast in 2019 and 2020 on the three main radio stations in Portugal were analysed.

The research method used in this study is content analysis. This is a method commonly used in social sciences to research various forms of human communication, as is the case with videotapes and/or audiotapes (Berg 2009). Through this method, the programmes were analysed in detail and systematically, using broadcasts from 2019 and 2020 included in the radio programming of the three main information radios in Portugal: TSF, Antena 1, and Renascença (RR), and whose thematic area falls within the field of tourism.

We chose to analyse Portugal because of the tourism sector's growing importance in the country and its increasing visibility in national and international media. Domestic tourism has been encouraged by governmental entities in the face of a global pandemic. Furthermore, it was decided to address the radio sector.

The radio panorama in Portugal consists of broadcasters with national, regional, and local coverage. Within this classification, we found thematic radio stations, which are dedicated to a specific theme (musical, sports, and information) and generalist radio stations, those with a diversified programme. We can also classify Portuguese radio stations as public, as they are part of the state's audiovisual sector and have a public service and private function. Also noteworthy is the strong presence of the Catholic Church in the Portuguese radio sector. The Catholic Church owns one of the main radio groups with national coverage and many others with local coverage.

For the present study, on the one hand, the choice of radio stations is determined by those that, in the national context, have more presence and are dedicated to informative content, with more programmes reporting on tourism. On the other hand, the choice of these radio stations provides a sample of what is broadcast on a general public service radio (Antena 1), Catholic generalist radio (Renascença), and private newsradio (TSF). We analysed the content of five programmes on TSF, two on Antena 1, and one on RR.

Table 4.1 Criteria and parameters used for the analyses of radio programmes

Criteria	Parameters
Characteristics of the programmes	Definition
	Schedule
	Subject
	Duration (time)
Partnership	Tourism institutions/enterprises
	Political entities
	Public institutions linked to heritage
Voices	Politicians
	Destination management organization
	Host/journalist
	Building heritage specialists
	Restaurant owners
	Local population
Themes	Building heritage
	Cultural events
	Religious heritage
	Natural heritage
	Tourist destination
	Health and well-being
	Sport and adventure
	Gastronomy and wines
	Local traditions
Language and sound narrative	Interview
	Local sounds
	Voice (of the host or journalist)
	Local music
	Others music

Taking the objectives of the study into account, the following criteria and parameters were defined for analysis (Table 4.1).

Results and Discussion

Characterization of the Programmes

The observations made allowed us to identify various periods of the day for the broadcasting of programmes on tourism; however, there was a trend towards broadcasting programmes at night or weekends. The length of such programmes ranged between 15 and 45 minutes. Also, we found programmes of shorter duration, albeit in smaller numbers, which aim to provide listeners with a brief overview of specific locations, restaurants, or events. Such programmes do not exceed five minutes in length, since they are broadcast in the morning when the radio is mainly aimed at an active audience, on the move from home to work or in the workplace. Our sample also revealed that there is no fixed timing for this type of programme. Half of such content is broadcast daily and the other half weekly (Table 4.2).[1]

Most of the radio programmes studied that deal with tourism promotion result from partnerships with organizations linked to the sector or local politics. Thus, in the corpus analysed, we found programmes on the radio in partnership with city councils (Oeiras Cultural Agenda), the specialized press (Essência do Vinho), regional entities in the tourism sector, and structures for preserving cultural heritage—as is the case of the Serralves Foundation.

We can, however, divide partnerships into two types. In permanent partnerships, the programme is co-produced with the radio and circumstantial partnerships that provide support for the production of certain programmes. Therefore, the entities change from programme to programme. This type of partnership can be seen in the programme "*Terra a Terra*".

Programmes without identification of partnerships are mainly those that are based on tips for visits, gastronomy, shows, and so on, as is the case of "*Boa vida*" and "*TSF à mesa*".

The Voices of Tourism

As devices of social representation, the media find one of their main roles in society in the diversity and plurality of discourses, which is to serve as a stage for the discussion and representation of themes of public interest. The call for protagonists from different walks of life in society helps to

---

[1] The titles of the programmes were freely translated in Table 4.1. The original titles, in Portuguese, will be used in the text.

Table 4.2 Characterization of the corpus

Rádio Radio	Programme	Characterization	Schedule	Duration of the programme
TSF (Private radio. News-radio)	"*Encontros com o Património*" (Encounters with Heritage)	Programme that addresses places with history, landscapes, and people, past and the present.	Suspended in July 2020.	40 minutes
	Agenda Cultural 30 dias em Oeiras (Oeiras Cultural Agenda)	Programme focused on cultural, built heritage and gastronomic initiatives that take place in Oeiras.	Weekly. Wednesday. 7:45 a.m.	4–5 minutes.
	"*Terra a Terra*" (Land to Land)	Conversations and reports reveal the wonders of the landscape, the heritage, and the stories and characters from all corners of the country. Traditional knowledge, gastronomy, past and modern.	Saturdays in the morning. Since October 20, 2020, and for 12 weeks, it started being broadcast on Tuesdays and entirely dedicated to the theme Lisbon "Green European Capital".	120 minutes. Weekly. In the special edition dedicated to the theme Lisbon "European Green Capital", it lasts 60 minutes.
	"*Magazine Serralves*" (Serralves Magazine)	Exhibitions, music, dance, cinema, family programmes promoted by the Serralves Foundation.	Weekly. Thursdays at 5:45 p.m.	4–5 minutes.
	"*TSF à Mesa*". (TSF at the Table)	Brief information about gastronomy and restaurants.	Daily. 12:45 pm. The programme was suspended in July 2020.	3 minutes.

(*continued*)

Table 4.2 (continued)

Rádio Radio	Programme	Characterization	Schedule	Duration of the programme
	"Boa Vida" (Good Life)	Restaurants, hotels, exhibitions, activities, new trends, bars, places, foods, wines, what is in fashion but also the most hidden stories.	Weekly. Thursday. 6:45 p.m.	8–10 minutes.
Antena 1 (Public radio)	*"Vou ali e já Venho"*, (I'm Going There, and I'll Be Back Soon)	Local people. Activity promoters. "European cultural heritage, we will discover people and places, even those that exist only in tales or legends".	Monday to Friday 2:10 p.m.	2 minutes.
	"Visita Guiada" (Guided Tour)	Television and radio programme about the treasures of Portuguese cultural heritage.	Weekly. Wednesdays. Midnight	45 minutes.

(*continued*)

Table 4.2 (continued)

Rádio Radio	Programme	Characterization	Schedule	Duration of the programme
RR (Catholic radio)	"*A Essência do Vinho*" (The Essence of Wine)	Programme where wine, gastronomy, and culture are talked about. Here, you will discover stories told in the first person, in conversations with producers, winemakers, chefs, sommeliers, writers, artists, and thinkers from various areas and explore and communicate the best that is done in Portugal.	Weekly. Tuesdays. 11:30 p.m.	15 minutes.

create a favourable environment for a better perception of the events reported.

The media in general, and radio in particular, build information by giving space to information sources as a strategy for crediting messages. This logic is particularly important when it comes to themes that refer to a significant degree of specialization. The approach that the radio programmes analysed take to tourism refers to that same specialization by giving priority to history, heritage, gastronomy, and wines; for this reason the use of specialists in these areas is evident in the programmes analysed. It is through these voices that the interpretation of a given topic is defined. Thus, it is important to understand who is speaking in order to understand the framework the programme is utilizing and, also, because they are the ones that guide and transmit information.

In the case of the programmes we analysed, we found a proliferation of experts' voices in the areas being addressed. In this regard, we often found historians, university professors in the area of heritage, researchers, and curators, among others. These voices appear mainly in the programmes on built heritage, such as "*Encontros com o Património*" or "*Visitas Guiadas*".

We also found, with some frequency, voices from the local political field. Mayors appear in the programmes "*Agenda Cultural em Oeiras*" and "*Terra a Terra*", promoting activities and events that take place in the area of their municipality. This role of the mayor is sometimes mixed with the function of organizing events, thus increasing their presence on the radio waves through these types of programmes.

On the one hand, the evidence found in the programmes analysed is in line with media standards, whereby the media include sources from the political field that presumably strengthen their institutional power. The presence of voices from the political field is justified by their almost permanent availability to the media and, on the other hand, by signifying the reproduction of popular representation and decision centres for citizens (Meditsch 1999). The media coverage of the political field (Serrano 2002) translates into the demand on the part of politicians for participating in media spaces and thus gaining visibility for their actions. This happens in the programmes analysed in which politicians appear, giving a voice to events that are organized by them or in the geographic space that they manage.

There is also space in these programmes for entrepreneurs in the area of tourism, wines, and restaurants. These sources of information thus represent the tourism sector itself more directly and give a voice to those directly connected to the business.

A significant feature of these programmes that seems worthwhile underlining is the limited presence of voices from local populations. We find these voices mainly in the programme "*Vou ali e já venho*", by Antena 1 and in "*Terra-a-Terra*", by TSF. With regard to the promotion of the regions, priority thus goes to the mayors, local event organizers, and tourism promoters.

The reduced presence of voices from the population is echoed in some critical media studies that note the lesser presence of popular voices in the news and in the media in general, pointing to an underrepresentation of the community in the media space. As a rule, the media reproduce a closed circuit between politicians, businessmen, and advisers (Reiffel 2003). The radio programmes analysed are in line with this perception, giving priority to institutional and political voices and, in doing so, reducing the possibilities of a wider reproduction of the traditions and experiences of the community and places—which is relevant when the objective is promoting tourism. This aspect was also identified by Ledhesma when he mentioned that it is almost impossible to see programmes committed to local populations: "The goal always seems to be for companies and the government to pay for radio space and wages whenever possible" (Ledhesma 2014, 17).

The Themes of the Programmes

Listening to the programmes that make up our sample allows us to make a first observation. The radio spaces related to tourism in Portugal have, in their entirety, thematic diversity, ranging from built heritage to gastronomy and including sport and leisure, environment, and wines. This does not mean, however, that all programmes have this thematic scope. On the contrary, in our sample we found several programmes dedicated to exploring only one theme, such as "*A Essência do Vinho*" or "*Magazine Serralves*". Programmes dedicated to built, religious, and natural heritage were also found.

Heritage programmes are, in fact, of great relevance within our case studies, especially with regard to built heritage. These are programmes that address historical monuments, museums, castles, palaces, and that work, in many cases, to explore stories around characters and certain places. Even though such programmes often explore different elements, their starting point is heritage, in particular built heritage.

Cultural events, such as exhibitions, musical concerts, or theatre shows also occupy an important space on Portuguese radio waves, as a result of the institutional partnerships that radio stations have made. Of equal importance, the presence of gastronomy and wines is a constant in several programmes analysed, doing justice to the enormous tourism potential of the Portuguese gastronomy and wine sector.

The strategy for Tourism 2027 developed by Tourism of Portugal (TP 2017) reinforces the diversity of tourism resources existing in the country as a strong point. Cultural heritage, including gastronomy, culture, and the hospitality of the Portuguese people, are differentiating elements of tourism in Portugal and are highly valued by the people who visit us. The national marketing strategy focuses on people (residents, industry professionals, and visitors), and its aims for the future are for the sector to resume post-COVID-19 with the construction of a sustainable and safe destination (TP 2020b).

In line with this strategy, the regional tourism entities (there are seven in the country) and city councils (there are 308)—who are also public tourism agents—define their strategies and operational plans, based on the tourist resources and products with potential development in their territories.

From the analyses carried out, we found that the themes addressed reflect the tourist potential of the place, with an emphasis on built cultural heritage but also, on cultural events and activities that take place more regularly. Therefore, it is necessary to proceed with its dissemination among potential visitors in order to channel public interest and mobilize it for their enjoyment.

Less common in the programmes studied is the presence of lifestyle, health, and sport. In addition to TSF's "*Boa Vida*" programme, references to these themes are made only occasionally. An important feature that our analysis revealed is that the themes and focus of the programmes are local or national. We did not find any international approach or programmes with the theme of sustainability.

The Expressiveness of Radio and Tourism

Radio is a medium that constructs reality through sounds, be it via words, music, silence, or ambient noise (Crisell 1994; Hendy 2000; Balsebre 2004). This sound construction of reality has the effect of generating mental images in the listener from what he hears, and, in so doing, transporting him symbolically to the reported places, which may work as an excellent form of tourism promotion.

The combination of these expressive elements of the radio with the listener themselves creates semiotics of sound (Balsebre 2004) that translates into the sound reproduction of reality that is then interpreted in an image-based/visual way by those who listen. The sound of waves suggests a coastal location to listeners. The accuracy of the reproduction of places and events in the radio message is, therefore, dependent on the sound codes that it deploys, as well as on the fact that it will find in the listener a receiver able to decode and reconstruct that reality according to his/her cultural repertoire. Through sound messages, listeners recreate places and spaces.

The programmes we analysed, as they deal with themes related to places, spaces, and buildings, would benefit from the more assiduous presence of the various expressive elements of the radio language, insofar as, in the absence of the image, they would facilitate the creation of mental images in the listeners, taking advantage of the suggestive character of the sound (Soengas 2003). However, the observation made did not lead us that way. In fact, the analysis of our case studies allows us to see that such sound potential is not exploited by their authors. While it is true that most programmes have background music behind the voice, others present small musical excerpts during the breaks between interviews or as a separator of themes within the programme. However, we found that the presence of ambient sounds is practically non-existent in the programmes analysed, with the exception of the programme "*Vou ali e já venho*" from Radio Antena 1.

The analysed programmes rely, above all, on the voice: the voice of the presenter (who is sometimes a journalist) and the interviewees who are invited to the programme. In several examples, the interviewee assumes the role of a "*tour guide*" who guides the listener through the "route" of the space or building that is the subject of the programme.

The programmes analysed do not greatly explore the sound tools of radio language. There are very few programmes with the introduction of ambient sounds from the places, which is very important in the sense of transporting the listeners to the places of action. Radio is not enhanced in these programmes in its ability to generate contexts of imagination in the listeners about the spaces that are being reported. The absence of ambient sounds in most programmes is somewhat compensated—although not fully—by the descriptions of the locations, whether by the announcer/journalist or by the interviewees.

Music is also frequently used and appears as a background sound for the statements of the protagonists, or as a way to create a rupture between the radio spaces in the programme. Very rarely, traditional music from the places reported was used.

Most programmes use a similar formula that includes statements by the protagonists, descriptions of places, spaces, monuments, dishes, and so on by announcers/journalists. The statements of the protagonists appear in the programmes, sometimes with brief excerpts, alternated by the interventions of the announcers, sometimes in a running interview.

That is, in the absence of ambient sounds that allow the mental recreation of places by listeners, the role of this construction is played by words, which are the most used resource for the transmission of messages on the radio (Balsebre 2004). The programmes analysed adopted a dialogical strategy; that is, they promote interaction and dialogue between the actors in the programmes and this conveys emotion and closeness at the same time as, through the constant descriptions of the space, helping the listeners to mentally recreate the places of the events.

Conclusion

The aim of this exploratory study is to characterize the way in which Portuguese radio represents and promotes tourism, through the analysis of programmes that focus on this theme on the radio stations TSF, Antena 1, and RR.

We concluded that the theme most often addressed is built heritage. Concretely, most programmes are focused on promoting historic buildings, namely castles, museums, palaces, and historic villages. In terms of approach, we found that the programmes focused on a local and national context, with the aim of publicizing the tourism potential and cultural activities in each territory. We did not find any programmes dedicated to destinations or tourist resources outside the country.

The vision transmitted through the analysed programmes is that of public and political entities. In addition to these, tourism in radio is translated by specialists, especially in historical heritage. Local people rarely have a voice in these programmes. The programmes analysed are based on conversations with interviewees and tips from the presenters. Sound narratives were very rarely used.

On the one hand, this study will contribute to an understanding of the importance and the role of radio in the dissemination of resources, activities, and tourist destinations. On the other hand, the study can also contribute to understanding media coverage and trends in the selection of content for tourism dissemination, which, in view of the influential power of the media, can help stakeholders in the sector to understand consumer behaviour in tourism.

This is an exploratory study; to our knowledge there is no other study that has addressed this topic. A limitation of the study was the sample size used, as it was only possible to analyse a selection of programmes. For future investigations, it would be important to extend this analysis to more programmes from these radio stations in order to consolidate these results and to use other methodological approaches, namely interviews, to have the perception of the authors of programmes and/or tourism organizations.

Acknowledgements This work was financially supported by the research unit on Governance, Competitiveness, and Public Policy (UIDB/04058/2020) + (UIDP/04058/2020), funded by national funds through FCT—Fundação para a Ciência e a Tecnologia.

Works Cited

Al-khasawneh, Nermin. 2018. The Role of Tourism Media in the Promotion of Domestic Tourism in Jordan (Governorate of Irbid as A model). *Journal of Tourism, Hospitality and Sports* 37: 36–47.

Arino, Didier. 1999. Communication Image et Communication Produit. Comment Optimiser les Retombées? In *Communication Touristique des Territoires edited by Frédérique Fau and Michel Tiard*, 6–12. Paris: ESPACES.

Arnheim, Rudolf. 1986. *Radio*. New Hampshire: Ayer Company Publishers.

Baldissera, Rudimar. 2010a. Comunicação Turística: A Comunicação das Secretarias Municipais de Turismo da Rota Romântica, Vale do Sinos e Vale do Paranhana (RS). *Conexão—Comunicação e Cultura* 9 (17): 67–83.

Baldissera, Rudimar. 2010b. Comunicação Turística. *Revista Rosa dos Ventos* 2 (1): 6–15.

Balsebre, Armand. 2004. *El Lenguage Radiofónico*. Madrid: Cátedra.

Brandão, Vanessa. 2001. "Comunicação e Marketing na Era Digital: A Internet Como Mídia e Canal de Vendas". XXIV Congresso Brasileiro de Ciências da Comunicação—Campo Grande. Sociedade Brasileira de Estudos Interdisciplinares da Comunicação (INTERCOM).

Chebli, Amina, and Foued Ben Said. 2020. The Impact of Covid-19 on Tourist Consumption Behaviour: A Perspective Article. *Journal of Tourism Management Research* 7 (2): 196–207.

Conceição, Cristina Palma. 1998. Promoção Turística e (Re)construção Social da Realidade. *Sociologia- Problemas e Práticas, no.* 28: 67–89.

Crisell, Andrew. 1994. *Understanding Radio*. London: Routledge.

Daye, Marcella. 2005. Mediating Tourism- An Analysis of the Caribbean Holiday Experience in the UK National Press. In *The Media and the Tourist Imagination: Converging cultures*, ed. David Crouch, Rhona Jackson, and Felix Thompson, 14–24. New York: Routledge.

Fakeye, Paul, and John Crompton. 1991. Image Differences between Prospective, First Time and Repeat Visitors to the Lower Rio Grande Valley. *Journal of Travel Research* 30 (2): 10–16.

Fodness, Dale, and Brian Murray. 1999. A Model of Tourist Information Search Behavior. *Journal of Travel Research* 37 (3): 220–230.

Francesconi, Sabrina. 2014. *Reading Tourism Texts: A Multimodal Analysis*. Bristol: Channel View Publications.

Gotardo, Ana Teresa. & Ferreira Freitas, Ricardo. 2017. "Aquarelas do Brasil: Um Estudo Sobre as Campanhas Internacionais de Comunicação e o Turismo no Brasil". Anais do XI Congresso Brasileiro Científico de Comunicação Organizacional e Relações Públicas. https://bit.ly/38qowVT.

Heitmann, Sine. 2011. Tourist Behaviour and Tourism Motivation. In *Research Themes for Tourism*, ed. Peter Robinson, Sine Heitmann, and Peter Dieke, 31–44. UK: CAB International.

Ledhesma, Miguel. 2014. "Los Programas de Radio y el Turismo". https://www.academia.edu/27209570/Los_Programas_de_Radio_y_el_Turismo

Marktest. 2020. Bareme Rádio—3ª Vaga de 2020. https://bit.ly/2IaGmSd.

Marujo, Maria Noémi. 2008. *Turismo & Comunicação*. Castelo Branco: RVJEditores.

Marujo, Maria Noémi, and Fernanda Cravidão. 2012. Turismo e Lugares: Uma Visão Geográfica. *PASOS-Revista de Turismo y Patrimonio Cultural.* 10 (3): 281–288.

Meditsch, Eduardo. 1999. *A Rádio na Era da Informação*. Coimbra: Minerva.
OECD. 2020. "OECD Policy Responses to Coronavirus (COVID-19): Tourism Policy Responses to the Coronavirus (COVID-19)". https://bit.ly/2ZUlQv0.
Okaka, Wilson. 2007. "The Role of Media Communications in Developing Tourism Policy and Cross-Cultural Communication for Peace, Security for Sustainable Tourism Industry in Africa". Paper Presented at the *4th International Institute of Peace through Tourism African Conference on Peace through Tourism at Educators' Forum*, Uganda.
Park, Jihwan. 2015. "The Impact of Different Types of Media on Tourists' Behavioral Intentions". PhD diss, Florida International University, https://digitalcommons.fiu.edu/etd/1757/.
Reisinger, Yvette, and Lindsay Turner. 2004. *Cross-cultural Behaviour in Tourism: Concepts and Analyses*. Burlington: Butterworth-Heinemann.
Ruschmann, Doris. 2006. *Marketing Turístico: Um Enfoque Promocional*. 2nd ed. São Paulo: Papirus.
Schafer, Raymond Murray. 1969. *The New Soundscape*. New York: Associated Music Publishers.
Serrano, Estrela. 2002. *As Presidências Abertas de Mário Soares*. Coimbra: Minerva.
Soengas, Xosè. 2003. *Informativos Radiofónicos*. Madrid: Cátedra.
Tasci, Asli, and William Gartner. 2007. Destination Image and Its Functional Relationships. *Journal of Travel Research* 45 (4): 413–425.
Turismo de Portugal (TP). 2017. *Estratégia de Turismo 2027*. Lisboa: Turismo de Portugal.
———. 2020a. "Desempenho Turístico. https://bit.ly/32r7ZNR.
———. 2020b. Plano Turismo + Sustentável 20-23". https://bit.ly/3s6fTXd
UNWTO. 2017. "UNWTO Tourism Highlights: 2017". https://bit.ly/3jRvpS9.
———. 2020. UNWTO World Tourism Barometer May 2020 Special focus on the Impact of COVID-19 (Summary). https://bit.ly/30C6wlS
Xiang, Zheng, Dan Wang, Joseph T. O'Leary, and Daniel Fesenmaier. 2015. Adapting to the Internet: Trends in Travelers' Use of the Web for Trip Planning. *Journal of Travel Research* 54 (4): 511–527.
Yeoman, Ian. 2008. *Tomorrow's Tourist*. Amsterdam: Elsevier.

5

Digital Content Creation and Storytelling at the Time of COVID-19: Tourism Ireland's Online Film *I Will Return*

Alessandra De Marco

Introduction

The outbreak of the COVID-19 pandemic in March 2020 has had a devastating impact on the tourist industry. With travel restrictions in place in most nations, grounded air carriers and the forced closure of hospitality facilities, several countries went from "overtourism to no tourism in a matter of days" (Richards 2020, np). In May 2020, international tourist arrivals had gone down by 98% with US $300 million in losses (UNWTO 2020), while air companies had lost $419 billion in total revenues by October 2020 (IATA 2020). In the summer, with the easing of travel restrictions, people timidly returned to forms of tourism guaranteeing safety and social distancing, such as "staycations," local travel, and holidays in the outdoors (Vowinkel 2020). However, because of the duration of the pandemic, the future of the tourism industry continues to remain bleak (Gretzel et al. 2020).

A. De Marco (✉)
Cosenza, Italy

Lockdowns, social distancing, and other forms of restrictions redefined pre-COVID-19 consumers' habits, needs, education, work routines, and sociality, leading to an unprecedented growth in online shopping, entertainment, Internet, and social media usage (Donthu and Gustafsson 2020). Digital platforms became the privileged tools for coping with the unfolding crisis and the emotional distress derived from home isolation, fear of the virus, and other stressors. They became the primary source of information to navigate the highly unstable COVID-19 landscape; they offered a substitute for established lifestyles and forms of sociality (Garfin 2020). Within such a scenario, businesses in various sectors—including tourism and travel—sought to increase or maintain online visibility, brand awareness, and customer relationships. To this aim, they incremented their communication activities and produced new or updated content able to generate consumer sentiment and engagement due to its relevance to the moment of crisis (Balis 2020).

IT, the Internet, and social media provide the infrastructure through which every facet of the travel process—from place promotion to information-seeking and decision-making—occurs. Therefore, tourism and travel organizations were among the most active players catering to increased users' demand for digital travel content (Gretzel et al. 2020). In effect, digital content marketing aimed at providing prospective tourists with inspirational information at the pre-travel stage (and initiating the customer journey) is central to the industry (Minazzi 2015; Jiménez-Barreto et al. 2019). National tourism organizations (NTOs) generally use Web 2.0 and mobile apps content (360° videos, mini-films, Instagram stories, online exhibitions, image galleries, blog articles) or virtual reality to provide a preliminary experiential encounter between destinations and tourists able to generate a positive—albeit technologically mediated—tourism experience (Jiménez-Barreto et al. 2019). During lockdowns, virtual tourism on digital channels became a proxy for actual travel (Gretzel et al. 2020). Thus, NTOs updated, modified, or implemented their online content to offer users a variety of virtual travel experiences catering to various tourist segments.

For example, Great Britain's official tourism website www.visitbritain.com became the departure point for an "armchair journey" that could still offer users a "true taste of Britain" and transform the current moment of forced immobility into one of discovery and inspiration (Visit Britain 2020). The website featured expanded thematic sections with updated online editorial and image content (e.g. "Stories," "Local Flavours," "Adventure," "Culture," "Discovery," "Relaxation," "Unexpected," and "Fun") capturing selected distinguishing elements of the destination (Visit Britain 2020). Tourism Portugal, instead, readapted its early 2020 promotional video "Can't Skip Portugal," releasing it with a new voice-over and the title "Can't Skip Hope." The video treated an end to travel as an act of social responsibility, necessary to defeat the virus and to return to an improved normality (Visit Portugal 2020). Tourism Ireland devised a similar initiative, launching a short online film entitled *I Will Return* (Tourism Ireland 2020) to offer grounded travellers inspirational material for future journeys or, as the hashtag accompanying both this and the former video summarized, an opportunity to #DreamNowTravelLater.

These initiatives effectively demonstrate a generalized marketing approach to the crisis that sought to ensure brand visibility by offering stories that appealed to users' need to make sense of the COVID-19 crisis as a unifying experience equally affecting everyone (Sobande 2020). Arguably, storytelling provides a compelling way to organize and, possibly, understand experience, to generate connection among people, and to affect consumer behaviour via seductive, appealing narratives (Moin et al. 2020). Those stories, including travel ones, tapped into and built on what some call a digitally mediatized flow of affect (Döveling et al. 2018). The flow of emotions circulating through social media during lockdown articulated people's need to overcome loneliness and their subjective fears by finding human connection, a sense of community, and to share their hope for a quick return to an old, improved normality (Sobande 2020).

Within such a context, the present chapter will investigate the film *I Will Return* through a multidisciplinary approach grounded in digital marketing, destination branding, and social semiotic multimodality. The aim is to discuss how destination marketing officers (DMOs) used tourism audiovisual content to market Brand Ireland during the early COVID-19 pandemic by crafting a story that appeals to an imagined community of grounded tourists and their wanderlust. In addition to examining the film's formal and thematic features, the analysis will investigate the meanings and discourses it generates and disseminates about the destination, and will question whether it envisions any changes in tourism in the post-lockdown world. In effect, the COVID-19 pandemic has been challenging the dominant economic model and culture-ideology of hyper-consumerism, upon which tourism as an economic activity is premised, exacerbating the inequalities, the vulnerabilities, and the environmental unsustainability it produces (Harvey 2020; Higgins-Desbiolles 2020). Recovery from this crisis will therefore entail, among other things, reviewing tourism cultural paradigms, practices, and behaviours—not only to accommodate biosecurity requirements in the shorter run, but also, as tourism and hospitality scholars have been advocating, to render tourism more equitable and sustainable for local communities and the environment in the long term. To this aim, new stories and narratives are also required to imagine and communicate change in the way destinations construct and promote themselves (Gössling et al. 2021, Richards 2020, Stefanie et al. 2020, Sigala 2020).

However, this tourism film and the institutions that produced it do not envisage new travel stories and emotional configurations for a post-pandemic world. Indeed, the film does not reveal a preoccupation with the transformative impacts of the crisis on the industry. Rather, it appears to advocate a return to pre-COVID tourism models, and reaffirms consolidated discursive constructions of the destination, its people, and culture.

Tourism Ireland's Online Film *I Will Return*: Context and Theoretical Approach

On May 1, 2020, Tourism Ireland released a short online film entitled *I Will Return*, featuring a specially written poem on its major social platforms (Facebook, Twitter, and YouTube) (Tourism Ireland 2020a). The film, aimed at maintaining brand awareness through online visibility, showcases the "unspoilt beauty" of the country, and invites prospective visitors and fans to continue dreaming of travelling to Ireland during lockdown and to plan a visit to the country when travel is permitted again (Tourism Ireland 2020a). This initiative is part of the destination marketing campaign called "Fill your Heart with Ireland," launched at the end of 2018 to promote the country overseas through a mix of official brand and user-generated online content. According to the Board, as of September 2020, the campaign had achieved 143 million impressions, 25 million video views, and over 3 million engagements on Facebook and Instagram (Tourism Ireland 2020b).

Destination brands, such as Ireland, make extensive use of digital content marketing that features online promotional audiovisual material in order to construct, develop, and consolidate their Unique Destination Proposition (UDP) and to promote affiliation towards the destination (Morgan et al. 2004). Enticing, meaningful content is paramount to engage and attract tourists with the destination's promise of value—be it social, emotional, or experiential (Kotler and Gertner 2004). Indeed, videos are especially suitable for communicating both the physical and the emotional attributes attached to a destination brand and to shape visitors' perceptions of a destination by offering affective images of a place. As John Urry (2000) posits, videos make the intangible destination tangible, concrete, and visible. Thus, they deliver the promise of a meaningful experience that will arise from visiting. For this reason, more than other media texts, tourism audiovisuals are able to produce a strong emotional connection and a profound relationship between viewers and the destination (Hudson and Brent Ritchie 2009). DMOs use various types of audiovisual material across several channels to create a unique, coherent, and powerful destination brand image that sends authoritative messages about its values, attributes, and equity. Furthermore, audiovisuals most successfully realize the Attraction-Interest-Desire-Action (AIDA) model, which in tourism marketing ultimately serves to trigger prospective or returning visitors' interest in, and desire towards, the destination, to initiate their customer journey and finally to urge them to take action (i.e. to travel to the destination) (Morgan et al. 2004). Official tourism websites and social media accounts (primarily Instagram, Facebook, and YouTube) multiply the opportunities for encounter and interaction between tourists and destinations (Minazzi 2015; Jiménez-Barreto et al. 2019), foster brand affiliation through users' participation, user-generated content (UGC), and eWOM—electronic word of mouth—via content sharing. UGC, in particular, has proven an especially prolific form of brand promotion and of "cultural co-creation," whereby "co-created meanings (among both producers and consumers) fold back into the culture" (Tuten and Solomon 2015, 171).

From an academic perspective, a useful contribution to the investigation of tourism audiovisual promotion (Leotta 2020) as a distinct form of media texts can come from social semiotic multimodal analysis. Social semiotic multimodality provides a multidisciplinary approach to communication, and seeks to understand the social and ideological communicative role of a plurality of texts (from videos to toys), each using multiple semiotic resources with different affordances or representational possibilities (Kress and Van Leeuwen 2006; Van Leeuwen 2005; Kress 2010). This field of enquiry, pioneered by Hodge and Kress (1988), is based on M.A.K. Halliday's Systemic Functional Linguistics (developed in 1960), which studies language as a semiotic process, arising within a specific context, and fulfilling a social function. Just like language, other semiotic resources realize social functions, namely ideational, interpersonal, and textual (Eggins 2004). A text's communicative aim is to construct our experience of the world, create logical connections into it, and establish social relations, while at the same time organizing the message (Kress 2010). Social semiotics seeks to understand how sign-makers communicate their interests within a specific social, historical, and cultural context and, in turn, how communication creates an alignment between their views and those of an ideal (or as in the case of destination marketing, profiled) audience (Kress 2010). To this aim, it can make use of Critical Discourse Analysis (CDA) to unravel the ideological content of apparently multimodal neutral communicative texts (Machin and Mayr 2012). CDA, for example, has been applied to investigate the tourism audiovisual promotion of South Korea (Pan et al. 2016) and of New Zealand (De Marco 2017).

Several scholars have attempted to develop a social semiotic multimodal theoretical and methodological approach to videos and films using transcription and microanalysis (Iedema 2001; Baldry and Thibault 2006; Bateman and Schmidt 2012). Their efforts aimed at devising a sort of grammar of the moving image (Burn 2013) in order to capture the interplay of different modes from the smallest level of unit (the shot) to the largest (the video as a whole). Burn, for example, uses what he calls the *kinekoic* to analyse videos along two axes, the diachronic and the syntagmatic, at the level of shot and including speech, music, action, filming, and editing. Francesconi (2017) and De Marco (2017) have used this type of microanalysis for the analysis of tourism videos.

This approach compounds theoretical and methodological attempts in other disciplines to understand and describe the characteristic features of tourism audiovisuals. These include, among others, Pan's (2011) analysis of the structural components of a TVC and their role in the construction of a destination image; Pan et al.'s (2011) investigation of the *mise-en-scène*, its primary elements of signification, and their use in the construction of selected frames (salient aspects of a destination) to represent a destination's image and its attributes. Campelo et al. (2011) used content analysis to explore the visual rhetoric through which a destination conveys its sense of place. A useful combination of both the social semiotic multimodal microanalysis and the kind of content and macro-analyses mentioned above informs De Marco's (2017) study of the 100% Pure New Zealand TV commercials. The author critically examined how such TVCs signify destination brand New Zealand through highly mediatized images and narratives, carrying their specific discursive (ideological, political, cultural) dimensions relayed via their structuring modes and attendant affordances.

In what follows, a multidisciplinary macro-analysis and discussion of the online film *I Will Return*—inspired by the social semiotic multimodal approach—will be carried out in order to explore the peculiar combination of various modes and their affordances in this film, and how they realize Tourism Ireland's brand marketing interests in the current historical moment.

I Will Return: Analysis and Discussion

The online film *I Will Return* was created by the London agency Publicis-Poke, who brought together existing aerial footage of famous Irish locations (including Tara, Glendalough, Kylemore Abbey, and Powerscourt estate in Co Wicklow) and footage from the Official Tourism Ireland campaign video series, "Fill Your Heart with Ireland." In this latter series, released between 2018 and 2019 for TV, cinema, and online distribution, an actual Swedish couple of tourists, selected by the Board, travels around the country filming their journey via head-mounted cameras. The couple, equipped with wearable technology, recorded their physical responses and emotional reactions to various sites and sights. The tourism commercials eventually included footage of the locations that produced the highest heart rate responses in the couple (Tourism Ireland 2018). The video's originality emerges primarily from its use of tourists' biometric data, and more significantly, from the fact that it constitutes a hybrid between user-generated and branded content, which is meant to resonate more closely with prospective visitors and viewers. Indeed, the couple embody the ideal travellers to Ireland, personifying the primary target audience for the destination; at the same time, however, because they are real tourists visiting the country for the first time, viewers can identify with the video protagonists, who thus lend authenticity to the brand and to the online experience of the destination. Authenticity is constructed through a combination of actual and perceived attributes of the country and its people. According to Publicis' ECD, these include history and glorious landscapes that can generate the kind of dreamy mood required to escape the bleak reality of lockdown, a penchant for verse, and resilience in the face of adversity (Shots 2020).

For the purpose of the present analysis, I will use the term "online film" in keeping with that coined by Tourism Ireland. I see this type of film as a mini-video, that is tourism audiovisual promotion meant primarily to entertain online users during lockdown, while at the same time functioning as a form of advertising for the country. This type of "advertisement" has become increasingly common in the marketing of branded content, including that of destinations (Gong and Tung 2016). Based on Pan and Hanusch (2011) and Pan et al. (2011), the online film's main elements are video and soundtrack in the form of verse narration and musical score, and its duration is 50 seconds. Analysis focuses on the shot as the most basic unit (Iedema 2001). Manual transcription recorded 22 shots, lasting between 2 and 2.30 seconds, alternating aerial views of spectacular natural locations (10 shots) with those of the Swedish couple, their actions, and their emotional responses to the sites and views (12 shots). Transitions between location-only shots and those featuring the couple signal specific moments in the poem, thus contributing to expanding and enhancing the voice-over narration through the distinctive affordances of the moving image. As regards the *mise-en-scène*, several meaning-making elements of signification emerge that contribute to the country's representation. According to Pan et al. (2011), these include dominant elements, shot and camera proxemics, angle, colour values, density, composition, framing, character placement, and position.

At a social semiotic multimodal level, the video produces meaning through three main functions: ideational, interpersonal, and textual. The first function pertains to the construction of experiential meaning, that is an experience of the destination through its represented participants and the actions they perform (Jewitt and Oyama 2001). These include places or landscapes, people, and things. In particular, this film uses natural landscapes as *Carriers* of the destination's actual and symbolic attributes and values, as the *Goal* of the protagonists' actions, and as the *Phenomenon* to observe and feel. The two human represented participants, the Swedish couple, act as both *reactors* in front of the landscape and *actors* performing a number of tourist activities. The video is conceptual in nature, insofar as it offers a depiction of a country and of its actual and symbolic attributes. However, it is also narrative, as it provides a story of a past or imagined journey appropriate for a time of crisis. Interpersonal meaning, instead, explains the way participants interact either with each other or with the represented world of the analysed text, and the attitudes and opinions they develop towards the destination. It also clarifies the way they interrelate with viewers, and suggests the standpoint that the ideal viewers (primary, but also secondary, target audience) should adopt towards what is being represented (Kress and Van Leeuwen 2006). Finally, the combination of different modes across a diachronic and syntagmatic pattern (intersemiosis) creates textual or compositional meaning; consequently, video, sound, and voice-over mutually relay and multiply meanings through their co-occurrence and unfolding in time (Jewitt and Oyama 2001).

In this film, camera angle, movement, and size of frames create ideational and interpersonal meanings. The angle varies depending on the subject of the shot. Long to very long shots, through aerial cameras, are crucial for landscape and historical sites in order to capture the dramatic, awe-inspiring beauty and variety of the natural resources the country offers. These shots alternate with some eye-level angle shots using a panning camera, as in the case of a team of wild horses running. The Swedish couple are filmed through head-mounted cameras, which use eye-level (or slightly above the eye-level) angle with long to medium shots to either focus on the people immersed within the landscape or to capture their emotional responses through bodily language. The participants appear mostly frontally, centre-staged, using frontality to generate maximum involvement with viewers, or obliquely, to shift the attention away from them and onto the landscape (Jewitt and Oyama 2001). The man and the woman are either moving or performing a number of fun activities, such as cycling, hiking, camping, or rowing. According to Kress and Van Leeuwen (2006), when looking at the camera, represented participants *demand* the ideal viewers' attention in order to invite the latter to travel with them and share their actions and emotions, expressed through the couple's gestures and facial mimicry. By contrast, when they turn their back to the camera they present an *offer* to the ideal viewer by focusing on what the destination offers at an experiential or emotional level. Bird's-eye view, instead, liberates the viewers' imagination, allowing them to experience a virtual flight over the country, a virtual escape from their homes, and a form of symbolic power over the constraints imposed by lockdowns.

Cuts mark shot transitions. Light and colours vary, capturing the landscape at different times of the day and in different weather conditions. Only one night shot is present, with the wife pointing her camera from inside her tent towards her husband sitting outside by a fire. Overexposure occurs in an aerial shot of sunrise over the hills of Tara (00:11-00:12), in one shot showing the man on the top of a hill facing the sun (00:16-00:18), in the sunrise over Glendalough monastery (00:22-00:24), and in the closing shot with the slogan "Fill your Heart with Ireland" alongside a shamrock logo. Overexposure, as Pan et al. (2011) indicate, can contribute to a fantasy atmosphere, entirely in keeping with the dreamlike ambience of the film. On the contrary, the green of the gardens, of the hills, and of the meadows, the blue of the cloudless skies, the grey of the clouds, the high variability of the Irish weather, the white of the stone constructions and of the sheep fleece, provide a realistic representation of the country. The skilful deployment of the destination's iconographic assets, such as the colour green as the national colour, and sheep and wild horses as endemic fauna of the country, helps to construct the authenticity of the experiential representation.

Most shots have a stark density, that is, images do not present too many details. This tends to enhance the fleetingness of memories and dreams, although some shots may contain more elements, such as the view of the gardens with its flowers and garden landscaping (00:08-00:10), or that of Glendalough with its ruins. Shots with the couple mostly have moderate density and the frames reveal their ability to move freely, without impediment. They appear immersed in the landscape or interacting with it. This element conveys an extreme sense of liberty in harmony with nature, and presents the Irish landscape as an ideal destination to escape crowds, live a romantic adventure, or indulge in the silence of nature.

Soundscape is fundamental to the construction of ideational meaning through storytelling. It anchors and relays the meanings emerging from the visual mode, increasing their power of signification, identification, and engagement. Voice-over constitutes the most prominent aural element, working as a "figure," while the piano score continues to play in the background as the "field" (Van Leeuwen 1999). The actor's gentle, rolling Irish lilt lends local colour to the film; coupled with the soothing, relaxing tempo of the piano/string score, voice-over, and music work together to create a favourable atmosphere for dream and recollection, predisposing viewers to the film's message, and making the destination more memorable (Pan et al. 2011).

The verses recite as follows:

> I will return into her arms/Gently into the fold/To see her waters and her hills/And all the beauty she beholds/To feel the earth beneath my feet/The warmth against my face/And be welcomed in at every turn/Into her kind embrace/But alas for now I'll have to wait/To see my true love's form/But we all know that these green lands/Have weathered tougher storms/The wandering lanes and rugged cliffs/Her fields laced with streams/Will still be there after I awake/But for now they're in my dreams.

The poem deploys several verbal techniques proper of the poetic genre to hook the viewers. Its use of first person "I" seeks to offer a personal account that speaks of an affective and cognitive condition with which viewers can identify, while the "we" in line 11 instead refers to Irish people. Verses use rhyme, parallelism, and alliteration to create a lulling atmosphere, one in which you can close your eyes and visualize the country with all its distinctive traits (the wandering lanes, the rugged landscape). The story is of a dream, of memory and recollection, of a land, Ireland, personified as a woman, a now distant lover. The poem revolves around the structuring opposition presence/absence. Memory makes the loved one present through sensory recollection of physical presence, the latter supported by images. These include the embrace of the hills and ruins at Glendalough, the man standing with his feet firmly planted onto the ground (00:14-00:16) or raising his open arms towards the sun on the top of a hill (00:16-00:18), the welcoming of a flock of sheep surrounding the man in their embrace while cycling along a country road (00:19-00:20). You can even perhaps hear the water gurgling in the streams. Yet, this is nothing but a fantasy, a dream since the narrator cannot physically travel to his beloved and enjoy her in her true form.

The multimodal analysis of the film allows us to see how DMOs use the film's various modes and affordances to create experiential, interpersonal, and textual meanings to advertise the destination while telling a story. Yet, when considering the film in its entirety, it also helps to reveal its ideological function. Indeed, while leveraging the COVID-19 crisis to promote the destination, the film reinforces and circulates an institutionalized knowledge (Van Leeuwen 2005) of Ireland and conceptions of tourism pre- and post-COVID-19, which reflect established cultural tourism models and practices that the crisis challenges.

The video uses a recurring visual cultural repertoire to depict the destination based on a consolidated brand identity and image. These are the product of the politics of destination branding, whereby NTOs choose selected aspects of the nation, its history, and people to mobilize imaginaries of the destination with a strong emotional resonance (Van Ham 2001). As Clancy (2011) argues, Brand Ireland has been constructing its unique image as a rural, timeless, ethnically pure country, celebrating empty breathtaking landscapes and the friendliness of its people. This has now become a sanctioned and legitimate construction of the destination firmly grounded in visitors' minds. However, this depiction clashes with the actuality of a post-industrial, urban, secular, immigrant society suffering from population and consumption growth, overtourism, pollution, and environmental issues (Clancy 2011). In its branded form, the country becomes a sum of emotional and affective values that at the same time promise and realize tourists' quests for pleasurable and self-fulfilling experiences (Lynch and De Chernatony 2004). As such, Ireland caters to tourists' need for adventure, nature, escapism, and romance. The film frames the destination as a place where you can escape from the hustle and bustle of daily life, a land devoid of people and rich in wildlife. The tourist gaze (Urry 2000) is clearly at work in the depiction of an emptied-out landscape, as is a gendered, feminized version (Pritchard and Morgan 2000) of Ireland as a supple, sensuous lover yielding her secrets and her beauty to the male represented participant. Indeed, the husband appears in 10 of the 12 shots featuring the couple. When pitted against the ghostly landscape produced by the lockdown, such constructions gain further currency as the empty landscape and the sense of isolation it generates regain positive connotations.

Furthermore, to make the brand more appealing, DMOs piggyback and capitalize on the flow of affect produced by the disruption of travel and of sociality to confection a story that voices feelings of desire, powerlessness, deep yearning, and discomfort. The film exploits the theme of separation from loved ones resulting from lockdown, and the emotional responses that such a separation may produce, to confection a story about separated lovers, that is the destination and its visitors. Thus, the film builds on emotions such as separation, loss, and the desire to be reunited with our loved ones, to target individual tourists while fostering the notion of an imagined, global community of travellers all equally sharing the desire to resume travelling as in pre-COVID times. In doing so it mobilizes what Sobande (2020) calls commodified notions of connectivity and community, and legitimates a way of feeling about the pandemic as a temporary threat to the realization of the individual through travelling and sociality.

The hashtags accompanying the video on social media, particularly #DreamNowTravelLater and #WhenWeTravelAgain, further define this specific ideational, experiential, and textual narrative of the destination during lockdown. Indeed, in addition to being metadata used to group related content, facilitate topic searches, or draw attention, hashtags also constitute a technical affordance of the digital media, which fulfils all three metafunctions (Zappavigna 2015). In this case, DMOs use these hashtags to tag-mark the film because they represent a digital mode through which viewers articulate and share their views and emotions with other users, constructing an affective community. In so doing, the video participates in the proliferation of mediatized stories about the inability to travel at the time of COVID-19, while also substantiating specific constructions of the destination and projecting them onto the post-COVID-19 future.

The film speaks of an experience that has joined millions of people around the world; for this reason, it displays a heightened power to absorb and transport viewers who are prone to fantasize (Chen 2015). DMOs make the destination present in its absence by offering a form of entertainment that allows cognitive escape from lockdown. This brief story seems able to bestow order on uncertainty and, in keeping with the traditional story structure, envisions a "happy ending" (Moin et al. 2020) mutually reflecting and reinforcing then common expectations: a quick defeat of the virus, a return to embracing our loved ones, and a return to tourism as we knew it before the pandemic. In effect, the film does not envisage a change in established ways of tourism, and expresses nostalgia for a world unaffected by the impact that COVID-19 has had on local communities, biosecurity, tourism facilities, industry employment, and on travellers' financial situation. Rather, by directly addressing the individual viewer as a potential tourist, and by carrying the promise of a return to normality, the video appeals to the atomized consumer individualism that has been fuelling the tourism industry (Higgins-Desbiolles 2020). Consequently, this tourism film does not differ from pre-COVID-19 commercials, but rather uses COVID-19 as an element of storytelling that seeks to create an emotional alignment between users and brand values. As such, it continues to circulate virtual affective (re)presentations of destination Ireland as a branded place that fulfils consumers' aspirations for identity-construction through emotional and status-achieving tourism experiences (Morgan et al. 2004).

Conclusion

Tourism audiovisuals constitute a powerful tool in the hands of destination brands seeking to promote their values, affirm their online presence, and create engagement and affiliation among prospective and repeat tourists (Moin et al. 2020). The aim of the present chapter was to focus on the role and significance of tourism films as a digital content marketing tool to maintain destinations' online visibility and brand awareness during the early stage of the COVID-19 pandemic, when many countries were in lockdown. Within this purview, the online film *I Will Return*, released by Tourism Ireland during spring 2020, was selected and examined. A social semiotic multimodal analysis of the film was performed to investigate the structural features of the film, and to understand how it signifies and fulfils specific communicative goals about Brand Ireland through the co-occurrence of different meaning-making modes and their affordances at a precise historical moment. The analysis evidenced that the film promotes a narrative of separation and longing for travelling that caters to home-confined tourists' need for positive and heart-warming travel stories. This virtual journey through Ireland provides a technologically mediated experience that, by offering counter-narrative to the travel restrictions imposed by the virus containment efforts, also productively advertises the destination and its unique values. DMOs use the affect generated by the pandemic as a hook to connect viewers to the destination via a story that addresses and speaks to an imagined global community of travellers. However, by advocating a return to pre-COVID-19 normality, the film does not offer a meditation on the challenges and the disruptions that tourism as a socio-economic activity faces because of the combined effects of the pandemic and of the industry's structural flaws. The film thus fails to produce new and alternative narratives of the post-COVID phase that might eventually lead to innovative ways to envision and practice tourism and to promote destinations.

While focusing on one video at an early stage of the pandemic constitutes a limitation of this study, nonetheless, it aims to offer some reflections and to initiate further research, on the unique institutional, and communicative, actual and potential role of tourism films as official destination marketing tools in the current time, and for the post-COVID-19 tourist world.

Works Cited

Baldry, Anthony, and Paul J. Thibault. 2006. *Multimodal Transcription and Text Analysis: A Multimedia Toolkit and Coursebook*. London: Equinox.

Balis, Janet. 2020. "Brand Marketing Through the Coronavirus Crisis". *Harvard Business Review*, April 6. https://hbr.org/2020/04/brand-marketing-through-the-coronavirus-crisis. Accessed 28 Jan 2021.

Bateman, John A., and Karl-Heinrich Schmidt. 2012. *Multimodal Film Analysis: How Films Mean*. New York: Routledge.

Burn, Andrew. 2013. The Kineikoic Mode: Towards a Multimodal Approach to Moving Image Media. *National Centre for Research Methods Working Paper* 3: 1–25.

Campelo, Adriana, Robert Aitken, and Juergen Gnoth. 2011. Visual Rhetoric and Ethics in Marketing of Destinations. *Journal of Travel Research* 50 (1): 3–14.

Chen, Tsai. 2015. The Persuasive Effectiveness of Mini-Films: Narrative Transportation and Fantasy Proneness. *Journal of Consumer Behaviour* 14 (1): 21–27. https://doi.org/10.1002/cb.1494.

Clancy, Michael. 2011. Re-presenting Ireland: Tourism, Branding and National Identity in Ireland. *Journal of International Relations and Development* 14 (3): 281–308.

De Marco, Alessandra. 2017. *Destination Brand New Zealand. A Social Semiotic Multimodal Analysis*. Perugia: Morlacchi UP.

Donthu, Naveen, and Anders Gustafsson. 2020. Effects of COVID-19 on Business and Research. *Journal of Business Research* 117: 284–289. https://doi.org/10.1016/j.jbusres.2020.06.008.

Döveling, Katrin, Anu A. Harju, and Denise Sommer. 2018. From Mediatized Emotion to Digital Affect Cultures: New Technologies and Global Flows of Emotion. *Social Media + Society* 1: 1–11. https://doi.org/10.1177/2F2056305117743141.

Eggins, Susan. 2004. *An Introduction to Systemic Functional Linguistics*. London: Continuum.

Francesconi, Sabrina. 2017. Dynamic Intersemiosis as Humor Enacting Trigger in a Tourist Video. *Visual Communication* 16 (4): 395–425.

Garfin, Dana Rose. 2020. Technology as a Coping Tool During the COVID-19 Pandemic: Implications and Recommendations. *Stress & Health* 36 (4): 555–559.

Gong, Tianyi, and Vincent Wing Sun Tung. 2016. The Impact of Tourism Mini-Movies on Destination Image: The Influence of Travel Motivation and Advertising Disclosure. *Journal of Travel & Tourism Marketing* 34 (3): 1–13. https://doi.org/10.1080/10548408.2016.1182458.

Gössling, Stefan, Daniel Scott, and C. Michael Hall. 2021. Pandemics, Tourism and Global Change: A Rapid Assessment of COVID-19. *Journal of Sustainable Tourism* 29 (1): 1–20. https://doi.org/10.1080/09669582.2020.1758708.

Gretzel, Ulrike, Matthias Fuchs, Rodolfo Baggio, Wolfram Hoepken, Rob Law, Julia Neidhardt, Juho Pesonen, Markus Zanker, and Xiang Zheng. 2020. E-Tourism Beyond COVID-19: A Call for Transformative Research. *Information Technology & Tourism* 22: 187–203. https://doi.org/10.1007/s40558-020-00181-3.

Harvey, David. 2020. "Anti-Capitalist Politics in the Time of COVID-19". *Jacobin*. https://jacobinmag.com/2020/03/david-harvey-coronavirus-political-economy-disruptions. Accessed 28 January 2021.

Higgins-Desbiolles, Freya. 2020. "The End of Global Travel As We Know It: An Opportunity for Sustainable Tourism". *The Conversation*, March 17. https://theconversation.com/the-end-of-global-travel-as-we-know-it-an-opportunity-for-sustainable-tourism-133783. Accessed 12 October 2020.

Hodge, Robert, and Gunther Kress. 1988. *Social Semiotics*. Ithaca, NY: Cornell University Press.

Hudson, Simon, and J.R. Brent Ritchie. 2009. Branding a Memorable Destination Experience. The Case of 'Brand Canada'. *International Journal of Tourism Research* 11 (2): 217–228.

Iedema, Rick. 2001. Analysing Film and Television: A Social Semiotic Account of Hospital: An Unhealthy Business. In *Handbook of Visual Analysis*, ed. Theo Van Leeuwen and Carey Jewitt, 183–206. London: SAGE.

International Air Transport Association. IATA. https://www.iata.org/. Accessed 15 October 2020.

Jewitt, Carey, and Rumiko Oyama. 2001. Visual Meaning: A Social Semiotic Approach. In *Handbook of Visual Analysis*, ed. Theo Van Leeuwen and Carey Jewitt, 134–156. London: SAGE.

Jiménez-Barreto, Jano, Natalia Rubio, and Sara Campo. 2019. Destination Brand Authenticity: What an Experiential Simulacrum! A Multigroup Analysis of its Antecedents and Outcomes through Official Online Platforms. *Tourism Management* 77: 10–24. https://doi.org/10.1016/j.tourman.2019.104022.

Kotler, Philip, and David Gertner. 2004. Country as Brand, Product and Beyond: A Place Marketing and Brand Management Perspective. In *Destination Branding. Creating the Unique Destination Proposition*, ed. Nigel Morgan, Annette Pritchard, and Roger Pride, 2nd ed., 40–56. Oxford: Butterworth Heinemann.

Kress, Gunther. 2010. *Multimodality. A Social Semiotic Approach to Contemporary Communication*. London: Routledge.

Kress, Gunther, and Theo Van Leeuwen. 2006. *Reading Images. The Grammar of Visual Design*. 2nd ed. London: Routledge.

Leotta, Alfio. 2020. 'This isn't a Movie … It's a Tourism ad for Australia': The Dundee Campaign and the Semiotics of Audiovisual Tourism Promotion. *Tourist Studies* 20 (2): 203–221. https://doi.org/10.1177/1468797619894462.

Lynch, Joanne, and Leslie De Chernatony. 2004. The Power of Emotion: Brand Communication in Business-to-Business Markets. *Journal of Brand Management* 11 (5): 403–419.

Machin, David, and Andrea Mayr. 2012. *How to Do Critical Discourse Analysis. A Multimodal Introduction*. London: SAGE.

Minazzi, Roberta. 2015. *Social Media Marketing in Tourism and Hospitality*. Switzerland: Springer International Publishing.

Moin, S.M.A., Sameer Hosany, and Justin O'Brien. 2020. Storytelling in Destination Brands' Promotional Videos. *Tourism Management Perspective* 34: 1–12. https://doi.org/10.1016/j.tmp.2020.100639.

Morgan, Nigel, Annette Pritchard, and Roger Pride. 2004. Introduction. In *Destination Branding. Creating the Unique Destination Proposition*, ed. Nigel Morgan, Annette Pritchard, and Roger Pride, 2nd ed., 3–16. Oxford: Butterworth Heinemann.

Pan, Steve. 2011. The Role of TV Commercial Visuals in Forming Memorable and Impressive Destination Images. *Journal of Travel Research* 50 (2): 171–185.

Pan, Steve, and Folker Hanusch. 2011. Tourism TV Commercials: A Delicate Balance between Aural and Visual Information Load. *Journal of Travel & Tourism Marketing* 28 (5): 465–480.

Pan, Steve, Henry Tsai, and Jinsoo Lee. 2011. Framing New Zealand: Understanding Tourism TV Commercials. *Tourism Management* 32 (3): 596–603.

Pan, Steve, Carla Santos, and Seongseop Kim. 2016. Promoting Tourism, Projecting Power: The Role of Television Commercials. *Journal of Travel & Tourism Marketing* 34 (2): 192–208. https://doi.org/10.1080/10548408.2016.1156610.

Pritchard, Annette, and Nigel Morgan. 2000. Privileging the Male Gaze. Gendered Tourism Landscapes. *Annals of Tourism Research* 27 (4): 884–905.

Richards, Greg. 2020. "Tourism and Resilience: From Overtourism to No Tourism. Paper presented at the Summer School on the Management of Creativity". University of Barcelona, 30th June. https://www.academia.edu/43480944/Tourism_and_Resilience_Greg_Richards_June. Accessed 15 September 2020.

Sigala, Marianna. 2020. Tourism and COVID-19: Impacts and Implications for Advancing and Resetting Industry and Research. *Journal of Business Research* 117: 312–332.

Sobande, Francesca. 2020. 'We're All in This Together': Commodified Notions of Connection, Care and Community in Brand Responses to COVID-19. *European Journal of Cultural Studies* 23 (6): 1033–1037.

Benjamin, Stefanie, Alana Dillette, and Derek H. Alderman. 2020. "We Can't Return to Normal": Committing to Tourism Equity in the Post-pandemic Age. *Tourism Geographies* 22 (3): 476–483. https://doi.org/10.1080/14616688.2020.1759130.

Tourism Ireland. 2018. "Tourism Ireland Unveils the World's First Tourism Campaign Created by the Hearts of Its Visitors". Press Release, December 20. https://www.tourismireland.com/Press-Releases/2018/December/Tourism-Ireland-unveils-the-world%E2%80%99s-first-tour-1. Accessed 20 September 2020.

———. 2020. *I Will Return*. YouTube Video. 00:50. https://www.youtube.com/watch?v=K6Uj97nTFws&feature=youtu.be. Accessed 30 May 2020.

———. 2020a. "Tourism Ireland Invites Prospective Visitors to Dream of Future Adventures on the Island of Ireland". Press Release, May 1. https://www.tourismireland.com/Press-Releases/2020/May/Tourism-Ireland-invites-prospective-visitors-to-dr. Accessed 10 September 2020.

———. 2020b. "Tourism Ireland Seeks Inspirational Content to Share with Future International Visitors". Press release, September 9. https://www.tourismireland.com/Press-Releases/2020/September/Tourism-Ireland-seeks-inspirational-content-to-sha . Accessed 15 September 2020.

"Tourism Ireland Launches I Will Return Film from Publicis Poke". *Shots*, May 6, 2020. https://www.shots.net/news/view/tourism-ireland-launches-i-will-return-film-from-publicispoke. Accessed 10 October 2020.

Tuten, Tracy L., and Michael R. Solomon. 2015. *Social Media Marketing*. 2nd ed. London: SAGE.

United Nation World Tourism Organization. 2020. "International Tourism and COVID-19". https://www.unwto.org/international-tourism-and-COVID-19. Accessed 30 September 2020.

Urry, John. 2000. *The Tourist Gaze*. 2nd ed. London: Routledge.

Van Ham, Peter. 2001. The Rise of the Brand State: The Postmodern Politics of Image and Reputation. *Foreign Affairs* 80 (5): 2–6.

Van Leeuwen, Theo. 1999. *Speech, Music, Sound*. Basingstoke: Macmillan.

———. 2005. *Introducing Social Semiotics*. Abingdon: Routledge.

Visit Britain. https://www.visitbritain.com/gb/en. Accessed 20 October 2020.

Visit Portugal. *Can't Skip Hope*. YouTube Video. 02:18. 21 March 2020. https://www.youtube.com/watch?v=lFlFkGV207A. Accessed 5 October 2020.

Vowinkel, Susie. 2020. "Safe Escapes: How Consumers Are Traveling During the Pandemic". Think with Google. https://www.thinkwithgoogle.com/consumer-insights/consumer-trends/escaping-locally-summer-travel-trends/. Accessed 20 September 2020.

Zappavigna, Michele. 2015. Searchable talk: The Linguistic Functions of Hashtags in Tweets About Schapelle Corby. *Global Media Journal* 9 (1): 27–37. https://www.hca.westernsydney.edu.au/gmjau/?p=1762. Accessed 12 October 2020.

6

Virtual Tourism in the Age of COVID-19: A Case Study of the Faroe Islands' 'Remote Tourism' Campaign

Alfio Leotta

Since the 1990s there has been a growing attention, both within the industry and academia, to tourism applications of immersive digital technologies, such as Augmented Reality (AR) and Virtual Reality (VR). While AR overlays computer-generated perceptual information on real-world environments, VR creates virtual environments by the provision of either computer-generated or 360-degree real-life captured content (Beck et al. 2019, 586). Recently, a number of scholars have pointed out how technological advances in the field of VR can provide tourists with both a 'taste' of the tourism experience and a set of rich and trustworthy information (Rainoldi et al. 2018; Beck et al. 2019; Sarkady et al. 2021; Schiopu et al. 2021). From this point of view, VR has demonstrated significant potential in terms of the marketing and promotion of tourism destinations and experiences. The impact of the COVID-19 pandemic on the global tourism industry throughout 2020 generated even further interest in tourism applications of VR. While in the first half of 2020 international

A. Leotta (✉)
Victoria University of Wellington, Wellington, New Zealand
e-mail: alfio.leotta@vuw.ac.nz

© The Author(s), under exclusive license to Springer Nature Singapore Pte Ltd. 2021
D. Bonelli, A. Leotta (eds.), *Audiovisual Tourism Promotion*,
https://doi.org/10.1007/978-981-16-6410-6_6

air travel shrank by 90% (Debusmann Jr 2020), Google searches for virtual tourism increased sevenfold (Begley Bloom 2020). Some VR producers have attempted to create experiences capable of replacing traditional tourism activities. For example, Japan-based First Air, which bills itself as the first 'virtual aviation facility,' offers virtual flights, complete with boarding passes and in-flight meals from Tokyo to international destinations such as New York, Rome, and Hawaii (Debusmann Jr 2020). Although companies such as First Air are becoming increasingly popular, some scholars and practitioners remain sceptical about the ability of VR and other immersive technologies to fully replace physical tourist experiences (Itani and Hollebeek 2021). Mura et al. for example, suggest that although VR engages vision and hearing, tourists often seek multisensorial bodily experiences that also stimulate smell, taste, and touch (2017, 115). Similarly, Dewailly points out that VR is better suited to promote traditional tourism rather than replace it (1999, 41).

During the COVID-19 pandemic many Destination Management Organisations (DMOs) deployed VR as a marketing tool in efforts to plan for the gradual recovery of their tourism industries. Petra Hoderfer, the Chief Executive of the German National Tourism Board, which in 2020 launched a series of 360° videos of popular tourist destinations for Oculus Rift, claimed that: "VR and AR applications are essential elements in keeping interest in Destination Germany alive during travel restrictions, […] providing inspiration for real-world travel" (Debusmann Jr 2020). During the same period a number of other tourism boards, museums, and theme parks utilised VR, conceived for either web-based applications or head-mounted devices, for marketing and promotional purposes. However, most of these initiatives failed to get the striking international media visibility achieved by the Faroe Islands with their 'Remote Tourism' campaign.

Shortly after the beginning of the global pandemic crisis in April 2020, the Faroe Islands Tourism Board launched a new virtual travel tool called Remote Tourism. Remote Tourism consisted of a micro-website which allowed prospective visitors to control a local guide via a live video stream. More specifically, virtual tourists were invited to use a digital remote control to request the Faroese guide, who wore a hard hat with a GoPro camera mounted on it, to walk, turn, and jump within local attractions.

The Remote Tourism campaign made the headlines of news providers around the globe and was considered a major success as 700,000 online visitors, five times the number of people who visited Faroe in 2019, participated in a live stream tour of the islands between April and June 2020 (Visit Faroe Islands 2020).

This chapter will discuss the aesthetic, cultural, and technological factors responsible for the global success of the Remote Tourism campaign. The examination of the Remote Tourism virtual tours illustrates the ways in which immersive digital technologies can be effectively deployed to market certain destinations. This chapter will also discuss how the specific characteristics of the Faroe Remote Tourism campaign problematise existing definitions and understandings of virtual tourism.

Virtual Tourism

There is not yet a universally accepted definition of virtual tourism, as scholarly attempts to engage with this notion are often discordant (Mura et al. 2017). According to Bittarello (2008), virtual travel, understood broadly as the ability to move through place and space without the body, has been part of human history since prehistoric times. Mura et al. suggest that reading a book or watching a theatrical representation can be considered forms of virtual tourism as they allow readers/viewers to escape their mundane reality and enter alternative worlds (2017, 157). Similarly, building upon the work of Urry (2002), Larsen deploys the concept of 'imaginative mobility' to describe "armchair travel through books, images and television" (2006, 242). As Mura et al. suggest, virtual tourism has always had a presence in traditional tourism literature as theories on tourist motivation implicitly assume that corporeal travels are often anticipated by 'unbodied' journeys (2017, 147). Technology, however, has played a crucial role in enhancing access and opportunities for virtual tourism. Traditionally, research on this topic has connected the concept of 'virtuality' to technological hardware and software and, more specifically, online and digital tools. Robinson, for example, argues that the development of Street View on Google Earth allowed users to explore a virtual world and arguably dwell within it (2016, 163).

More recent discussions about virtual tourism, however, have been associated with the notion of VR. In the academic literature on tourism the term VR has been used inconsistently to refer to both specific technological devices and the experience itself (Beck et al. 2019, 589). In one of the first studies on the application of VR to tourism, Hobson and Williams provided the following definition: "VR is the computer-generated medium that gives people the feeling that they are being transported from a physical world to a world of imagination" (1995, 128). Beck et al. point out that historically VR has been associated with computer-generated virtual worlds (2019); however, more recently, real-world panoramic 360° images, also known as 360° VR, have become increasingly popular (Slater and Sanchez-Vives 2016). Slater and Sanchez-Vives (2016) claim that what distinguishes VR from other media are the concepts of immersion and presence. While immersion is a measurable aspect of display technology related to its ability to surround users and exclude physical reality, presence is not bound to any specific technology and describes the feeling of 'being there' (Riva et al. 2003). Some studies have found that higher levels of VR technological sophistication correlate to a higher degree of immersion (Diemer et al. 2015). Recently, several studies have engaged with the application of VR to tourism (Beck et al. 2019). Building upon their review of this area of study, Beck et al. formulated the most comprehensive definition of VR in tourism to date:

> Virtual Reality (VR), in a tourism context, creates a virtual environment (VE) by the provision of synthetic or 360-degree real life captured content with a capable non-, semi-, or fully-immersive VR system, enabling virtual touristic experiences that stimulate the visual sense and potentially additional other senses of the user for the purpose of planning, management, marketing, information exchange, entertainment, education, accessibility or heritage preservation, either prior to, during or after travel. (2019, 591)

Hobson and Williams (1995) and Sussmann and Vanhegan (2000) have pointed out how VR can allow tourists to visit protected or dangerous sites that cannot normally be accessed. However, significant questions have been raised about the authenticity of virtual travel and, more specifically, about its ability to replace traditional tourism experiences (Beck et al. 2019). Although VR has so far failed to become a widespread substitute to corporeal tourism, it is said to be especially beneficial for tourism marketing and promotion (Rainoldi et al. 2018). As a useful resource to preview distant destinations and experiences, VR can have a significant influence on tourists' decision-making process (Robinson 2016, 164). Rainoldi et al. found that VR is a more effective promotional tool than traditional visual media (such as tourism brochures) as it creates more realistic expectations about the destination (2018, 63). Similarly, building upon Cheong (1995), Rainoldi et al. also concluded that by providing a clearer perception of place, VR can increase the desire to visit the locations it depicts (Rainoldi et al. 2018, 63).

A number of scholars have conducted research on the best ways to construct VR worlds to attract tourists. Huang et al., for example, suggested that the effectiveness of VR experiences as promotional tools is determined by both their ease of use and their perceived usefulness, particularly in terms of gathering information about a given destination (2016). By contrast, Rainoldi et al. claim that the most effective VR experiences in a tourism marketing context should engage multiple senses and stimulate an emotional response while conveying information in a fast and clear way (2018, 64). Finally, Mura et al. argue that the perceived authenticity of the location is an important factor in the success of virtual marketing tools, and emphasise the importance of interactive digital tourist spaces in which destinations are promoted by virtual guides (2017, 157–158). The following sections of this chapter will examine Faroe Islands' unique application of VR to tourism promotion. Particular attention will be devoted to the specific cultural, technological, and aesthetic features of the Remote Tourism campaign.

Tourism Marketing and Promotion in the Faroe Islands

The Faroe Islands are a small archipelago located in the North Atlantic between Norway and Iceland with a population of just over 53,000 people. As a self-governing region of the Kingdom of Denmark, the Faroe Islands have an autonomous trade policy and an independent destination marketing organisation, Visit Faroe Islands. Since the late 1990s, the

Arctic region has been attracting growing numbers of visitors due to media attention to climate change (Kaltenborn 1998; Maher 2017), however, until the mid-2010s visitor numbers to the Faroe Islands remained among the lowest in Europe (Maher et al. 2014). Recently, the islands have attempted to diversify the local economy, which is heavily reliant on fishing, by transforming tourism into one of the country's key economic sectors (Visit Faroe Islands 2019). In 2013 the Faroese authorities introduced a new destination brand, 'Unspoiled, Unexplored and Unbelievable' with the goal of turning the country into a more visible tourism destination. The rebranding of the Faroe was complemented by an effort to improve local tourism facilities and increase accessibility to the islands, but most importantly, by the development of a series of innovative tourism marketing campaigns.

As Glen Croy points out, DMOs with limited financial resources need to capitalise on non-conventional-publicity tools (2004). The marketing department of Visit Faroe Islands comprises only five people and has a budget of US $2.2 million (ten times less than the estimated destination marketing budget available to their Icelandic counterparts) to cover both staff costs and advertising (Deighton 2020). According to Bárður Eklund, the digital marketing manager at Visit Faroe Islands:

> We see some other countries ... making films with the story of 'this is a great destination—come and visit us once you can', we cannot make those movies and push through those channels—we don't have those budgets. ... We can never compete with them. We have to think differently. (Eklund cited in Deighton 2020)

Most of the tourism marketing campaigns launched by Visit Faroe Islands since 2016 relied on both an unusual and innovative use of digital media and the strong involvement of the local community. According to Scheyvens and Momsen (2008), due to the small size of their countries, the DMOs of small island states can better incorporate local values into their policy and therefore facilitate the involvement of wider sectors of society in tourism development.

The first major campaign developed since the creation of the 'Unspoiled, Unexplored and Unbelievable' brand was 'Google Sheep View'. In April 2016 Visit Faroe Islands started campaigning for the country to be mapped by Google Street View (Hadderingh 2020). According to Durita Andreassen, the creator of the campaign: "When we started this project, we wanted Google Street View available in the Faroe Islands so we could share our beautiful country with the world" (cited in Hadderingh 2020). As part of this project the marketers decided to attach a 360° camera to the back of a sheep to capture images of the islands in Google Street View fashion. As well as being an important part of Faroese culture and economy, sheep are the main symbol of the country, as Faroe translates as 'Sheep Island'. In June 2016 Visit Faroe Islands posted the first sheep-made 360° video on their website and uploaded five 360° photos to Street View to Google Api. The marketers also circulated a press release together with Faroe Islands-branded Google cardboard glasses to some of the major news outlets around the world. The campaign went viral in just a few days, generating more than 7000 news stories, 42,000 web mentions, and estimated 2,000,000,000 media impressions (Visit Faroe Islands 2016). Google responded positively to the viral campaign by sending technicians and equipment to map the islands in street view. Both local people and tourists were also enlisted to capture footage by car, on foot, and other means of transportation (Visit Faroe Islands 2016). Google Sheep View won over 30 marketing awards, generated an estimated PR value of around 40 million euros, and led to an immediate surge in tourism to the islands (Hadderingh 2020).

Google Sheep View was followed in October 2017 by 'Faroe Islands Translate', another project which took as its premise the lack of Google's involvement in the country. The campaign took as its starting point the fact that Google Translate does not offer translations into Faroese, a language spoken by only approximately 80,000 people around the world. Due to the growing tourism market, the Faroese tourism board felt that there was an increasing need for this service, which would allow visitors to immerse themselves further in local culture. Visit Faroe Islands then partnered with Atlantic Airways, the national air carrier, to create Faroe Islands Translate. As part of this project, the words or sentences typed in by users in the Faroe Islands Translate website were translated by local Faroese volunteers for free. The volunteers recorded their translations as videos with their smartphones and uploaded them onto the website, thus creating a video translation database. Each time different users requested the translation of the same word, the same video would be shown (Visit

Faroe Islands 2017). Once again, the campaign circulated virally across the web generating further awareness of Faroese unique language and culture. Despite the success of the campaign, however, Google did not include Faroese into its translation services.

The success of the marketing campaigns created by Visit Faroe Islands led to a rapid and significant increase in the number of tourism arrivals to the country, which went from 68,000 in 2013 to over 110,000 in 2018 (Dickinson 2019). Similarly, international awareness of the Faroe Islands as a tourism destination increased drastically:

> Within the last few years, the Faroe Islands has developed from being small dots in the North Atlantic with little global awareness to a destination on the bucket list of travellers from all over the world. (Visit Faroe Islands 2019, 9)

In order to manage the potential negative effects of over-tourism, which in the late 2010s had been particularly apparent in similar destinations such as Iceland, in 2019 Visit Faroe Islands launched the 'Closed for Maintenance, Open for Voluntourism' campaign. In early 2019 the Faroese tourism board announced the country would close to the public a number of its most popular tourist sites for three days in order to protect their fragile ecosystems. At the same time, the country asked for applications from 100 volunteers, who in return for food and accommodation would take part in maintenance projects to help preserve the islands. The campaign was very successful as the tourism board received over 3500 applications for 2019. 'Closed for Maintenance, Open for Voluntourism' provided an opportunity for in-depth cultural exchanges between locals and visiting volunteers, but it also doubled up as a marketing campaign to encourage future visitors to respect the islands' delicate ecosystem (Dickinson 2019). Due to its success, Visit Faroe Islands decided to turn 'Closed for Maintenance' into an annual event, and the following year the tourism board received nearly 6000 applications. The 2020 edition of the event, however, had to be postponed due to the COVID-19 pandemic, as in March of that year the Danish authorities decided to close the national borders, a decision which also affected the Faroe Islands as a territory of the kingdom of Denmark (Hadderingh 2020).

Remote Tourism

In late 2019 Atlantic Airways announced the beginning of non-stop flights from New York to the small Vágar airfield, and 2020 tourism arrivals to the Faroe Islands were expected to reach record-breaking numbers (Leigh 2019). The country prepared accordingly by opening two new hotels earlier in the year, thus doubling the existing bed capacity. As already mentioned, however, the emergence of the COVID-19 pandemic in early 2020 forced the closure of the borders and caused a sudden halt to tourism in the Nordic archipelago. In order to maintain the strong global awareness of the country generated by previous marketing campaigns, Visit Faroe Islands launched the 'Remote Tourism' project. The Remote Tourism website allowed users from around the world to virtually visit the islands by controlling a local guide equipped with a live-action video camera. The virtual tours were scheduled at set times on the Remote Tourism website (www.remote-tourism.com) between April and June 2020 and lasted around an hour each. Users were presented with both a point-of-view video stream from the perspective of the local guide and a digital joypad which allowed them to control his/her movements in a 360° range. The joypad also featured a 'run' and a 'jump' button which let virtual tourists request the corresponding movements. Users took turns controlling the guide for a minute each and their movement requests were transformed into audio inputs communicated live to the guide through earphones. All the virtual tours were also recorded and uploaded onto both Vimeo and the Visit Faroe Islands Facebook page. The Remote Tourism website thus described the virtual tour experience:

> Just like a real-life computer game, you—the main player—will control the moves of the Faroese islander, who will not only explore locations on foot, but also take to the skies by helicopter, giving virtual visitors a bird's eye perspective on our beautiful island nation's steep grassy slopes, our 80,000 sheep and our unspoilt, wild and natural countryside. (Visit Faroe Islands 2020)

The campaign proved to be a major success, attracting 700,000 virtual tourists in 6 weeks and circulating virally on social media and international media providers. The Remote Tourism website was particularly popular among key markets such as the USA (54,983 visits), Russia (38,830 visits), and Italy (19,360 visits) (Southan 2020). The campaign won several awards and the Faroe Islands were given a place in the Community Connection category of the prestigious Lonely Planet Travel list for 2021 (Barlow 2020).

The success of the Remote Tourism campaign may be explained by its ability to simultaneously deploy an innovative use of immersive digital technology and satisfy psychological needs such as autonomy, relatedness, and the yearning for authentic experiences. The tourists' quest for authenticity has been the main focus of a large number of studies in tourism scholarship. In his seminal work on this topic, Dean MacCannell claims that tourists constantly seek authentic experiences; however, in most cases they encounter staged representations of events and cultures created by the tourism industry to meet their desires and expectations (1976). Building upon MacCannell, Wang (1999) suggests that tourists' perceptions of authenticity are the result of negotiated experiences between the tourist selves and the toured objects. According to Shaw and Williams, one of the major characteristics of the contemporary shift from mass tourism to post-Fordist modes of tourism consumption is the increased emphasis on the accumulation of social and cultural capital from the holiday experience (2004, 132). Contemporary travellers are demanding increasingly higher levels of authentic, experientially oriented opportunities involving more meaningful interactions with locals (Grayson and Martinec 2004). Paulauskaite et al. (2017) claim that the sharing economy, exemplified by companies such as Airbnb, emerged partly as a response to these new consumer trends which value interaction with and immersion in the local culture. Shaw and Williams (2004) also suggest that one of the defining features of the 'new' or 'post' tourist is a willingness to integrate technology in the consumption processes. Technology, however, does not necessarily hinder perceptions of authenticity, as post-tourists construct their own tourist experience by combining overlapping and disjunctive elements: the imagined (dreams, screen cultures), the real (actual travels, guides), and the virtual (myths, internet) (Campbell 2005, 203).

It could be argued that one of the unique elements of the Remote Tourism campaign which contributed to its success was the foregrounding of a technologically mediated, yet profoundly authentic, tourist experience. The VR experience offered by Remote Tourism is very unusual as it is not made possible by the 360° capability of the video camera, but rather by the users' ability to fully control and immerse themselves into the body and gaze of a local islander equipped with a traditional action camera. In other words, the uniqueness of the Remote Tourism experience is determined by the overlap and merging of the tourist gaze and the local gaze. The conflation between tourist and local gaze is enhanced by the gamification of the virtual experience. Deterding et al. (2011) define gamification as the process of contextualising game design outside its original domain. Similarly, Zichermann and Cunningham (2011) suggest gamification engages users and influences their behaviour by using game mechanics in areas other than a traditional gaming context. Visit Faroe Islands explicitly presented Remote Tourism as a gamified experience, the main appeal of which consisted of the possibility to control a local guide ("Just like a real-life computer game, you—the main player—will control the moves of the Faroese islander").

In their examination of the gamification of tourism, Xu et al. suggest that "in a carefully designed gamified system, tourists […] have the freedom to play someone else, to enhance their fantasy experiences in a fun, and more stimulating way, leading to a higher level of satisfaction" (2017, 249). Similarly, Poncin and Garnier (2012) argue that the presence of an avatar is crucial to the gaming experience as the player imagines the avatar as a substitute for himself or herself. While serving as surrogate of the player, the avatar is also the mechanism through which s/he can experiment with multiple identities and allow for the expression of an authentic self (Xu et al. 2017). The gamification of the Remote Tourism virtual experience is further emphasised by both the foregrounding of a digital joypad, which simulates the appearance of a traditional game console controller, and the use of the first-person point of view (POV). The subjective POV camera shot is a common visual storytelling technique used in film and TV. The reliance on an avatar's first-person POV is also a key element of contemporary video games design and experiences. The adoption of an avatar's POV provides gamers with the opportunity to represent themselves in the video game environment. In turn, scholars have suggested such representations are crucial to both improve game immersion and increase users' involvement in the overall experience (Ferchaud and Sanders 2018). At the visual level, the first-person POV is realised through the use of an action video camera mounted on the local volunteer's hard hat. The most common image used to promote the Remote Tourism campaign was a photo of a local young woman wearing a traditional Faroese woollen jumper and yellow hard hat with a GoPro mounted on it. The GoPro and, implicitly, the view of the land offered by it, became a crucial visual signifier of the campaign, thus contributing to the conflation of the tourist and local gaze. According to Chalfen (2014), the GoPro camera allows users to capture 'exciting' and unexpected scenes of actions and locations seldom seen, and offers fresh, original, and memorable perspectives. While the tourist gaze tends to domesticate touristscapes by making them seem easily reachable and familiar, the GoPro Gaze strives to maintain the 'wildness' of a site by actively selecting seemingly untamed places (Vannini and Stewart 2017, 153). From this point of view, the GoPro Gaze enhances the notion of presence and being, thereby 'allowing a viewer to believe he/she is/was there' (Chalfen 2014) together with or even in lieu of the producers of the footage (Vannini and Stewart 2017).

The combined deployment of local volunteer guides, an interactive and gamified virtual experience, and the aesthetics of the GoPro Gaze contributed to enhance the authenticity of Remote Tourism. But as well as catering to virtual visitors' yearning for authenticity, Remote Tourism was also capable of fulfilling other important psychological needs. In their study about the application of Self-Determination Theory (SDT) to the understanding of VR technology in tourism marketing, Huang et al. suggest that the satisfaction of certain psychological needs leads to sustained engagement in virtual contexts (2016). SDT posits that the fulfilment of psychological needs such as competence, autonomy, and relatedness determines the underlying motivational mechanism that energises individuals to pursue an activity, therefore directing their behaviour (Huang et al. 2016). Wang et al. define autonomy as the need to feel ownership of one's behaviour, competence as the need to experience mastery of a given situation, and relatedness as the need to connect with others (2019).

Remote Tourism permitted users to feel ownership of their behaviour as it allowed them to move relatively freely within the Faroese landscape. Although the freedom of exploring local space was limited by the need to preserve the physical safety of the guide, users were able to actively subvert established or suggested itineraries and go 'off the beaten tracks'. While in their verbal description of the local landscape the guide often implicitly or explicitly suggested certain directions, the design and anonymity of the user interface allowed users to counter the local's preferred path. Users often opted to pause hikes or retrace their steps to have another look at certain attractions. In other instances, by contrast, virtual tourists wanted to explore objects or areas located at the periphery of the frame. The ease of use of Remote Tourism, which capitalised on users' familiarity with video games' interfaces, reinforced the virtual tourists' sense of technological competence. In turn, through the mediation of the gamified experience and the framing of the land as a playground, Remote Tourism also provided users the opportunity to cognitively and symbolically master a wild and unfamiliar environment. Finally, the mechanics of the virtual tourist experience fostered relatedness, as users were asked to interact with the local guides and, implicitly, with other virtual tourists too. As already mentioned, users took turns controlling the local avatar, and new users were routinely acknowledged and welcomed by the guides when they took control of their movements. The guides talked about the significance of the physical environment in their immediate field of view and often provided users with suggestions about potential itineraries (i.e. "if we go right we would be able to see"). At times users complied with the guide's suggestions while in other instances they overtly subverted them, but the interface always fostered either implicit or explicit exchange between guides and tourists. Similarly, while waiting for their turn to control the local avatar, users often witnessed the interaction between the guide and other users. Such observations would also offer opportunities for indirect and mediated interactions between virtual tourists. For example, by requesting the guide to retrace their steps and spend more time contemplating a certain view, users had the opportunity to undo or resist the choices of other virtual tourists.

The videos of the completed virtual tours were uploaded onto the Visit Faroe Islands Vimeo channel and Facebook page, where they could be freely accessed by other users after the end of the campaign. As such, the videos gained a hybrid status situated in between amateur tourist videos and official promotional material. The Faroe Islands reopened their borders to neighbouring countries such as Denmark, Norway, Iceland, and Germany without the need to quarantine on 15 June 2020, a few days before the end of Remote Tourism, and although at the time of writing the country is only expected to receive 20–30% of the annual visitors forecasted at the beginning of the year, the director of the Tourism Board Gudrid Hoejgaard remained optimistic about the future (Murray 2020). The viral success of the Remote Tourism campaign played a crucial role in reinforcing the country's destination image in a moment of crisis, and it is very likely that in the near future it will provide the Faroe Islands with a competitive edge over other locations in the sub-arctic region.

Conclusions

Remote Tourism launched by Visit Faroe Islands in the wake of the global crisis caused by the COVID-19 pandemic has been one of the most innovative VR marketing campaigns in the industry's recent history. The innovative nature of Remote Tourism is a direct consequence of the financial 'poverty' of the local tourism board that needs to rely heavily on both non-conventional publicity tools and the involvement of the local community. Since the mid-2010s the Faroe Islands have created for themselves a strong reputation in innovative tourism marketing which capitalises on both new digital media and the islands' own political, geographical, and cultural marginality within the global market. The development of Google Sheep View and Faroe Islands Translate is strictly connected to the process of (symbolically and literally) putting the country on the map. In turn, the success of these campaigns (as well as 'Closed for Maintenance, Open for Voluntourism') was made possible by the fact that they provided a strong sense of interaction between tourists and the local community. Similarly, Remote Tourism builds upon the country's reputation as a distant and geographically small destination that can offer truly authentic travelling experiences.

Remote Tourism is innovative in technological and aesthetic terms. At the technological level, the Remote Tourism tool is able to offer an immersive virtual tourism experience without relying on the technological apparatuses (360° cameras, 3D computer-generated imagery, etc.) traditionally associated with the notion of VR. At the aesthetic level, Remote Tourism problematises established notions of the tourist gaze by conflating video game mechanics, GoPro aesthetics, and interaction with the landscape. In Remote Tourism immersive digital technology is deployed to foster the perception of an authentic encounter with the land and its inhabitants. In turn, the promise of such virtual encounters contributed to and generated further international awareness about the Faroe Islands as a destination and reinforced its 'Unspoiled, Unexplored and Unbelievable' brand. From this point of view, the examination of the Remote Tourism campaign sheds new light on the way in which virtual tourism experiences can be used as effective marketing tools by small DMOs.

Works Cited

Barlow, Nigel. 2020. "The Faroe Islands Set to Transform Travel, According to the Lonely Planet Best in Travel List 2021." *About Manchester*, 17 November 2020. https://aboutmanchester.co.uk/the-faroe-islands-set-to-transform-travel-according-to-the-lonely-planet-best-in-travel-list-2021/

Beck, Julia, Mattia Rainoldi, and Roman Egger. 2019. Virtual Reality in Tourism: A State-of-the-art Review. *Tourism Review* 74 (3): 586–612. https://doi.org/10.1108/TR-03-2017-0049.

Begley Bloom, Laura. 2020. "Ranked: The World's 15 Best Virtual Tours to Take During Coronavirus." *Forbes*, 27 April 2020. https://www.forbes.com/sites/laurabegleybloom/2020/04/27/ranked-worlds-15-best-virtual-tours-coronavirus/

Bittarello, Maria Beatrice. 2008. Another time, Another Space: Virtual Worlds, Myths and Imagination. *Online—Journal of Religions on the Internet* 3 (1): 246–266. https://doi.org/10.11588/rel.2008.1.396.

Campbell, Neil. 2005. Producing America. In *The Media and the Tourist Imagination*, ed. David Crouch, Rhona Jackson, and Felix Thompson, 198–214. London: Routledge.

Chalfen, Richard. 2014. 'Your Panopticon or Mine?' Incorporating Wearable Technology's Glass and GoPro into Visual Social Science. *Visual Studies* 29: 299–310. https://doi.org/10.1080/1472586X.2014.941547.

Cheong, Roger. 1995. The Virtual Threat to Travel and Tourism. *Tourism Management* 16 (6): 417–422. https://doi.org/10.1016/0261-5177(95)00049-T.

Croy, W. Glen. 2004. The Lord of the Rings, New Zealand, and Tourism: Image Building with Film. *Monash University Department of Management Working Paper* Series 1, no. 21.

Debusmann Jr, Bernd. 2020. "Coronavirus: Is Virtual Reality Tourism about to Take Off?." *BBC*, 30 October 2020. https://www.bbc.com/news/business-54658147

Deighton, Katie. 2020. Meet the Former Journalist Marketing the Faroe Islands on a Shoestring. *The Drum* (27 April 2020) https://www.thedrum.com/news/2020/04/27/meet-the-former-journalist-marketing-the-faroe-islands-shoestring.

Deterding, Sebastian, Dan Dixon, Rilla Khaled, and Lennart Nacke. 2011. "From Game Design Elements to Gamefulness: Defining 'Gamification'." In *Proceedings of the 15th International Academic MindTrek Conference: Envisioning Future Media Environments*, 9-15.

Dewailly, Jean-Michel. 1999. Sustainable Tourist Space: From Reality to Virtual Reality? *Tourism Geographies* 1 (1): 41–55. https://doi.org/10.1080/14616689908721293.

Dickinson, Greg. "The Faroe Islands to 'Close for Maintenance' in 2020." *Telegraph*, 12 November 2019. https://www.telegraph.co.uk/travel/destinations/europe/faroe-islands/articles/faroe-islands-overtourism-closed-for-maintenance/

Diemer, Julia, Georg W. Alpers, Henrik M. Peperkorn, Youssef Shiban, and Andreas Mühlberger. 2015. The Impact of Perception and Presence on Emotional Reactions: A Review of Research in Virtual Reality. *Frontiers in Psychology* 6 (26): 1–9. https://doi.org/10.3389/fpsyg.2015.00026.

Ferchaud, Arienne, and Meghan S. Sanders. 2018. Seeing Through the Avatar's Eyes: Effects of Point-of-View and Gender Match on Identification and Enjoyment. *Imagination, Cognition and Personality* 38 (2): 82–105. https://doi.org/10.1177/0276236618761372.

Grayson, Kent, and Radan Martinec. 2004. Consumer Perceptions of Iconicity and Indexicality and their Influence on Assessments of Authentic Market Offerings. *Journal of Consumer Research* 31 (2): 296–312. https://doi.org/10.1086/422109.

Hadderingh, Ellen. 2020. "Making places: How the Faroe Islands Became a Visible Tourist Destination." MSc Tourism, Society and Environment, Wageningen University.

Huang, Yu Chih, Kenneth Frank Backman, Sheila J. Backman, and Lan Lan Chang. 2016. Exploring the Implications of Virtual Reality Technology in Tourism Marketing: An Integrated Research Framework. *International Journal of Tourism Research* 18 (2): 116–128. https://doi.org/10.1002/jtr.2038.

Itani, Omar S., and Linda D. Hollebeek. 2021. Light at the end of the tunnel: Visitors' Virtual Reality (versus in-person) Attraction Site Tour-related Behavioral Intentions During and post-COVID-19. *Tourism Management* 84: 1–12. https://doi.org/10.1016/j.tourman.2021.104290.

Kaltenborn, Bjørn P. 1998. Effects of Sense of Place on Responses to Environmental Impacts: A Study among Residents in Svalbard in the Norwegian High Arctic. *Applied Geography* 18 (2): 169–189. https://doi.org/10.1016/S0143-6228(98)00002-2.

Larsen, Jonas. 2006. Geographies of Tourist Photography. In *Geographies of Communication: The Spatial Turn in Media Studies*, ed. André Jansson and Jesper Falkheimer, 241–257. Gothenburg: Nordicom.

Leigh, Gabriel. 2019. "Faroe Islands Tourism Boom: Nonstop New York Flights Coming Soon." *Forbes*, 27 November 2019. https://www.forbes.com/sites/gabrielleigh/2019/11/27/faroe-islands-tourism-boom-nonstop-new-york-flights-coming-soon/?sh=1a91e0ed6d64

MacCannell, Dean. 1976. *The Tourist: A New Theory of the Leisure Class*. London: Macmillan Press Ltd.

Maher, Patrick T. 2017. Tourism Futures in the Arctic. In *The Interconnected Arctic—UArctic Congress 2016*, ed. Kirsi Latola and Hannelle Savela, 213–220. Cham: Springer.

Maher, Patrick T., Hans Gelter, Kevin Hillmer-Pegram, Gestur Hovgaard, John Hull, G. T. Jóhannesson, A. Karlsdóttir, Outi Rantala, and Albina Pashkevich. 2014. "Arctic Tourism: Realities and Possibilities." *Arctic Yearbook 2014*, 290-306. https://arcticyearbook.com/arctic-yearbook/2014

Murray, Adrienne. 2020. "The Islands that Want Tourists as well as Fish." *BBC*, 5 August 2020. https://www.bbc.com/news/business-53593137

Paulauskaite, Dominyka, Powell Raymond, J. Andres Coca-Stefaniak, and Alastair M. Morrison. 2017. Living like a Local: Authentic Tourism Experiences and the Sharing Economy. *International Journal of Tourism Research* 19 (6): 619–628. https://doi.org/10.1002/jtr.2134.

Poncin, Ingrid, and Marion Garnier. 2012. Avatar Identification on a 3D Commercial Website: Gender Issues. *Journal of Virtual Worlds Research* 5 (3): 1–20. https://doi.org/10.4101/jvwr.v5i3.6321.

Rainoldi, Mattia, Veronika Driescher, Alina Lisnevska, Daria Zvereva, Anna Stavinska, Jennifer Relota, and Roman Egger. 2018. Virtual Reality: An Innovative Tool in Destinations' Marketing. *The Gaze: Journal of Tourism and Hospitality* 9: 53–68. https://doi.org/10.3126/gaze.v9i0.19721.

Riva, Giuseppe, Fabrizio Davide, and Wijnand A. Isselsteijn. 2003. *Being There: Concepts, Effects and Measurement of User Presence in Synthetic Environments.* Amsterdam: IOS Press.

Robinson, Peter. 2016. Developing the E-mediated Gaze. In *Mediating the Tourist Experience: From Brochures to Virtual Encounters*, ed. Jo-Anne Lester and Caroline Scarles, 155–170. London: Routledge.

Sarkady, Daniel, Larissa Neuburger, and Roman Egger. 2021. Virtual Reality as a Travel Substitution Tool During COVID-19. In *In Information and Communication Technologies in Tourism 2021*, ed. Wolfgang Wörndl, Chulmo Koo, and Jason L. Stienmetz. Cham: Springer. https://doi.org/10.1007/978-3-030-65785-7_44.

Scheyvens, Regina, and Janet Momsen. 2008. Tourism in Small Island States: From Vulnerability to Strengths. *Journal of Sustainable Tourism* 16 (5): 491–510. https://doi.org/10.1080/09669580802159586.

Schiopu, Andreea F., Remus I. Hornoiu, Mihaela A. Padurean, and Ana-Maria Nica. 2021. Virus Tinged? Exploring the Facets of Virtual Reality Use in Tourism as a Result of the COVID-19 Pandemic. *Telematics and Informatics* 60: 1–20. https://doi.org/10.1016/j.tele.2021.101575.

Shaw, Gareth, and Allan Williams. 2004. *Tourism and Tourist Spaces.* London: Sage.

Southan, Jenny. 2020. "Faroe Islands Welcomes Thousands of Virtual Tourists via Live Video Stream." *Globetrender*, 7 June 2020. https://globetrender.com/2020/06/07/faroe-islands-virtual-travel-remote-tourism/

Sussmann, Silvia and Hugo Vanhegan. 2000. "Virtual Reality and the Tourism Product: Substitution or Complement?" In *Proceedings of the 8th European Conference on Information Systems* 2, edited by Hans Robert Hansen, Martin Bichler and Harald Mahrer, 1077-1083.

Urry, John. 2002. *The Tourist Gaze.* London: Sage.

Vannini, Phillip, and Lindsay M. Stewart. 2017. The GoPro Gaze. *Cultural Geographies* 24 (1): 149–155. https://doi.org/10.1177/1474474016647369.

Visit Faroe Islands. 2016. "Sheepview PR & Case Films." https://visitfaroeislands.com/sheepview360/sheepview-pr-case-films/

———. 2017. "Faroe Islands Translate." https://www.faroeislandstranslate.com/#!/en/about-the-project

———. 2019. "Join the Preservolution! A Sustainable Tourism Development Strategy for the Faroe Islands Towards 2025." https://www.visitfaroeislands.com/join-the-preservolution/strategy/

———. 2020. "Remote Tourism." https://visitfaroeislands.com/remote-tourism/

Wang, Ning. 1999. Rethinking Authenticity in Tourism Experience. *Annals of Tourism Research* 26 (2): 349–370. https://doi.org/10.1016/S0160-7383(98)00103-0.

Wang, C.K. John, Woon Chia Liu, Ying Hwa Kee, and Lit Khoon Chian. 2019. Competence, Autonomy, and Relatedness in the Classroom: Understanding Students' Motivational Processes Using the Self-Determination Theory. *Heliyon* 5 (7): e01983. https://doi.org/10.1016/j.heliyon.2019.e01983.

Xu, Feifei, Dimitrios Buhalis, and Jessika Weber. 2017. Serious Games and the Gamification of Tourism. *Tourism Management* 60: 244–256. https://doi.org/10.1016/j.tourman.2016.11.020.

Zichermann, Gabe, and Christopher Cunningham. 2011. *Gamification by Design: Implementing Game Mechanics in Web and Mobile Apps*. Newton, MA: O'Reilly Media, Inc.

Part II

Recent Developments
in Screen-Induced Tourism

7

Fabulous Locations: Tourism and Fantasy Films in Italy

Giulia Lavarone

Introduction

Fiction films and TV series are used extensively for the purposes of tourism promotion, and their potential to induce tourist flows is widely recognized (Tooke and Baker 1996; Riley et al. 1998; Beeton 2005). Compared to non-fiction works, their handling of place is generally less concerned with the needs of verisimilitude. This brings challenges for their exploitation in terms of tourism promotion, as well as the development of tourist products and the sustainable management of heritage sites used for filming. The fantasy genre, free to reach the highest degree of fictionality, represents an interesting starting point to discuss some relevant questions related to the research on tourism induced by films, such as the search for authenticity in the tourist experience and the relationship of film tourists with the identity and heritage of the place. Since Beeton's (2005) seminal work on film-induced tourism, fantasy films and

G. Lavarone (✉)
Università di Padova, Padova, Italy
e-mail: giulia.lavarone@unipd.it

TV series have been widely discussed by the academic literature in this field, with a specific focus on film series such as *The Lord of the Rings* (Jackson 2001–2003) (hereon *LotR*) in New Zealand, *Harry Potter* (Columbus; Cuarón; Newell; Yates 2001–2011) in Great Britain, and *Star Wars* (Lucas; Kershner; Marquand 1977–1983) in Tunisia, or the HBO television series *Game of Thrones* (2011–2019) (hereon *GoT*), filmed across several European countries.

In the first part, this chapter will briefly introduce film tourism, defined as tourist phenomena linked to film and TV programmes, often stimulated by deliberate actions of audiovisual tourism promotion. It will then discuss some pivotal issues emerging within this interdisciplinary research field (Connell 2012), with a specific focus on the fantasy genre. Film tourism will be mainly discussed from a cultural perspective, as this chapter situates itself in the disciplinary framework of film studies, yet insights into tourist marketing and management will also be provided. The aim is to critically review selected academic literature in order to point out how specific genre features might impact the use of these films for tourism promotion, as well as their impact on product development, heritage management, and tourists' experiences.

The second part will provide an exploration of the relationship between tourism and fantasy films in the contemporary Italian context. After introducing the cases of two American fantasy movies used to promote local heritage in Italy, attention will be focused on Italian productions (and co-productions). Italian cinema has often been associated with a realist canon (O' Leary and O' Rawe 2011; Scaglioni 2020) and national fantasy attempts belong to a minority course, suffering from an endemic scarcity of resources and culturally perceived as a sort of foreign body in national cinema (Crespi 2014; Venturini 2014). In recent years, however, the global popularity of the fantasy genre has led some directors—counting on unusually high budgets—to try to find a balance between international models and the search for an 'Italian way.' The simultaneous increase of national interest in the film and tourism nexus, together with the exposure of fantasy-related international tourist phenomena, has generated high expectations for these films' potential within tourism promotion. This only occasionally led to the actual development of tourist products which, in some cases, brilliantly take advantage of the specific features of the genre for devising original tourist experiences.

Challenging Authenticity, Place Identity, and Heritage? Film Tourism and the Fantasy Genre

The term film-induced tourism (Beeton 2005) defines several possible connections between the world of cinema and television and that of tourism. It may refer to tourist visits to filming locations, or to settings declared in the narrative when they differ from the places used for shooting (*mistaken identities*) (Beeton 2005). It also includes visits to production studios, film-related theme parks, celebrity homes, Walks of Fame, film museums or exhibitions, and even tourist movements to participate in events like film festivals, film premières, and fan conventions (Beeton 2005; Beeton 2015). Broader terms such as screen tourism or media tourism aim at including other audiovisual products, such as videogames or web content (Månsson and Eskilsson 2013).

Film tourism can refer to participation in organized tours or to individual visits, either spontaneous or resulting from complex strategies of tourism promotion developed by institutional and commercial subjects operating at the destination (Beeton 2005; Connell 2012). Film tourists can show a high degree of fandom and purposely organize their trip, but they can also be tourists less interested in the movie and who just participate in film-related activities while at a destination (Macionis 2004). These tourists often include visits to film locations as part of broader itineraries, showing an interest in toured places that signal beyond their connection with media products (Roesch 2009). Film tourism is often integrated with other forms of tourism, such as adventure tourism (e.g., Leotta 2011; Çelik Rappas and Baschiera 2020) or heritage tourism, of which film tourism has sometimes been described as a possible form (among others: Schofield 1996; Martin-Jones 2014). Agarwal and Shaw (2018, 34) have identified a nexus between heritage, screen, and literary tourism, as they all entail "the consumption and production of a tourism landscape that is associated with people (real or fictional, living or dead), events (past or present, fact or fantasy) and/or place (real of fictional)," deeply involving the tourist in the co-creation of the experience. Film and TV production itself has been understood in relation to British period dramas of the 1980s as part of a broader "heritage industry," aimed at exploiting economic and symbolic profit associated with national heritage (Higson 2003). If historical accuracy is a distinguishing trait of the so-called heritage films (Higson 2003), the nonchalant treatment of history typical of adventure movies—particularly those featuring fantastical elements—generates sharper tensions between film tourism and heritage promotion, which might manifest in different ways. In the Cambodian archaeological site of Angkor Wat, the enhancement of "high quality, cultural tourism" pursued by transnational heritage bodies has clashed with the use of the site for filming *Lara Croft: Tomb Raider* (West 2001), favoured by a national government longing for increases of (any type of) tourism. The film has been accused of conveying an undesired image of the site, rendered as an Orientalist pastiche and virtually destroyed within a narrative centred on grave robbing (Winter 2002).

Fantasy is a genre potentially more inclined to move away from the 'reality' of a place, even if this varies from one film to another, since in some cases the most accurate portrayal of the 'ordinary' is creating a contrast with fantastical elements. The move away from reality is apparent at both the narrative level—even more so if the setting is an imaginary world—and the visual level. The introduction of the extraordinary, in fact, often requires an extensive reliance on special and digital effects, sometimes deeply affecting the representation of places. During the tourist experience on-site, spatial discrepancies between actual locations and filmic spaces (due to multiple reasons, e.g., framing choices, use of certain lenses, and non-existing topographies created through editing), are usually recognized by film tourists (Couldry 2000; Roesch 2009; Reijnders 2011). This may either produce disappointment or additional pleasure, as it generates a "restless movement" between actual and virtual worlds which finally "provide the [film and] TV tourist with his/her destination" (Torchin 2002, 250). These discrepancies become even more apparent in the fantasy genre. According to Carl et al. (2007, 58) disappointment in the *LotR* tours is due to unmet expectations often concerning the feeling that "landscapes did not match the grandeur of those featured in the films" precisely because of digital "enhancements." Roesch (2009) reports diverse reactions generated by different kinds of alterations: disappointment, provoked by the on-site absence of spectacular statues digitally added to movie images; indifference, for the presence of 'disturbing' buildings which had been removed digitally; or excitement, for the discovery of digital flippings of some shots (i.e., when a film image is reversed 180° across its axis).

Digital alterations obviously concern fantasy narratives set both in the real world and in imaginary universes. In respect to the latter, the choice of location filming often derives from the desire to physically anchor the fictional world in the 'real' world in order to make it more believable or, using Wright's (2000, 53) words about *LotR*, "enable an 'authentication' of the illusion by the very real presence of the spectacular New Zealand landscape." Landscape itself is so inextricably linked to the imaginary world, that it becomes per se more appreciated by film tourists than any remaining pieces of the actual film set, especially if the latter is not well preserved (Carl et al. 2007; Roesch 2009).

The explicit 'falseness' of fantasy universes appears particularly apt to exemplify film tourism's questioning of the notion of authenticity in the contemporary tourist experience. These fantasy worlds evidently challenge a simplistic idea of authenticity of the toured objects, measured through objective criteria, but an understanding only in terms of existential authenticity, that is, the existential value assumed by the tourist experience (Wang 1999), does not appear satisfying either. According to Buchmann et al. (2010), who have studied the *LotR* tourist experiences, authenticity results from a complex relationship between these two understandings of the concept because the place itself must be recognized as the 'authentic' one where the shooting was made. Moreover, it must provide an 'authentic' encounter, both physically and socially, as a result of apparently sincere relationships with other tourists or with the guide. Somehow paradoxically, the 'authentication' of the tourist experience and its successful bridging to imaginary worlds passes through the physical encounter with the actual place, enhanced by discomfort, as for the bad weather conditions in *LotR* tours, the extreme heat in a *Star Wars* canyon in Tunisia (Roesch 2009), or the staging of an exhibition in the Italian Caserta Palace visited by *Star Wars* pilgrims (Boni 2010). At times, by contrast, this same physical encounter might inhibit the immersion into the desired atmosphere. As an example, tourists sleeping above the Tasmanian bakery connected to Hayao Miyazaki's *Kiki's Delivery Service* (1989) sometimes complain about the noises of the actual baking activity, making the place different from the "idealized version of a bakery" provided by the film (Norris 2013).

Interestingly, the "restless movement" between actual and virtual worlds at the core of the film tourist experience has been described using metaphors borrowed precisely from science fiction and fantasy. Brooker (2007), in his analysis of *X-Files* (1993–2002), *Smallville* (2001–2011), and *Battlestar Galactica* (2004–2009) fan pilgrimages in Vancouver, uses the metaphor of parallel universes. He understands fan tourism as a potentially carnivalesque use of spaces, like office buildings meant for everyday work subversively employed by media pilgrims as "gateways into alternative worlds" (442). This also happens when fantasy movies are set, and not only shot, in those same places, which are given an extraordinary value through the embedding of fantastical narratives. A famous example is that of King's Cross Station in London, chosen by J.K. Rowling as the site of *Harry Potter*'s 9 ¾ platform: in this case an ordinary place therefore ends up hosting the ultimate gateway into a magical world (Lee 2012).

These creative practices, nevertheless, are not always welcome by residents (Beeton 2005; Tzanelli 2007; Provenzano 2007). Many disadvantages of film-induced tourism, including relevant issues of over-tourism, will not be discussed in this chapter, while other concerns on cultural and social sustainability will be raised. Post-colonial readings of Hollywood films often point out local communities' potential distress in the face of perceived stereotyping of landscape and culture by global simplified narratives, whose outreach is amplified when extensive tourism marketing or substantial film tourism phenomena appear (Tzanelli 2007; Buchmann and Frost 2011). Within the fantasy genre, the *LotR* case comes again to the fore for its complexity. Tensions concern, on the one hand, the Hollywood origin of the project and its New Zealand appropriation, and on the other hand, the image of the country conveyed through the fantasy transfiguration of actual places into mythical worlds. Despite being a Hollywood project based on English books and set in an imaginary Middle Earth, a sort of "national authenticity" has been fabricated in New Zealand through a complex cultural process, analysed by Jones and Smith (2005) through a survey of the movies' media coverage, along with texts produced by the government and by the local tourism industry.

Film tourism had a pivotal role, because "national identity as established in the *LotR* project lend[ed] authenticity to tourism rhetoric, and [wa]s itself reinforced by tourism rhetoric" (927). Recurring arguments include Peter Jackson's New Zealand nationality and his presumed "Kiwi character," as the man who brought to New Zealand a Hollywood production to work with the local creative industries. The latter have realized 'authentic' artefacts and some sets were physically built despite the possibility of creating them through digital effects (935). All this, together with the same high-tech digital technologies, has marked the project with distinctive New Zealand creativity. This image of a high-tech New Zealand paradoxically contrasts with the pre-historical one conveyed by the typical fantasy narrative and by the use of natural landscape in the film itself (Jones and Smith 2005; see also Leotta 2011), a simplistic, exotic, mythical image "different to those which communities and governments would wish to disseminate" (Buchmann and Frost 2011, 52). More specifically, *LotR*, while contributing to New Zealand's international reputation as the 'Home of Middle Earth,' erases any traces of the indigenous Māori population from the cultural geography of the country (Leotta 2011).

Momentarily putting aside issues of cultural sustainability, when it comes to tourism marketing, the main challenge of imaginary settings is the same as other cases of so-called *mistaken identities*, namely to connect the film to its actual shooting locations. Sue Beeton defines *mistaken identities* as instances of film tourism in which the movie is filmed in places different from the explicit setting (2005, 10). However, marketing strategies appear more effective when they aim at establishing a connection with imaginary worlds instead of places which physically exist elsewhere, as New Zealand has experienced with the different outcomes of the tourism marketing campaigns associated with *The Last Samurai* (Zwick 2003), set in Japan, and the *LotR*, set in the fantasy world of Middle Earth. While the latter's effects on boosting tourism are widely recognized, *The Last Samurai* failed to induce tourism to New Zealand in the long term, mainly because of an 'authentic' Japan existing elsewhere. New Zealand landscapes in *The Last Samurai* lack any "sense of distinctiveness" that *LotR*, despite digital alterations and the imaginary setting, still safeguards (Leotta 2011, 157). In a similar way, an imaginary setting might allow an easier integration of local heritage in film-related tourist products, especially if the fantasy film or series itself includes reworked references to history or traditions, like *Game of Thrones* (Waysdorf and Reijnders 2017). In Northern Ireland, the creation of *GoT*-inspired artefacts with local materials, like the tapestry exposed at Ulster Museum in Belfast weaved with linen coming from an ancient mill, or the pub doors carved with wood of the Dark Hedges trees felt down, represent fascinating attempts to integrate screen tourism with the promotion of natural and cultural heritage. This approach has the potential to produce a double advantage: on one hand, fostering a deeper connection between film tourism and the local context, aimed at prolonging its effects in time; on the other hand, injecting a new life to heritage, enhancing its attractiveness for larger groups of tourists (Çelik Rappas and Baschiera 2020).

The fear of film tourists wiping out the actual identity of the place whilst pursuing only its fantasy counterpart, for example visiting the Croatian historical city of Dubrovnik merely as *GoT* King's Landing, is often expressed by scholars (e.g., Violante 2016). Nevertheless, research conducted on screen tourists' experiences both in Northern Ireland and in Dubrovnik highlights the coexistence of several readings of the place involving different types of imagination, either connected to the fictional world, to the series' actual production process, or to historical narratives of the site (Waysdorf and Reijnders 2017). This awareness influences the design of commercial tours and the speeches proposed by guides who intentionally provide historical information about the place (Waysdorf and Reijnders 2017). Managers of heritage attractions used for filming must face challenges in meeting different expectations, those of tourists more (or only) interested in the actual history of the 'real' location and those more (or only) interested in the film, and take delicate decisions concerning the "heritage interpretation" provided (Bakiewicz et al. 2017). During guided tours to Alnwyck Castle, used for the shooting of *Harry Potter*, historical and fictional accounts are assembled (Bakiewicz et al. 2017). The negotiation between the two sometimes expresses local communities' concerns about the protection of national narratives, like in the case of Dracula tourism in Romania (Reijnders 2011). In Lee's (2012, 58) words, "the imaginary geography," drawn by multiple, diverse literary and screen narratives, "adds further layers to the existing landscape," which is not merely "writ[ten] over (replacing one image with another)"

(61). This process, by the way, resonates with the specific functioning of fantasy (literary and filmic) texts such as *Harry Potter*, based on the coexistence of ordinary and extraordinary elements (Lee 2012).

When *Harry Potter* tour guides in the UK combine fictional stories with official history, legends, and folklore—providing an "enchanted" image of the country—they somehow "level" them "*as narrative*" (Lee 2012, 60). There is no need to recall that history itself is made of narratives which are often conflicting, as demonstrated in the aforementioned case of Dubrovnik. Its official tourist narrative based on the Old City heritage, in fact, underplays not only the *Game of Thrones* connection, but also the references to wars in former Yugoslavia and to the 1991 siege of the city—the historical fact of foremost relevance in the lives of residents (Joyce 2019). Essentialist approaches to place identity, counterposing a monolithic 'authenticity' to presumedly 'inauthentic' fictional narratives, should be avoided, partly because "the 'established' real place is often already a site of contested interpretations as different interest groups struggle for control of the place's meaning" (1389). In any case, what differentiates film tourists from other tourists is obviously the stronger influence played by the specific text on their "historical imagination," as clearly stated by Waysdorf and Reinders (2017, 185):

> historical imagination is never neutral. It takes a particular form depending on the text being de-mediated. This separates film tourists from 'regular' tourists, insofar that even if they are interested in aspects of the location that are not strictly part of filming process, the contours of their imaginative experience are shaped by a notion of history provided by popular culture. Just as *Lord of the Rings* fans see New Zealand as timelessly pastoral and spectacular, so *Game of Thrones* fans frame Dubrovnik and Northern Ireland as part of a mythic-medieval world.

The common features of fantasy films and TV series, heightening the narrative and visual discrepancies between actual locations and their filmic counterparts, may magnify some of the difficulties normally faced in tourism promotion through fiction films in the development of film-related tourist products and in the management of heritage sites used for shooting. Nevertheless, their specific features might also inspire creative initiatives, giving new life to local heritage, without necessarily implying the demise of the multiple pre-existing identities and narratives of the place. In the next section, this opportunity will be explored within the Italian context, where recent attempts have been made to exploit the tourist potential of Italian fantasy films, dealing with a genre that is relatively unpopular within national cinema.

An Unfamiliar Taste: Tourism and Fantasy Films in Italy

Interest in the complex relationship between film and tourism has recently increased in Italy, both at a regional and national level. The 2016 national law on the audiovisual sector finally institutionalized film commissions, namely the public (or public-private) bodies in charge of attracting and supporting audiovisual projects, facilitating the relationships between audiovisual companies and host territories, and favouring audiovisual tourism promotion. In 2017, within the framework of the national Strategic Plan for Tourism, the website Italy for Movies was released. The latter represents a welcome attempt to create a national film location database, to collect information about regional funds and services, and to suggest tourist itineraries across film locations.

This interest in audiovisual tourism promotion originated from the exposure of several international and national cases of increased tourist flows in film and TV locations (for Italy, see Provenzano 2007). Before discussing Italian fantasy productions, I would like to focus on two relevant examples of tourism promotion and practices connected to American fantasy films shot in Italy, belonging to the two popular sagas *Star Wars* and *Twilight*. These cases provide interesting, additional examples of initiatives aimed at promoting local heritage through fantasy narratives.

Italian locations like the Caserta Palace and the Balbianello Villa on Como Lake were used to stand in for the enchanted land of Naboo in two episodes of the second *Star Wars* trilogy (*The Phantom Menace* 1999 and *Attack of the Clones* 2002, both directed by George Lucas). Tourist flows induced by the movies have been observed in both locations (Boni

2010), and, together with other connections between Como Lake and the movie world (like the purchase of a villa on the lake by the popular American actor George Clooney), induced the local chamber of commerce to finance, in 2012, the creation of *The Stars of Lake Como*—both a guidebook and an app aimed at film tourists. However, the main focus here will be on the other Italian location used for the *Star Wars* second trilogy, the Caserta Palace. In 2018, in the wake of the subsequent (third) *Star Wars* trilogy release, the MANN Archaeological Museum in Naples—which in the last years has frequently resorted to media such as films, music videos, and videogames for its promotion—set up an exhibition titled *MANN@hero* assembling archaeological objects and *Star Wars* memorabilia from private fan collections, and focusing on the iconology of the hero across time. This capitalized on the connection to the nearby Caserta Palace, where it was possible to watch content related to *Star Wars* filming through VR headsets as part of the exhibition. As was the case for the *Game of Thrones*' related tapestry and doors, the aim of the organizers was to both refresh heritage and make it attractive for new groups of tourists. This has been more systematically pursued by the Tuscan city of Volterra, the setting of the most emotional scene in *Twilight* saga's book and movie *New Moon* (Weitz 2009)—even if the filming took place in the near city of Montepulciano. Both Volterra and Montepulciano, already established cultural tourist destinations, have reported a significant increase of tourists after the release of the film. In 2010, between 15% and 20% of Volterra tourists were induced by *Twilight* (Larson et al. 2013). Compared to the American city of Forks, where most of the narrative is set and where the *Twilight* connection has been totally embraced in order to boost tourism, Volterra and Montepulciano have adopted a strategy of "guarding place authenticity." They have, in fact, encouraged a socio-cultural sustainable tourism, introducing—albeit downplaying—the *Twilight* theme and finding creative ways to connect it with their heritage (Larson et al. 2013). At the time of writing, the tourist consortium Volterra Valdicecina, which manages the Volterra Tourist Board, is still organizing *Twilight* walking tours. Famous heritage sites, such as the Etruscan gate, or intangible heritage like the working of alabaster, are framed through their relation to the *Twilight* characters of Volturi and the leitmotif of mystery, assembling fictional and historical elements, regardless of the lack of actual shooting locations (yet taking advantage of references coming from the book). Heritage is thus given new life and revealed to *Twilight* tourists, whose "historical imagination" of the Etruscan past will be mediated by the *Twilight* text.

In more recent years, the growing awareness of the tourism potential of films and TV series has led to an even prompter tourist exploitation of other American fantasy movies. Two of the most recent Marvel and DC superhero movies shot in Italy, *Avengers: Age of Ultron* (Whedon 2015) and *Wonder Woman* (Jenkins 2017), have both been used for the creation of tourist itineraries, respectively in the regions of Valle d'Aosta and Basilicata (for Basilicata, see Colangelo 2018). However, the remaining part of this section will focus on the exploitation of fantasy Italian productions (or co-productions) for tourism purposes, where interest lies in their partial novelty and unfamiliarity in the Italian contemporary film landscape.

Fantasy as a screen genre has not flourished in Italian cinema, despite the abundance of fantasy elements in the Italian literature masterpieces since the Middle Ages (Crespi 2014). Although there are some exceptions, such as film adaptations of Collodi's *Pinocchio* and Dante's *Divine Comedy* (the latter limited to the silent era) (Crespi 2014) or Alessandro Blasetti's *The Iron Crown* (1941), most of the fantasy movies produced in Italian film history date from the specific context of popular B-movies shot in the 1950s and 1960s. In that period, mythological films (the so-called *pepla*) often included fantasy elements (Brunetta 1991), and, more specifically, an actual Italian fantasy-horror genre was born thanks to the creativity of Mario Bava and a few other directors. Despite their international circulation and commercial success, these films have suffered from endemic low budgets and an enduring limited critical appreciation in Italy, while being perceived as a sort of foreign body in Italian national cinema (Crespi 2014, Venturini 2014, Nazzaro 2019). The latter has been largely identified with a realist canon, encouraged by the valuable outcomes of Neorealism (O' Leary and O' Rawe 2011; Scaglioni 2020).

In recent years, due to the increasing global popularity of fantasy amongst the Italian audience (on the Italian reception of *LotR*, see Trobia 2008), significant attempts dealing with the fantasy genre have been made by Italian directors, whilst borrowing elements from international models. Among them, two films particularly stand out both for their production values and for being directed by two of the most renowned Italian authors: Gabriele Salvatores and Matteo Garrone. Salvatores tried to launch the first Italian superhero movie saga with *The Invisible Boy* (*Il ragazzo invisibile*, 2014) and its sequel *The Invisible Boy: Second Generation* (*Il ragazzo invisibile—Seconda generazione*, 2018); while Garrone set up an international co-production to adapt, with his *Tale of Tales* (*Il racconto dei racconti—Tale of Tales*, 2015), the Italian seventeenth-century collection of tales *Lo cunto de li cunti* by Giambattista Basile, before realizing a second fantasy literary adaptation with his *Pinocchio* (2020). All of these movies counted on extremely large budgets, particularly compared to the Italian standard (from *The Invisible Boy*'s 8 million euros to *Pinocchio*'s almost 15 million).

Despite the unfamiliar taste of national fantasy and the ultimately poor box office results, both *The Invisible Boy* and *Tale of Tales*, in different ways, have been explicitly intended as possible means of tourist promotion. This can be understood in relation to the recent enthusiasm for the tourism potential of films in Italy, as well as to the media exposure of the film-induced tourism phenomena connected to international fantasy works like *LotR*, *Harry Potter*, or *GoT*. The press discourses on the vast potential of audiovisual tourism promotion have involved, surprisingly, even an Italian *auteur* project like *Tale of Tales*, aiming at larger audiences than Garrone's previous films, yet unlikely to reach those of a blockbuster.

The Invisible Boy and *Tale of Tales* stand out as relevant case studies both because of their relevance and press exposure in Italy, and because they are exemplary of two different types of fantasy movies and of different types of related tourism promotion strategies. In one case the shooting location is given a fantasy aura by introducing extraordinary elements in a real setting (*The Invisible Boy*), while in the other case actual places are transfigured into imaginary worlds (*Tale of Tales*). Moreover, the two examples display different strategies and targets in terms of tourism promotion: *The Invisible Boy* has been used to develop tourist products aimed at promoting local heritage to national tourists and residents, while *Tale of Tales* aims at national as well as international audiences, to promote Italian heritage and national image at a broader level.

Tale of Tales is a fantasy movie set in entirely imaginary worlds devised by the writer Giambattista Basile. It was shot in around 20 spectacular natural and cultural heritage sites throughout Italy, carefully selected and eventually enhanced through visual and narrative strategies. The main aim is that of inducing awe in the eyes of the spectator, in order to visually achieve the effect of wonder pursued with literary means by Basile's stories. *Tale of Tales* has received financing from two of the regions involved in the production, Puglia and Lazio, whose funds aim at the economic benefits deriving from both hosting film productions and potential tourism spin-offs. The director Matteo Garrone, who often mentioned *Game of Thrones* as a source of inspiration, specifies nevertheless that his film should be described as *fiabesco* (fairy-tale) instead of fantasy, because it originates from actual shooting locations and does not create imaginary landscapes through studio shooting or digital effects, like many international fantasy films and series do (Garrone 2016). Both the press and the director himself continuously stressed this use of real (Italian) locations and never mentioned the digital effects employed to enhance the fantastic atmosphere, inspired by typically unrealistic Flemish landscape painting (Spaventa 2015). The other element highlighted by the press is the use of physical effects, created by Italian artists to realize the fantastic creatures, such as the dragon or the giant flea, instead of only relying on digital effects (for further details on the media coverage of the film, see Lavarone 2017). This has been described as a sort of 'Italian way' of doing fantasy, returning to the cliché of artisanal ability typically associated with the Made in Italy brand, but also highlighting the names of two Italian geniuses who worked on fantasy films. The first is Mario Bava, director of fantasy-horror B-movies known for their homemade special effects, while the second is Carlo Rambaldi, father of the alien creatures featured in Ridley Scott's *Alien* (1979) and Spielberg's *E.T.-The Extraterrestrial* (1982). This continuity with a presumed Italian tradition is often highlighted by the press, even if among the models acknowledged by the authors of the special effects there is also a reference from the other side of the world: that of Jackson's Weta and its work on *LotR* (Cosulich 2015).

Despite being an international co-production, shot in English and almost entirely casting foreign actors such as Salma Hayek or Vincent

Cassel, *Tale of Tales* has been described by the press as a totally Italian film, born of the courage of an Italian *auteur*, who has devised an Italian way for the unfamiliar genre of fantasy—and at the same time, has co-produced the film with his own money and managed to set up, and bring to Italy, a big international project. These arguments for the movie's Italian-ness have totally overtaken, for example, references to its literary origin. The press discourse thus testifies to a process of fabrication of a "creative authenticity" and a "national authenticity" strictly interconnected, partly reminiscent of the *LotR* case.

The project, targeted at international as well as national audiences, traces an enchanted image of Italy while celebrating Italian handcraft and creativity. The national and international press have explicitly read this movie through a tourist perspective, endlessly proposing lists of its numerous locations, and sometimes placing it in the 'travel,' instead of 'culture,' column (Lavarone 2017). It has often been compared to films which have induced dramatic tourist increases, in Italy and elsewhere, thus showing an enthusiasm that has, nevertheless, not been followed by an actual development of tourist products. The film is mentioned in the Tuscany and Puglia region tourist websites, and in itineraries proposed by the national portal Italy for Movies, but generally speaking, it has been poorly adopted for tourist promotion by public and private stakeholders operating at a local level. This limited exploitation of *Tale of Tales*' tourist potential, which also lies in its notable media exposure (see Roesch 2009) and has been confirmed by reported tourist increases in single locations (Lavarone 2017), may be due to several factors: on the one hand, the discouragement brought by its unsatisfying box office figures, and on the other hand, the general delay in commercial improvement of film tourism in Italy (di Cesare 2016), although the situation might be gradually evolving. Either way, the case of *Tale of Tales* and its media coverage reveals both the high expectations of the potential tourist use of fantasy films and an implicit awareness of the challenges that the genre might entail. The media discourse, in fact, has dealt with these challenges both on the narrative side—through the listings of locations aimed at connecting them with the movie's imaginary settings—and on the visual side, through downplaying the role of digital effects and stressing the high recognition values of the same locations. At the same time, it has constructed the national authenticity of the film, read as a paradigm of Italian creativity and a display of Italian tangible and intangible heritage, with the aim of marketing the country for international audiences.

The Invisible Boy project also originates from the will of 'domesticating' international models through the creation of the first Italian superhero: a 13-year-old boy who suddenly discovers his invisibility power. In order to further enable the identification of young Italian audiences—to which the film is targeted—with the main character, and to highlight the appearance of the extraordinary in everyday life, the film is purposely set and shot in an existing Italian city, Trieste. In the first scene, Trieste is described as the extremely 'ordinary' place where the magical baby, born in Russia, has randomly ended up. Even if the movie frequently relies on visual effects (supervised by Victor Perez, who had previously worked on digital compositing for the *Harry Potter* and *Star Wars* sagas), the locations generally remain recognizable. Among them, there is Porto Vecchio, a large area built in the nineteenth century to stock the goods arriving by sea to the port of Trieste. Fallen into disuse, its access is now forbidden to the general public and, in the later years, it has been the object of several discussions on possible redevelopment projects, as mentioned in the official website (portovecchio.comune.trieste.it). Because of its large empty spaces, it is often proposed as a film location by the Friuli Venezia Giulia regional film commission, having already been used in the past to film *The English Patient* (Minghella 1996)—where it stood for the Lybian city of Tobruk. Despite being used for *Invisible Boy* scenes set in Russia, Porto Vecchio also appears as itself in one scene within the second, and most exciting, part of the movie. This part includes thrilling rescue and fight sequences taking place inside a ship, and among the locations used there is also the floating crane Ursus (whose name is also clearly framed in a shot of the film)—a symbol of the city built in 1913, belonging to its maritime industrial heritage. Rather than proposing images of the city centre, the narrative and visual choices of the film highlight the importance of Trieste as a port and its industrial heritage, particularly apt to the fantasy turn of the film, thanks to Porto Vecchio's dark shadows and colour of rust (Grando 2014).

This has led the Friuli Venezia Giulia Film Commission, in collaboration with the institution Casa del Cinema (including all the associations dealing with film culture at a regional scope), to propose tours inspired by *The Invisible Boy* as one of the highlights in their limited yet interesting offer of movie tours, mostly targeted at residents and at national tourists. The itinerary also includes the rare opportunity to visit Porto Vecchio, often unknown even to the inhabitants of the city, during which the tour guide provides historical information about the site. These tours represent the only example in Italy of movie tours (by walking or by bus) realized with the additional support of VR headsets. Well beyond aiming at a mere novelty effect of surprise, VR technology is used in a highly functioning way with two objectives. The first one is to grant virtual access to places which cannot be open to the public, such as the interiors of the Ursus, which have thus been filmed purposely to insert the images into the VR headsets. The second one is to provide additional content concerning the technical details of film production, especially the perceived main feature of the film (namely special effects), but also the use of light in particular places—explained by interviews with the director in those same spaces. In all of the movie tours offered by the Casa del Cinema, particular attention is paid to the production process, through the direct participation of film professionals to the tours, or through providing additional filmed content such as interviews or images showing the work on the set. In the specific case of *The Invisible Boy*, typical fantasy elements such as the use of special effects thus become the core narrative of the tour, along with the discovery of places belonging to the industrial heritage of the city which are granted additional value by both the film itself and the tour. These both introduce extraordinary elements in ordinary spaces, like *Harry Potter*'s 9 ¾ platform in King's Cross, stimulating the audiences' and tourists' imagination thanks to the specific mix typical of the genre, devising a highly sustainable film tourism initiative. The latter, in fact, managed by local cultural institutions, allows the rediscovery of a neglected heritage—far from being an overcrowded tourist spot—in the eyes of both residents and tourists, providing historical information about the place whilst reading it through the lens of a fantastic narrative and visual effects, which provide it with new, extraordinary values.

In this case, the challenges posed by the fantasy genre to tourist promotion were mostly unproblematic at the narrative level, as the film is predominantly set in Trieste's actual shooting locations (except for the scenes set in Russia). By contrast, the challenges associated with the visual side, digital alterations which possibly affect the recognition of actual locations, have become one of the main components in the tour's narrative. An element of potential disappointment has thus been turned into a source of astonishment and pleasure, as per the aforementioned international examples.

Conclusions

Providing some of the most famous and discussed examples of film tourism, the fantasy genre represents an interesting case study to analyse this phenomenon. On the one hand, its very narrative premise, based on the creation of parallel universes (Brooker 2007) or the juxtaposition of ordinary and extraordinary elements (Lee 2012), strongly resonates with the "restless movement" between actual and virtual worlds (Torchin 2002) that underlies any film tourist experience. On the other hand, its typical features at both the narrative and visual level often magnify the discrepancies between movie images and shooting locations, whose perception is a pivotal element in this same experience. The evident detachment from the 'reality' of the place may also exacerbate the difficulties commonly faced in terms of heritage management and promotion when dealing with films shot on-site. The latter are often accused of conveying inaccurate images and of attracting undesired tourists, assumed to be careless of the historical value of the place. Actually, fantasy film tourists have often proved to be interested in the history of the destination, even if their "historical imagination" is strongly mediated by the film text itself (Waysdorf and Reijnders 2017), rather than other (historical) narratives, which would still not allow the definition of a monolithic, 'authentic' place identity. Fantasy films and TV series can thus inspire creative attempts at integrating local heritage in initiatives and products aimed at film tourists, as in Northern Ireland for *GoT*, as well as in the Italian examples of the MANN exhibition in Naples, or, in a longer-term perspective, *Twilight* tours in Volterra. The latter's strategy of "guarding place authenticity" has been described, in this sense, as an example of sociocultural sustainability in film tourism (Larson et al. 2013). However, the potential communities' distress when facing stereotypical images conveyed by movies, enhanced by their extensive use in tourist promotion and tourist products, is also a potential issue. While not being a property of fantasy films, it must be acknowledged that the latter's typical transfiguration of living places into enchanted, pre-historical lands often raises problematic issues, as for New Zealand and *LotR* (Buchmann and Frost 2011).

The interest of exploring the Italian context lies in its traditional unfamiliarity with the genre, and in the desire to deal with it in the wake of its global popularity. The high-budget fantasy films by two of the most important Italian directors have arrived at the same time as the first strong signals of interest in film tourism by the national government. Despite their unsatisfying box office results, the awareness of the tourist potential for fantasy films and TV series—raised by the exposure of international cases such as *LotR* or *GoT*—has led to the use of both these films for the purposes of tourism promotion. Even an *auteur* project like *Tale of Tales* has raised high expectations for its tourist potential.

In both cases, the peculiar features of the fantasy genre, that is, its explicit move from the 'reality' of the place both at the narrative and visual level, are explicitly addressed in order to manage their 'otherness' in the Italian context, as well as their possible shortcomings in terms of tourism promotion. Two different communicative strategies are employed. The first one (*Tale of Tales*) consists of downplaying the presence of digital effects, stressing the high recognition values of the 'real' locations used. The second one (*The Invisible Boy*) consists, on the contrary, of emphasizing the choice of using digital effects and in placing them at the heart of the tours' narrative, thanks to a brilliant employment of AR and VR technologies to provide technical explanations. Both of these cases reiterate the potential of fantasy's typical creativity (in terms of narratives and visual effects) to confer extraordinariness to the shooting locations and to inspire original attempts of promoting heritage, without necessarily neglecting the multiple pre-existing identities of the place, which is particularly evident in the second case.

Tangible and intangible Italian heritage are on display in *Tale of Tales*, promoting an enchanted image of the entire country thanks to the visual and narrative strategies employed by Garrone to convey the sense of wonder generated by Basile's original stories. Analyses of the film's media coverage reveal that the peculiar creative values of the genre are also used to achieve a combined cultural construction of "creative authenticity" and "national authenticity," such as in the *LotR* case (Jones and Smith 2005), turning creativity into a national asset which contributes to nation branding and tourist promotion at an international level. Nevertheless, in a context still mainly unprepared for the commercial exploitation of film tourism (di Cesare 2016), enthusiasm does not always result in the actual development of tourist products.

An original tourism product was instead developed through the *Invisible Boy* tours in Trieste, which focus their narrative on the creative values of the fantasy genre, digital effects included. Favoured by the film being mostly set in the city, the embedding of extraordinary elements into an ordinary world typical of the fantasy genre is replicated in the tour thanks to virtual and augmented reality, which allows both tourists and local residents to look with new eyes at the industrial heritage of Trieste. Narrative and visual elements perceived as 'foreign' in Italian culture are thus integrated into local neglected heritage, in order to give it new life. VR and AR technologies are used to virtually visit inaccessible parts of the sites, on which historical information is provided. Far from inducing undesired forms of tourism, the *Invisible Boy* tours, developed by local cultural institutions, have turned some specific features of the fantasy genre into a source of inspiration for a highly sustainable form of tourism promotion through films.

Works Cited

Agarwal, Sheela, and Gareth Shaw. 2018. *Heritage, Screen and Literary Tourism*. Bristol-Blue Ridge Summit: Channel View.

Bakiewicz, Justyna, Anna Leask, Paul Barron, and Tijana Rakic. 2017. Management Challenges at Film-Induced Tourism Heritage Attractions. *Tourism Planning & Development* 14: 548–566. https://doi.org/10.1080/21568316.2017.1303540.

Beeton, Sue. 2005. *Film-Induced Tourism*. Clevedon: Channel View.

———. 2015. *Travel, Tourism and the Moving Image*. Clevedon: Channel View.

Boni, Federico. 2010. Pellegrinaggi mediatici. Itinerari architettonici nel turismo cinematografico e televisivo. In *Altri turismi. Viaggi, esperienze, emozioni*, ed. Ezio Marra and Elisabetta Ruspini, 43–67. Milano: Franco Angeli.

Brooker, Will. 2007. Everywhere and Nowhere: Vancouver, Fan Pilgrimage and the Urban Imaginary. *International Journal of Cultural Studies* 10: 423–444. https://doi.org/10.1177/1367877907083078.

Brunetta, Gian Piero. 1991. *Cent'Anni di Cinema Italiano*. Roma-Bari: Laterza.

Buchmann, Anne, and Warwick Frost. 2011. Wizards Everywhere? Film Tourism and the Imagining of National Identity in New Zealand. In *Tourism and National Identities: An International Perspective*, ed. Elspeth Frew and Leanne White, 52–64. London: Routledge.

Buchmann, Anne, Kevin Moore, and David Fisher. 2010. Experiencing Film Tourism. Authenticity & Fellowship. *Annals of Tourism Research* 37: 229–248. https://doi.org/10.1016/j.annals.2009.09.005.

Carl, Daniela, Sara Kindon, and Karen Smith. 2007. Tourists' Experiences of Film Locations: New Zealand as 'Middle Earth'. *Tourism Geographies* 9: 49–63. https://doi.org/10.1080/14616680601092881.

Çelik Rappas, Ipek A., and Stefano Baschiera. 2020. Fabricating "Cool" Heritage for Northern Ireland: *Game of Thrones* Tourism. *The Journal of Popular Culture* 53: 648–666. https://doi.org/10.1111/jpcu.12926.

Colangelo, Delio. 2018. *Cinema in Basilicata: Impatti su Economia e Turismo*. Milano: Fondazione Eni Enrico Mattei.

Connell, Joanne. 2012. Film Tourism—Evolution, Progress and Prospects. *Tourism Management* 33: 1007–1029. https://doi.org/10.1016/j.tourman.2012.02.008.

Cosulich, Oscar. 2015. Effetti speciali, ora il mostro è tra gli attori. *L'Espresso*, June 30.

Couldry, Nick. 2000. *The Place of Media Power. Pilgrims and Witnesses of the Media Age*. London-New York: Routledge.

Crespi, Alberto Ed. 2014. Gli alieni i cavalier l'arme gli orrori. *Bianco e nero* 579: 7–151. https://doi.org/10.7371/77998.

di Cesare, Francesco. 2016. Se bastasse un Oscar a far arrivare turisti. *Il Capitale Culturale* 4: 21–27. https://doi.org/10.13138/2039-2362/1406.

Garrone, Matteo. 2016. *Le fiabe sono vere. Conversazione con Italo Moscati*. Roma: Castelvecchi.

Grando, Elisa. 2014. Salvatores a Trieste «Penso al sequel del mio super-eroe». *Il Piccolo*, December 9.

Higson, Andrew. 2003. *English Heritage, English Cinema. Costume Drama Since 1980*. Oxford: Oxford University Press.

Jones, Deborah, and Karen Smith. 2005. Middle-earth Meets New Zealand: Authenticity and Location in the Making of *The Lord of the Rings*. *Journal of Management Studies* 42: 923–945. https://doi.org/10.1111/j.1467-6486.2005.00527.x.

Joyce, Stephen. 2019. Media Tourism and Conflict Heritage in Dubrovnik, Westeros. *The Journal of Popular Culture* 52: 1387–1407. https://doi.org/10.1111/jpcu.12854.

Larson, Mia, Christine Lundberg, and Maria Lexhagen. 2013. Thirsting for Vampire Tourism: Developing Pop Culture Destinations. *Journal of Destination Marketing & Management* 2: 74–84. https://doi.org/10.1016/j.jdmm.2013.03.004.

Lavarone, Giulia. 2017. Fantasy, *Film-Induced tourism* e patrimonio nazionale. *Il racconto dei racconti* di Matteo Garrone. *La Valle dell'Eden* 30: 115–121.

Lee, Christina. 2012. 'Have Magic, Will Travel': Tourism and *Harry Potter*'s United (Magical) Kingdom. *Tourist Studies* 12: 52–69. https://doi.org/10.1177/1468797612438438.

Leotta, Alfio. 2011. *Touring the Screen: Tourism and New Zealand Film Geographies*. Bristol: Intellect.

Macionis, Niki. 2004. Understanding the Film-Induced Tourist. In *International Tourism and Media Conference Proceedings. 24th–26th November 2004*, ed. Warwick Frost, Glen Croy, and Sue Beeton, 86–97. Melbourne: Tourism Research Unit, Monash University.

Månsson, Maria, and Lena Eskilsson. 2013. *Euroscreen: The Attraction of Screen Destinations. Baseline Report Assessing Best Practice*. Rzeszów: Pracownia Pomysłów.

Martin-Jones, David. 2014. Film tourism as heritage tourism: Scotland, diaspora and *The Da Vinci Code* (2006). *New Review of Film and Television Studies* 12: 156–177. https://doi.org/10.1080/17400309.2014.880301.

Nazzaro, Giona A. 2019. Schermi delle nostre brame. L'insostenibile singolarità di un cinema di genere (che forse non è mai esistito). In *Ieri, oggi e domani. Il cinema di genere in Italia*, ed. Pedro Armocida and Boris Sollazzo, 179–191. Venezia: Marsilio- Fondazione Pesaro Nuovo Cinema Onlus.

Norris, Craig. 2013. A Japanese Media Pilgrimage to a Tasmanian Bakery. *Transformative Works and Cultures*. https://doi.org/10.3983/twc.2013.0470.

O' Leary, Alan, and Catherine O' Rawe. 2011. Against realism: on a 'certain tendency' in Italian film criticism. *Journal of Modern Italian Studies* 16: 107–128. https://doi.org/10.1080/1354571X.2011.530767.

Provenzano, Roberto, ed. 2007. *Al cinema con la valigia. I film di viaggio e il cineturismo*. Milano: Franco Angeli.

Reijnders, Stijn. 2011. *Places of the Imagination. Media, Tourism, Culture*. Furnham-Burlington: Ashgate.

Riley, Roger, Dwayne Baker, and Carlton S. Van Doren. 1998. Movie-induced tourism. *Annals of Tourism Research* 25: 919–935. https://doi.org/10.1016/S0160-7383(98)00045-0.

Roesch, Stefan. 2009. *The Experiences of Film Location Tourists*. Bristol-Buffalo-Toronto: Channel View.

Scaglioni, Massimo, ed. 2020. *Cinema made in Italy. La circolazione internazionale dell'audiovisivo italiano*. Roma: Carocci.

Schofield, Peter. 1996. Cinematographic Images of a City: Alternative Heritage Tourism in Manchester. *Tourism Management* 17: 333–340. https://doi.org/10.1016/0261-5177(96)00033-7.

Spaventa, Simona. 2015. *La Repubblica*, November 19.

Tooke, Nichola, and Michael Baker. 1996. Seeing is Believing: The Effect of Film on Visitor Numbers to Screened Locations. *Tourism Management* 17: 87–94. https://doi.org/10.1016/0261-5177(95)00111-5.

Torchin, Leshu. 2002. Location, Location, Location. The Destination of the Manhattan TV Tour. *Tourist Studies* 2: 247–266. https://doi.org/10.1177/14687976020023002.

Trobia, Alberto, ed. 2008. *Sociologia del cinema fantastico. Il Signore degli Anelli in Italia: Audience, Media, Mercato*. Torino: Kaplan.

Tzanelli, Rodanthi. 2007. *The Cinematic Tourist. Explorations in Globalization, Culture and Resistance*. Abingdon-New York: Routledge.

Venturini, Simone. 2014. *Horror Italiano*. Roma: Donzelli.

Violante, Antonio. 2016. Quando la fiction produce turismo. Due località per il cinema fantasy a confronto. *Il Capitale Culturale* 4: 393–405. https://doi.org/10.13138/2039-2362/1429.

Wang, Ning. 1999. Rethinking Authenticity in Tourism Experience. *Annals of Tourism Research* 26: 349–370. https://doi.org/10.1016/S0160-7383(98)00103-0.

Waysdorf, Abby, and Stijn Reijnders. 2017. The Role of Imagination in the Film Tourist Experience: The Case of *Game of Thrones*. *Participations* 14: 170–191.

Winter, Tim. 2002. Angkor Meets *Tomb Raider*: Setting the Scene. *International Journal of Heritage Studies* 8: 323–336. https://doi.org/10.1080/13527250220000037218.

Wright, Andrea. 2000. Realms of Enchantment: New Zealand Landscape as Tolkienesque. In *New Zealand—A Pastoral Paradise?* ed. Ian Conrich and David Woods, 52–29. Nottingham: Kakapo Books.

8

How Do Video Games Induce Us to Travel?: Exploring the Drivers, Mechanisms, and Limits of Video Game-Induced Tourism

Jiahui (Yolanda) Dong, Louis-Etienne Dubois, Marion Joppe, and Lianne Foti

Despite the rapid growth of the video gaming industry in the last few decades—as well as mounting evidence of its impact, both positive and negative—on destinations (Dubois and Gibbs 2018; Dubois et al. 2020) and applications in tourism (Bahtiar and Segara 2020), research has yet to explain how video games *actually* induce individuals' emotions or actions towards a given destination at the pre-travel stage.

As such, this chapter attempts a first conceptualization of the key drivers and mechanisms of video game-induced tourism by investigating how known predictors of visit intention manifest in this particular context.

J. (Yolanda) Dong (✉) • M. Joppe • L. Foti
University of Guelph, Guelph, ON, Canada
e-mail: jdong13@uoguelph.ca; mjoppe@uoguelph.ca; foti@uoguelph.ca

L.-E. Dubois
Ryerson University, Toronto, ON, Canada
e-mail: le.dubois@ryerson.ca

© The Author(s), under exclusive license to Springer Nature Singapore Pte Ltd. 2021
D. Bonelli, A. Leotta (eds.), *Audiovisual Tourism Promotion*,
https://doi.org/10.1007/978-981-16-6410-6_8

More specifically, drawing from the stimulus-organism-response (SOR) theory (Mehrabian and Russell 1974), it considers the medium's particular influence of presence on the players' emotional reactions and in turn, on their behaviours towards or intention to visit game-related destinations.

Indeed, creating a strong sense of presence has become a key design consideration for video game developers for its capability to generate a positive attitude (Ho et al. 2017). Presence is defined as a psychological state of consciousness, describing to what extent users believe the virtual environment to be real (Lee 2004). While it may affect users' perceived reality in many ways, research has shown that when interacting with a virtual medium, the increase of users' presence may elicit or enhance their real-time emotional and behavioural responses (e.g. Tussyadiah et al. 2018). Further, given that popular destination-based game franchises such as *Yakuza*, *Watch Dogs*, and *Assassin's Creed* (Table 8.1) are set in distinctive historical periods, this chapter also considers the interplay between presence and nostalgia, and how it relates to game-induced tourism.

Last, despite a growing number of successful cases and promising applications, video games are also proving to be a less than perfect "selling machine" or promotional vehicle for destinations (Dubois et al. 2020). As such, this chapter concludes with a critical management discussion that outlines drawbacks, implications, and considerations for both game developers and destination marketers contemplating investing in destination-based video games or simply using them to prop up their brand.

The Rise of Video Game-Induced Tourism

Tourism scholars have long sought to determine what induces visitors to choose and travel to a destination (Um and Crompton 1990; Sirakaya and Woodside 2005; Beritelli et al. 2019). As a result, we know that such decisions often stem from a special meaning that tourists give to a destination (Ghosh and Sarkar 2016; Akgün et al. 2020), and that media

Table 8.1 Game descriptions

Games/franchises	Developer/publisher	Genre	Link to tourism
Assassin's Creed	Ubisoft	Role-playing/open-world adventure games	Exploration of ancient cities
Battlefield 1	DICE/electronic arts	First-person shooter	Setting in various locations during WWI
Bioshock	2 K games	First-person shooter (sets in a fictional city of rapture)	
Bloodborne	FromSoftware/SIE	Action role-playing game (depicts a fictional world of Yharnam)	
Call of Duty: WWII	Sledgehammer games/Activision	First-person shooter	Setting in real-life locations during WWII
Death Stranding	Kojima productions/SIE	Open-world action game	Setting in ruined cities that were the battlefields of WWII
Fallout	Bethesda Softworks	Role-playing games	Exploration of a post-apocalyptic America.
Far Cry 3	Ubisoft	First-person shooter	Exploration of island
Fun Nanjing	Runhe software	Monopoly game	Initiated by the Nanjing municipal government for promoting attractions of Nanjing City.
Grand Theft Auto	Rockstar games	Open-world action games	Exploration of fictional cities which are based on real-life locations (Los Angeles, Las Vegas, New York City)
Horizon Zero Dawn	Guerrilla games/SIE	Open-world & role-playing game	
Pokémon GO	Niantic	Location-based AR game	Used for the gamification in tourism
Shenmue	SEGA	Action-adventure games	Exploration of the city of Yokosuka

(continued)

Table 8.1 (continued)

Games/franchises	Developer/publisher	Genre	Link to tourism
Smile Land Game	TAT	Challenge game that explores the main attractions of the kingdom of Thailand	Specifically designed by tourism authority Thailand (TAT) as part of its digital marketing strategy, based on the tourism attractions of Thailand
Uncharted	Naughty dog/SIE	Action-adventure games	Exploration of international locations and ancient ruins (Istanbul, London, Tibet, etc.)
Watch Dogs	Ubisoft	Open-world game	Exploration of the cities of Chicago, San Francisco, or London
Yakuza	Ryu Ga Gotoku studio/SEGA	Action-adventure game	Exploration of the cities of Tokyo and Osaka

SIE Sony Interactive Entertainment Inc.

plays a central role in crafting that emotional connection (Kim 2010; Kim et al. 2019).

The concept of "media-induced tourism" is built on this understanding and describes visits that result from a destination being depicted in a film, series, or videos (Busby et al. 2013; Cardoso et al. 2017). Films can both attract tourists before their travel and increase willingness to revisit the destination or recommend it to friends at the post-travel stage (Báez-Montenegro and Devesa-Fernández 2017). When perceiving strong authenticity during media consumption, film tourists are also more likely to show a higher level of destination loyalty (Teng and Chen 2020). Interestingly, this phenomenon is not limited to a specific film genre, as portrayals in horror, action, or romance films equally appear to increase the popularity of a given destination, as well as broader consumer awareness about it (Busby et al. 2013).

For instance, New Zealand attracted many visitors after being featured in films such as *The Piano, Whale Rider,* and *The Lord of the Rings* (Zoladek 2017), much like Croatia's tourism and economy significantly benefited from HBO's *Game of Thrones* series (Tkalec et al. 2017). However, there remains some debate as to how media consumption triggers audiences' motivation to travel. While factors are likely multi-fold, antecedents such as authenticity (Buchmann et al. 2010), celebrity attachment (Teng and Chen 2020), and destination image (Chen 2018) are seen as having some influence on destination image and visitation in this context.

Similarly, many video game players have been shown to extend or replicate emotions previously experienced while consuming destination-based content by visiting said destination (Dubois and Gibbs 2018; Geraghty et al. 2019). Indeed, video games are proving to be powerful tools when it comes to promoting tourism destinations or to engaging with visitors on-site (Shen et al. 2020; Xu et al. 2016). Dubois and Gibbs (2018) analysed such testimonials left by destination-based "gamers" on popular travel websites and suggest that the medium's fast-rising cultural and economic relevance, as well as its broad demographic reach, are reasons for marketers to work alongside video game studios in shaping an enticing image. Specifically, by providing ways to explore sophisticated 3D renditions of existing built environments, the hope is that prospective tourists will grow more knowledgeable and attached to the local attractions and ultimately travel to said destination (Huang et al. 2016).

For example, the Yakuza franchise developers worked to digitalize real hotels (e.g. APA Hotel), eateries (e.g. Sushi Zanmai), and attractions (e.g. Shinjuku Toho Building), in turn helping to promote local brands. The Nanjing municipal government in China and Runhe Software jointly developed *Fun Nanjing*, a monopoly-like game in which players can travel between famous local attractions and "buy" virtual properties (Tao et al. 2016). Similarly, the Tourism Authority of Thailand (TAT) created the *Smile Land Game* featuring some of the country's iconic attractions, restaurants, and shops, as part of its digital marketing efforts to attract younger visitors (Xu et al. 2017). Meanwhile, the West Virginia Tourism Board formally teamed up with Bethesda to be featured in the studio's popular *Fallout* franchise's latest instalment. Despite this potential, it should be noted that the majority of destinations lucky enough to still find themselves in a popular video game often do so in a fortuitous manner, thereby missing out on a potential opportunity to intentionally affect the content and to better market to prospective visitors.

Perhaps more widespread are on-site applications of video games and of their core principles in tourism. Indeed, the concept of gamification has gained substantial interest in this sector in the last decade (Xu et al. 2017; Shen et al. 2020). Although there is still no agreement on the definition, it refers to an approach that uses game mechanics and game dynamics with a specific desired outcome in areas outside of traditional gaming (Reiners and Wood 2014). While it can be applied towards generating greater interest in a destination as Ontario Tourism did with its "Where Am I" campaign (Shen et al. 2020), it remains most frequently used to shape tourists' on-site behaviours through their mobile devices, engage them with the environment, and encourage them to embark on scavenger hunts (Xu et al. 2017). In this particular instance, game mechanics such as rules, feedbacks, and achievements help destinations develop immersive gamified experiences and to provide visitors with targeted, timely information (Shen et al. 2020). Gamification can even encourage cooperation or competition among tourists, increasing their engagement during the trip (Xu et al. 2017). More sophisticated location-based augmented reality (AR) games allow for interactions with the environment on their mobile devices and to complete simple tasks, helping tourists build a stronger connection with destinations.

Last, the rise of educational applications of destination-based video games may also indirectly benefit the tourism sector. For instance, Ubisoft introduced a non-violent *"Discovery Tour"* mode in its *Assassin's Creed: Odyssey* game to showcase their digital reconstruction of ancient Greece—as well as to allow players, generally elementary or high-school students, to experience the built environment, local culture, and rich history without having to actually engage with the game's central quests.

Investigating the Drivers and Mechanisms of Video Game-Induced Tourism

Unlike other forms of media-induced tourism, video games' interactive and immersive nature allows players to make independent choices and includes them as a part of the mediated world (Klimmt et al. 2009).

Thus, while playing in an "open-world" game (e.g. *Assassin's Creed, Grand Theft Auto, Uncharted*), players can freely explore the city, walk through a local bazaar, try local food, or even hold up their virtual mobile phone to take selfies. Gonzalez (2020) suggests that "video games of real-life places are like hearing a story from a friend" and wanting to visit the places afterwards because travelling makes others' stories become their own. In the case of *Shenmue*, an action-adventure game that depicts 1980's Yokosuka (Japan), players ended up building a robust online community, which in turn helped the town receive extensive media attention and additional visitors (Ramírez-Moreno 2019).

The Stimulus-Organism-Response (SOR) model (Mehrabian and Russell 1974) provides an interesting lens to understand tourists' decision-making process in this particular context. It posits that upon being stimulated by the external environment (S), individuals will experience an emotion (O), which in turn will lead them to take specific actions (R). The SOR model has been used before to predict consumer behaviour by examining their cognition and perceived service quality (Jacoby 2002). Hew et al. (2018) applied it in the context of mobile tourism shopping to explain how social presence as the environmental stimulus increases users' perceived enjoyment, and in turn, behavioural intention. SOR also predicts user behaviour when using other information and communication technologies. For instance, Kim et al. (2020) found that VR created more authentic experiences (S), leading to enhanced emotional involvement (O), and to a subsequent inclination to visit destinations (R).

Applied to destination-based video games, we posit that the environmental stimulus lies in the players' sense of presence. Indeed, the medium's complex renderings, combined with strong agency, impact the players' perceptions and blur the lines between the virtual and the real world (Blum et al. 2012; Tamborini and Skalski 2006). Gone are the days when destinations were only a distant skyline, the home of sports franchises or just the name of a mission, racetrack, or map in a given video game. According to Rardin (2020), some of today's video games "master iconic landmarks and capture the feel of their respective cities. It's especially fun to visit one of these cities in real life and have the feeling of being there before". Of interest is the fact that such a strong sense of presence has been shown to impact the players' emotional state and, in turn, their behavioural intention (Ravaja et al. 2006).

Presence and Nostalgia as Drivers and Mechanisms of Video Game-Induced Tourism

Enhancing the players' sense of presence has long been a priority for video game developers because of its impact on players' experience satisfaction (Tamborini and Skalski 2006). Likewise, several scholars have also sought to explain how humans interact with virtual environments using the construct of presence (e.g. Skalski et al. 2011; Yu and Wang 2019). Here, the term "presence" is derived from "telepresence" (Minsky 1980) and describes a phenomenon whereby media users are not able to differentiate between reality and the mediated or, as Sadowski and Stanney put it, "a sense of belief that one has left the real world and is now 'present' in the virtual environment" (2002, 791). Thus, presence can be understood in terms of "spatial presence", referring to feeling lost or immersed during media use, and to how individuals feel physically present in said environment (Schubert et al. 2001).

A growing body of evidence suggests that video games elicit a more intense feeling of 'being there' compared to other media such as film and television (e.g. Lombard and Ditton 1997; Dubois et al. 2020). This higher level of presence during virtual experiences generates greater enjoyment, which in turn forms a positive virtual destination image in the post-experience phase (Sylaiou et al. 2010; Weibel et al. 2008). Having a higher level of presence also reflects positively on dimensions such as local friendliness or infrastructure, and behavioural intentions such as booking travel products or purchasing travel itinerary packages (Hyun and O'Keefe 2012).

In addition to presence, destination-based video games have increasingly resorted to nostalgia in some of their popular franchises, especially in large "AAA" productions (Wulf et al. 2018). For instance, *Yakuza 0* depicts the real street scenery of Tokyo and Osaka in 1988, allowing players to experience that period's Japanese lifestyle by visiting karaoke bars, clubs, or arcades. This game also allows players to explore what the Japanese bubble-era economy looked like by completing side-stories such as investing in a local telephone club or writing letters to the radio station. In terms of mechanism, Kim et al. (2019) explain that such content evokes nostalgic feelings and generates an emotional connection with the featured destinations. This particular form of the stimulus also creates familiarity with destinations and elevates them to symbolic places with memories (Bandyopadhyay 2008), thereby influencing the decision-making process at the pre-travel stage (Caton and Santos 2007).

It should be noted that this nostalgia trend is also observed in other media, as exemplified by the recent successes of 1980s inspired film and television series (e.g. *Ready Player One, Stranger Things*). Such content has gained widespread popularity among Gen-Xers and Millennials who were either too young or not yet born to experience this era (Mccarthy 2019). Pickering and Keightley (2006) assert that nostalgia exists because people naturally long for things from the past. However, compared to traditional media, interactive media such as video games allow users to further focus on the content by enabling them to control their actions and visual angle, deriving a stronger emotional experience (Nelson et al. 2004; Poels et al. 2012).

Specifically, research indicates that "it is the ways in which video games are different that make them particularly suited as objects of nostalgia" (Fenty 2008, 24–25). For one, the intense sensory stimulation needed to yield a truly immersive experience generates stronger emotions than other leisure activities (Poels et al. 2012). The medium also benefits from the possibility to offer a range of nostalgic elements, be it using graphics, soundtracks, or narration, providing a more complete and meaningful experience than TV or film (Esposito 2005; Suominen 2008).

In summary, SOR theory suggests a mechanism by which tourists make travel decisions after experiencing video games: the medium and its content enhance users' sense of presence (stimulus) which contributes to their affective response (organism) and subsequently encourages them to travel (response). In other words, the more individuals are immersed in the virtual environment, the more intense emotions they will have for the past, which positively impacts travel-related behaviours. However, it is equally important to discuss the many ethical concerns and issues when using presence and nostalgia for tourism purposes. Attempting to elicit positive emotions or behaviours towards destinations through video games is one thing, but how players actually interpret and choose to react to the content in real life is another one.

The Risks and Limitations of Video Game-Induced Tourism

On the surface, exploiting history seems both very profitable for video game studios and enjoyable for players, while also generating positive externalities such as innovative educational material, awareness of a given historical event or character, as well as tourism revenues for featured destinations. Digitizing heritage sites and historical objects has also been shown to keep players engaged in the game longer and to help with restorative or preservation efforts. For instance, visual assets from *Assassin's Creed Unity*, set in eighteenth-century Paris, are proving to be crucial to the reconstruction of the Notre-Dame Cathedral (Hanussek 2019; de Ávila et al. 2020).

On the other hand, these same video games often face criticisms of cultural appropriation, of historical inaccuracy, or of insensitive representations (Balela and Mundy 2015). Case in point, *Assassin's Creed Unity* drew negative reviews for featuring anachronistic symbols such as the French flag and national anthem years before their actual inception. Likewise, Svensson (2017) noted that *Far Cry 3* was stereotyping Māori and Samoan cultures, while *Horizon Zero Dawn* borrowed symbolic elements from minority cultures and depicted Native Americans as "tribal" or "savage". Much like in the film industry, video game developers can always claim the right to creative freedom and artistic liberties. However, in the end, when pitting authenticity against enjoyability, developers appear to favour the latter and to use history to build a more entertaining game experience.

Using WWII elements is another example of how game developers inaccurately use historical events as a mere intellectual property bank. Instead of simply designing a random battlefield, some AAA franchises such as *Call of Duty*, *Battlefield*, and *Death Stranding* have decided to recreate (in)famous war zones or historical battles, often with troubling realism, while omitting the social-economic and human cost of war and delivering misleading messages. It is also important to at least recognize that history is usually told from the perspective of the 'winner', that representations of what happened are culturally biased, and that developers—even if well-intended—would only have partial knowledge as to events either because there were no recordings or the information was sealed for decades. Again, given the high level of immersion, players may not always be able to distinguish fact from fiction, not to mention the questionable ethics of using de facto cemeteries as virtual playgrounds.

In all fairness, video game developers owe very little to tourism boards and destinations that happened to be selected to host the next instalment of a given franchise. After all, few of the current cases of game-induced tourism, save for the recent West Virginia-Bethesda endeavour, are purposeful collaborations with clear visitation objectives. Destinations could not do much to fight it either. History is not mutually exclusive, and destinations would not have much of a case, even when negatively impacted by being chosen as the background to violent stories (Dubois et al. 2020). However, building realistic environments and time periods to emotionally bond with players—and yes, generate more initial or in-game purchases—comes with the responsibility of delivering authentic information about cultural heritage and actions to avoid widening the gap between minority and majority cultures. Without such principles and limitations in mind, developers are missing out on an opportunity to meaningfully encourage and engage their player base on what to actually seek out when visiting the games' various locations, instead merely affording them to "assassinate (their) way through history" (Politopoulos et al. 2019, 317). In the end, there is nothing wrong in using a fictional city, such as *Yharnam* (Bloodborne) or *Rapture* (Bioshock), when history and location come a far second to the narrative.

Even worse is when such insensitive behaviours in the virtual world, triggered by presence and nostalgia, negatively impact the modern-day featured destinations and communities. For instance, players reportedly feel the urge to push others when visiting places portrayed in the game (as they do when playing *Assassin's Creed* [de Gortari et al. 2011]), want to throw something to animals in the streets that allow them to be captured as in *Pokémon Go* (de Gortari 2018), or engage in a range of undesirable behaviours that mimic in-game action (Dubois and Gibbs 2018). Such observations are consistent with research that shows that gaming experiences impact almost all players' daily life, including their way of thinking and their actions (de Gortari et al. 2011). Thus, it is only natural to expect video game developers to consider that rather inappropriate content, or plots that include intense violence, is likely to increase subsequent players' on-site uncivil or deviant behaviours, and as such, to revisit the imperative to use a real destination as the backdrop for their story.

Other types of media-induced tourism have faced similar criticisms and can also at times negatively affect destination image, tourist satisfaction, and sustainability (Sharma 2017). Portrayals often encourage romanticized or stereotyped perceptions (Liu et al. 2020), thereby distorting the authentic identities of these places (O'Connor 2011). While a higher level of expectation often leads to a higher level of tourist satisfaction (Liu et al. 2017), discrepancies introduced by media between the expected image and the actual experience can decrease tourist satisfaction (Heitmann 2010). Further, the lack of collaboration with local residents and travel operators to properly plan for a sharp increase in tourist demand can also lead to shocks and sustainability issues (Thelen et al. 2020).

It is also worth considering the downsides of using a medium that is known to foster hostile actions (Gentile et al. 2004), increase future alcohol use (Wang et al. 2013), and engender aggressive responses (Lin 2013). However, video games have been shown to contribute to players' psychological well-being, vitality, and optimism (Wulf et al. 2018), and to increase feelings of connectedness during social isolation (Tamplin-Wilson et al. 2019). Thus, destinations contemplating video games as a potential promotion tool ought to carefully weigh the pros and cons of a medium whose mechanisms rely on creating an intense feeling of presence, in a way that at times feels closer to addiction-like behaviours than just casual leisure. One way to potentially overcome these inherent limitations is to use video games to generate emotions other than just elation and actions other than shooting (Handrahan 2020).

Conclusion

This chapter adds to an emerging body of literature on the linkage between video games and tourism by providing the first conceptualization of gaming's specific psychological drivers that induce behaviours and feelings towards a given destination. Understanding video games differ from other forms of media-induced tourism, and how it elicits travel allows destination marketers to fine-tune their promotional strategies. It also exposes the medium's inherent risks and calls for a prudent application to avoid undesirable behaviours, inaccuracies, or cultural appropriation.

Nevertheless, it remains that video games have become a mainstream fixture in households and popular culture and, as such, an unavoidable channel to reach potential visitors for destination marketers. While the tourism industry stands to further benefit from this medium, the hope is that destinations and developers come together to elicit more sophisticated and positive, yet equally powerful, emotional responses from players such as sadness, contemplation, and critical thoughts.

Works Cited

Akgün, A. E., Senturk, H. A., Keskin, H., & Onal, I. 2020. The relationships among nostalgic emotion, destination images and tourist behaviors: An empirical study of Istanbul. *Journal of Destination Marketing & Management* 16: https://doi.org/10.1016/j.jdmm.2019.03.009

Báez-Montenegro, Andrea, and María Devesa-Fernández. 2017. Motivation, Satisfaction and Loyalty In The Case Of A Film Festival: Differences Between Local And Non-Local Participants. *Journal of Cultural Economics* 41 (2): 173–195. https://doi.org/10.1007/s10824-017-9292-2.

Bahtiar, Arief Rais, and Alon Jala Tirta Segara. 2020. Design of Smart Gamification In Village Tourism: An Indonesian Case Study. *International Journal of Engineering Pedagogy* 10 (1): 82–93. https://doi.org/10.3991/ijep.v10i1.11522.

Balela, Majed S., and Darren Mundy. 2015. Analysing Cultural Heritage and its Representation in Video Games. In *DiGRA Conference*.

Bandyopadhyay, Ranjan. 2008. Nostalgia, Identity And Tourism: Bollywood In The Indian Diaspora. *Journal of Tourism and Cultural Change* 6 (2): 79–100. https://doi.org/10.1080/14766820802140463.

Beritelli, Pietro, Stephan Reinhold, and Jieqing Luo. 2019. "How Come You Are Here?" Considering the Context in Research on Travel Decisions. *Journal of Travel Research* 58 (2): 333–337. https://doi.org/10.1177/0047287517746017.

Blum, Lisa, Richard Wetzel, Rod McCall, Leif Oppermann, and Wolfgang Broll. (2012, June). The Final Timewarp: Using Form and Content To Support Player Experience and Presence When Designing Location-Aware Mobile Augmented Reality Games. In *Proceedings of the Designing Interactive Systems Conference*, 711–720.

Buchmann, Anne, Kevin Moore, and David Fisher. 2010. Experiencing Film Tourism: Authenticity and Fellowship. *Annals of Tourism Research* 37 (1): 229–248. https://doi.org/10.1016/j.annals.2009.09.005.

Busby, Graham, Rong Huang, and Rebecca Jarman. 2013. The Stein Effect: An Alternative Film-Induced Tourism Perspective. *International Journal of Tourism Research* 15 (6): 570–582. https://doi.org/10.1002/jtr.1875.

Cardoso, Lucília, Cristina M.S. Estevão, Ana Cristina Fernandes Muniz, and Helena Alves. 2017. Film Induced Tourism: A Systematic Literature Review. *Tourism & Management Studies* 13 (3): 23–30. https://doi.org/10.18089/tms.2017.13303.

Caton, Kellee, and Carla Almeida Santos. 2007. Heritage Tourism on Route 66: Deconstructing Nostalgia. *Journal of Travel Research* 45 (4): 371–386. https://doi.org/10.1177/0047287507299572.

Chen, Chien-Yu. 2018. Influence of Celebrity Involvement on Place Attachment: Role of Destination Image in Film Tourism. *Asia Pacific Journal of Tourism Research* 23 (1): 1–14. https://doi.org/10.1080/10941665.2017.1394888.

de Ávila, Camila, Aline Corso, and Gustavo Daudt Fischer. 2020. Preservation and Heritage at Play in Technoculture. *Journal of Digital Media & Interaction* 3 (7): 51–67. https://doi.org/10.34624/jdmi.v3i7.15559.

de Gortari, Angelica B. Ortiz. 2018. Empirical Study on Game Transfer Phenomena in a Location-Based Augmented Reality Game. *Telematics and Informatics* 35 (2): 382–396. https://doi.org/10.1016/j.tele.2017.12.015.

de Gortari, Angelica B. Ortiz, Karin Aronsson, and Mark Griffiths. 2011. Game Transfer Phenomena in Video Game Playing: A Qualitative Interview Study. *International Journal of Cyber Behavior, Psychology and Learning (IJCBPL)* 1 (3): 15–33. https://doi.org/10.4018/ijcbpl.2011070102.

Dubois, Louis-Etienne, and Chris Gibbs. 2018. Video Game–Induced Tourism: A New Frontier For Destination Marketers. *Tourism Review* 73: 2: 186–2: 198. https://doi.org/10.1108/TR-07-2017-0115.

Dubois, Louis-Etienne, Tom Griffin, Christopher Gibbs, and Daniel Guttentag. 2020. The Impact of Video Games on Destination Image. *Current Issues in Tourism* 24 (5): 1–13. https://doi.org/10.1080/13683500.2020.1724082.

Esposito, Nicolas. 2005. *How Video Game History Shows Us Why Video Game Nostalgia Is So Important Now*. University of Technology of Compiègne.

Fenty, S. 2008. Why Old School Is 'Cool': A Brief Analysis of Classic Video Game Nostalgia. *Playing the past: History and Nostalgia in video games*, 19-31. Nashville: Vanderbilt University Press.

Gentile, Douglas A., Paul J. Lynch, Jennifer Ruh Linder, and David A. Walsh. 2004. The Effects of Violent Video Game Habits on Adolescent Hostility, Aggressive Behaviors, and School Performance. *Journal of Adolescence* 27 (1): 5–22. https://doi.org/10.1016/j.adolescence.2003.10.002.

Geraghty, Lincoln, C. Lundberg, and V. Ziakas. 2019. Exploring the Popular Culture and Tourism Place Making Nexus. *Journal of Popular Culture (Boston)* 52 (6): 1241–1556. https://doi.org/10.1111/jpcu.12867.

Ghosh, Tathagata, and Abhigyan Sarkar. 2016. "To Feel a Place of Heaven": Examining the Role of Sensory Reference Cues And Capacity For Imagination In Destination Marketing. *Journal of Travel & Tourism Marketing* 33 (sup1): 25–37. https://doi.org/10.1080/10548408.2014.997962.

Gonzalez, B. 2020. Video Games Made Me Travel. https://medium.com/superjump/video-games-made-me-travel-95eb01638a32. Accessed 25 April 2020.

Handrahan, Matthew. 2020. Shawn Layden: "I Would Welcome a Return to the 12 to 15 Hour AAA Game." https://www.gamesindustry.biz/articles/2020-06-23-shawn-layden-gamelab. Accessed 30 July 2020.

Hanussek, Benjamin. 2019. Conducting Archaeogaming & Protecting Digital Heritage: Does the Future for Archaeology Lie in The Immaterial. *ISTE OpenScience*. London: ISTE Ltd. https://doi.org/10.21494/ISTE.OP.2019.0414.

Heitmann, Sine. 2010. Film Tourism Planning and Development—Questioning the Role of Stakeholders and Sustainability. *Tourism and Hospitality Planning & Development* 7 (1): 31–46. https://doi.org/10.1080/14790530903522606.

Hew, Jun-Jie, Lai-Ying Leong, Garry Wei-Han Tan, Voon-Hsien Lee, and Keng-Boon Ooi. 2018. Mobile Social Tourism Shopping: A Dual-Stage Analysis of a Multi-Mediation Model. *Tourism Management* 66: 121–139. https://doi.org/10.1016/j.tourman.2017.10.005.

Ho, Shirley S., May O. Lwin, Jeremy R.H. Sng, and Andrew Z.H. Yee. 2017. Escaping Through Exergames: Presence, Enjoyment, and Mood Experience in Predicting Children's Attitude Toward Exergames. *Computers in Human Behavior* 72: 381–389. https://doi.org/10.1016/j.chb.2017.03.001.

Huang, Yu Chih, Kenneth Frank Backman, Sheila J. Backman, and Lan Lan Chang. 2016. Exploring the Implications of Virtual Reality Technology in Tourism Marketing: an Integrated Research Framework. *International Journal of Tourism Research* 18 (2): 116–128. https://doi.org/10.1002/jtr.2038.

Hyun, Martin Yongho, and Robert Martin O'Keefe. 2012. Virtual Destination Image: Testing a Telepresence Model. *Journal of Business Research* 65 (1): 29–35. https://doi.org/10.1016/j.jbusres.2011.07.011.

Jacoby, Jacob. 2002. Stimulus-Organism-Response Reconsidered: An Evolutionary Step in Modeling (Consumer) Behavior. *Journal of Consumer Psychology* 12 (1): 51–57. https://doi.org/10.1207/S15327663JCP1201_05.

Kim, Sangkyun. 2010. Extraordinary Experience: "Re-enacting and Photographing at Screen Tourism Locations". *Tourism and Hospitality Planning & Development* 7 (1): 59–75. https://doi.org/10.1080/14790530903522630.

Kim, Seongseop, Sangkyun Kim, and James F. Petrick. 2019. The Effect of Film Nostalgia on Involvement, Familiarity, and Behavioral Intentions. *Journal of Travel Research* 58 (2): 283–297. https://doi.org/10.1177/0047287517746015.

Kim, Myung Ja, Choong-Ki Lee, and Timothy Jung. 2020. Exploring Consumer Behavior in Virtual Reality Tourism Using an Extended Stimulus-Organism-Response Model. *Journal of Travel Research* 59 (1): 69–89. https://doi.org/10.1177/0047287518818915.

Klimmt, Christoph, Dorothée Hefner, and Peter Vorderer. 2009. The Video Game Experience as "True" Identification: A Theory of Enjoyable Alterations of Players' Self-Perception. *Communication Theory* 19 (4): 351–373. https://doi.org/10.1111/j.1468-2885.2009.01347.x.

Lee, Kwan Min. 2004. Presence, Explicated. *Communication Theory* 14 (1): 27–50. https://doi.org/10.1111/j.1468-2885.2004.tb00302.x.

Lin, Jih-Hsuan. 2013. Do Video Games Exert Stronger Effects on Aggression Than Film? The Role of Media Interactivity and Identification on the Association of Violent Content and Aggressive Outcomes. *Computers in Human Behavior* 29 (3): 535–543. https://doi.org/10.1016/j.chb.2012.11.001.

Liu, Xiaoming, Jun Li, and Woo Gon Kim. 2017. The Role of Travel Experience in the Structural Relationships Among Tourists' Perceived Image, Satisfaction, and Behavioral Intentions. *Tourism and Hospitality Research* 17 (2): 135–146. https://doi.org/10.1177/1467358415610371.

Liu, Yong, Wei Lee Chin, Florin Nechita, and Adina Nicoleta Candrea. 2020. Framing Film-Induced Tourism into a Sustainable Perspective from Romania, Indonesia and Malaysia. *Sustainability* 12 (23): 9910. https://doi.org/10.3390/su12239910.

Lombard, Matthew, and Theresa Ditton. 1997. At the Heart of It All: The Concept of Presence. *Journal of Computer-Mediated Communication* 3 (2). https://doi.org/10.1111/j.1083-6101.1997.tb00072.x.

Mccarthy, Kayla. 2019. Remember Things: Consumerism, Nostalgia, and Geek Culture in Stranger Things. *Journal of Popular Culture* 52 (3): 663–677. https://doi.org/10.1111/jpcu.12800.

Mehrabian, Albert, and James A. Russell. 1974. *An Approach to Environmental Psychology*. Cambridge: The MIT Press.

Minsky, Marvin. 1980, June. Telepresence. *OMNI Magazine*.

Nelson, Michelle R., Heejo Keum, Ronald A. Yaros, and A. 2004. Advertisement Or Adcreep Game Players' Attitudes Toward Advertising and Product Placements in Computer Games. *Journal of Interactive Advertising* 5 (1): 3–21. https://doi.org/10.1080/15252019.2004.10722090.

O'Connor, Noëlle. 2011. A Conceptual Examination of the Film Induced Tourism Phenomenon in Ireland. *European Journal of Tourism, Hospitality and Recreation* 2 (3): 105–125.

Pickering, Michael, and Emily Keightley. 2006. The Modalities of Nostalgia. *Current Sociology* 54 (6): 919–941. https://doi.org/10.1177/0011392106068458.

Poels, Karolien, Yvonne De Kort, and Wijnand I. Jsselsteijn. 2012. Identification and Categorization of Digital Game Experiences: A Qualitative Study Integrating Theoretical Insights and Player Perspectives. *Westminster Papers in Communication and Culture* 9 (1): 107–129. https://doi.org/10.16997/wpcc.153.

Politopoulos, Aris, Angus A.A. Mol, Krijn H.J. Boom, and Csilla E. Ariese. 2019. "History Is Our Playground": Action and Authenticity in Assassin's Creed: Odyssey. *Advances in Archaeological Practice* 7 (3): 317–323. https://doi.org/10.1017/aap.2019.30.

Ramírez-Moreno, Carlos. 2019. Promoting Yokosuka via Video Game Tourism: The Case of the Shenmue Sacred Spot Guide Map. In *DiGRA 2019: The 12th Digital Games Research Association Conference*.

Rardin, Devin. (2020, March 15). *10 Most Realistic Recreations of Cities In Video Games*. TheGamer. https://www.thegamer.com/video-game-cities-most-realistic-assassins-creed-the-division/. Accessed Sept 2020.

Ravaja, Niklas, Timo Saari, Marko Turpeinen, Jari Laarni, Mikko Salminen, and Matias Kivikangas. 2006. Spatial Presence and Emotions During Video Game Playing: Does It Matter with Whom You Play?. *Presence: Teleoperators and Virtual Environments* 15 (4): 381–332. Spatial Presence and Emotions During Video Game Playing: Does It Matter with Whom You Play. https://doi.org/10.1162/pres.15.4.381.

Reiners, Torsten, and Lincoln C. Wood. 2014. *Gamification in Education and Business*. 2015th ed. New York: Springer International Publishing AG.

Sadowski, Wallace, and Kay Stanney. 2002. Presence in Virtual Environments. In *Human Factors and Ergonomics. Handbook of Virtual Environments: Design, Implementation, and Applications*, ed. Kay Stanney, 791–806. New Jersey: Lawrence Erlbaum Associates.

Schubert, Thomas, Frank Friedmann, and Holger Regenbrecht. 2001. The Experience of Presence: Factor Analytic Insights. *Presence: Teleoperators & Virtual Environments* 10 (3): 266–281. https://doi.org/10.1162/105474601300343603.

Sharma, Anukrati. 2017. Destination Marketing and Promotion Through Film Tourism: An Empirical Study of Hadoti Region of Rajasthan. *Journal of Applied Management and Investments* 6 (2): 118–129.

Shen, Ye Sandy, Hwansuk Chris Choi, Marion Joppe, and Sunghwan Yi. 2020. What Motivates Visitors To Participate In A Gamified Trip? A Player Typology Using Q Methodology. *Tourism Management* 78: 104074. https://doi.org/10.1016/j.tourman.2019.104074.

Sirakaya, Ercan, and Arch G. Woodside. 2005. Building and Testing Theories of Decision Making by Travellers. *Tourism Management* 26 (6): 815–832. https://doi.org/10.1016/j.tourman.2004.05.004.

Skalski, Paul, Ron Tamborini, Ashleigh Shelton, Michael Buncher, and Pete Lindmark. 2011. Mapping the Road to Fun: Natural Video Game Controllers, Presence, and Game Enjoyment. *New Media & Society* 13 (2): 224–242. https://doi.org/10.1177/1461444810370949.

Suominen, Jakko. 2008. The Past as the Future? Nostalgia and Retrogaming in Digital Culture. In *Proceedings of perthDAC2007. The 7th International Digital Arts and Cultures Conference. The Future of Digital Media Culture* 15: 18.

Svensson, Tova. 2017. *Cultural Appropriation in Games: A Comparative Study Between Far Cry 3 (2012), Overwatch (2016) and Horizon Zero Dawn (2017)*. Uppsala Universitet, Institutionen för speldesign.

Sylaiou, Stella, Katerina Mania, Athanasis Karoulis, and Martin White. 2010. Exploring the Relationship between Presence and Enjoyment in a Virtual

Museum. *International Journal of Human-Computer Studies* 68 (5): 243–253. https://doi.org/10.1016/j.ijhcs.2009.11.002.

Tamborini, Ron, and Paul Skalski. 2006. The Role of Presence in the Experience of Electronic Games. In *Playing Video Games: Motives, Responses, and Consequences*, ed. Peter Vorderer and Jennings Bryant, 225–240. Mahwah, NJ: Lawrence Erlbaum Associates Inc.

Tamplin-Wilson, Jay, Rebecca Smith, Jessica Morgan, and Pam Maras. 2019. Video Games as a Recovery Intervention for Ostracism. *Computers in Human Behavior* 97: 130–136. https://doi.org/10.1016/j.chb.2019.03.008.

Tao, Fei, Yiwen Wang, Ying Zuo, Haidong Yang, and Meng Zhang. 2016. Internet of Things in Product Life-Cycle Energy Management. *Journal of Industrial Information Integration* 1: 26–39. https://doi.org/10.1016/j.jii.2016.03.001.

Teng, Hsiu-Yu, and Chien-Yu Chen. 2020. Enhancing Celebrity Fan-Destination Relationship in Film-Induced Tourism: The Effect of Authenticity. *Tourism Management Perspectives* 33: 100605. https://doi.org/10.1016/j.tmp.2019.100605.

Thelen, Timo, Sangkyun Kim, and Elisabeth Scherer. 2020. Film Tourism Impacts: A Multi-Stakeholder Longitudinal Approach. *Tourism Recreation Research* 45 (3): 291–306. https://doi.org/10.1080/02508281.2020.1718338.

Tkalec, Marina, Ivan Zilic, and Vedran Recher. 2017. The Effect of Film Industry on Tourism: Game of Thrones and Dubrovnik. *International Journal of Tourism Research* 19 (6): 705–714. https://doi.org/10.1002/jtr.2142.

Tussyadiah, Iis P., Dan Wang, Timothy H. Jung, and M. Claudia tom Dieck. 2018. Virtual Reality, Presence, and Attitude Change: Empirical Evidence from Tourism. *Tourism Management (1982)* 66: 140–154. https://doi.org/10.1016/j.tourman.2017.12.003.

Um, Seoho, and John L. Crompton. 1990. Attitude Determinants in Tourism Destination Choice. *Annals of Tourism Research* 17 (3): 432–448. https://doi.org/10.1016/0160-7383(90)90008-F.

Weibel, David, Bartholomäus Wissmath, Stephan Habegger, Yves Steiner, and Rudolf Groner. 2008. Playing Games Against Computer-Vs. Human-Controlled Opponents: Effects on Presence, Flow, and Enjoyment. *Computers in Human Behavior* 24 (5): 2274–2291. https://doi.org/10.1016/j.chb.2007.11.002.

Wulf, Tim, Nicholas D. Bowman, John A. Velez, and Johannes Breuer. 2018. Once Upon a Game: Exploring Video Game Nostalgia and Its Impact on

Well-Being. *Psychology of Popular Media* 9 (1): 83–95. https://doi.org/10.1037/ppm0000208.

Xu, Feifei, Feng Tian, Dimitrios Buhalis, Jessika Weber, and Hongmei Zhang. 2016. Tourists as Mobile Gamers: Gamification for Tourism Marketing. *Journal of Travel & Tourism Marketing* 33 (8): 1124–1142. https://doi.org/10.1080/10548408.2015.1093999.

Xu, Feifei, Dimitrios Buhalis, and Jessika Weber. 2017. Serious Games and the Gamification of Tourism. *Tourism Management* 60: 244–256. https://doi.org/10.1016/j.tourman.2016.11.020.

Yu, Jian, and Yongbin Wang. 2019, July. User Interaction and Scenario-Based Experience Design for New Media Technology in Museum Spatial Experience. In *International Conference on Applied Human Factors and Ergonomics*, 263–270. New York and Cham: Springer. https://doi.org/10.1007/978-3-030-20444-0_25

Zoladek, Marek. 2017. On the Trail of Lord of The Rings. Pop-Culture Tourism in New Zealand. *Current Issues of Tourism Research* 5 (2): 44–47. bwmeta1.element.ekon-element-000171453417.

9

Screen Tourism on the Smartphone: A Typology and Critical Evaluation of the First Decade of Smart Screen Tourism

Cathrin Bengesser and Anne Marit Waade

The Convergence of Places in Smartphone-Based Screen Tourism

Screen tourism apps appeared on the market around 2009 (Leotta 2016), at about the same time museums and other destinations began to experiment with on-site uses of smartphone technology (Carson and Pennings 2020, 416). Over their first decade, many screen tourism apps disappeared from app stores and websites, highlighting their ephemeral nature. As a convergent media technology, the smartphone combines distinct services and practices all in one place, such as telecommunication, internet browsing, as well as the ability to play, produce, and share audiovisual material. For tourists, this multitude of 'applications' turns the smartphone into a one-stop-shop for previously distinct services used in the various phases of

---

C. Bengesser (✉) · A. M. Waade
Aarhus University, Aarhus, Denmark
e-mail: cbengesser@cc.au.dk; amwaade@cc.au.dk

tourism (Carson and Pennings 2020, 414). Because of its convenience and potential for gathering behavioural data, 'Smart Tourism' has become a buzzword in the tourism industry, ranging from the use of big data for city management to the development of mobile applications for tourists. As Gretzel et al. argue (2015, 180), there is a danger that 'suddenly everything is smart'. This warrants closer academic attention, and an effort to define and develop theories about the use of mobile technology in tourism experiences and their promotion. To analyse 'smart tourism' experiences, models are needed that are mindful of their specific contexts and uses, but still allow broader insights into the development of this trend.

This chapter assesses the use of 'smart' experiences in screen tourism to offer a typology that considers their mediation, their content, and the different ways of engaging with space they offer to screen tourists. Previous classifications of (screen) tourism apps have focused on either content or technology. Leotta's (2016) survey of movie apps grouped them according to the content they offer and their target audiences: guided tours and maps for tourists, quizzes for film buffs, and practical location information for film professionals. This overview is valuable for differentiating content offered to users and emphasises that there are far more film-related apps than the primarily tourism-oriented applications on which this chapter focuses. Still, grouping apps according to their content does not reveal much about the way they use smartphone technology to promote and develop tourism experiences.

From a technological point of view, screen tourism apps exist at the lower end of the 'smart' spectrum. Although they are not necessarily part of data-driven, smart city initiatives, smartphone-based screen tourism experiences use data from a location's infrastructure and the user's behaviour to create and/or enhance on-site experiences and facilitate forms of co-creation through user-generated content or sharing—all relevant to Gretzel et al.'s (2015, 181) definition of 'smart tourism'.[1] In 2014, Neuhofer, Buhalis, and Ladkin proposed a typology of the use of technology in tourism that groups the various applications according to two

---

[1] Gretzel et al. (2015, 181) define smart tourism as 'tourism supported by integrated efforts at a destination to collect and aggregate/harness data derived from physical infrastructure, social connections, government/organisational sources and human bodies/minds in combination with the use of advanced technologies to transform that data into on-site experiences and business value-propositions with a clear focus on efficiency, sustainability and experience enrichment'.

dimensions: the intensity of technology use and the level of the guest's involvement in the co-creation of the experience, in contrast to fully staged activities. These two dimensions may also be applied to smartphone-based screen tourism, since there are variants in the technologies' sophistication, and levels of customisation and interactivity. Yet, technology-focused models of the use of internet or mobile technology in tourism do not address the specificity of screen tourism as a practice.

Sue Beeton (2005, 11) defined screen tourism as 'the visitation to sites where movies and TV programmes have been filmed as well as to tours to production studios, including film related theme parks'. Stefan Roesch (2009, 7–8) refined this definition, indicating the necessity of distinguishing between the 'film location tourist' and tourists who have merely been inspired to visit a place because of a film or TV series. Whereas the former 'actively visits a precise on-location that has been used for shooting a scene or scenes that were portrayed on the cinema or television screen' (Roesch 2009, 8), the latter does not actively seek out location visits, studio tours, or on-site re-enactments. Also, there are visitors who only discover sites and activities related to film and TV once they arrive. Finally, Marion Schulze (2017) describes virtual 'screen screen tourism', in which tourists explore film locations online, either in preparation for, or in lieu of, travelling.

Given the considerable variation in how screen tourism may be defined, it is also impossible to pinpoint the impact of screen tourism on visitor numbers. A few blockbuster productions stand out. New Zealand reported a 23 per cent increase in foreign visitors over a three-year period following the release of *Lord of the Rings* (2001) (Leotta 2011, 163). The *Harry Potter* studio tour outside London has been attracting fans since 2010, but film-tourists also travel far beyond the metropolis, contributing to tourism in England's rural areas (Lee 2012). For example, half of the visitors to Alnwick Castle claim that its use as Hogwarts in the *Harry Potter* films was a contributing factor in their decision to visit (Olsberg SPI 2015, 60). More recently, *Game of Thrones* (2011–2019) inspired new ways in which Northern Ireland could promote its landscape and cultural heritage by using the *GoT* brand (Çelik Rappas and Baschiera 2020). Smartphone apps exist for all these big screen tourism properties, which range from location maps and trip-planning advice for *Lord of the*

Rings fans ('Middle Earth Explorer') to on-site augmented reality games in the *Harry Potter* Studio ('Wizarding World App') and 360° images allowing for virtual visits to the Northern Irish locations of *Game of Thrones* ('GoT Northern Ireland').

For the screen tourist, the smartphone can collapse the boundaries between their viewing of films or television series on their screens, their experience of the screen tourism destinations through which the phone navigates them, and their sharing of individual experience of places on social media, which in turn contributes to other (potential) visitors' imaginings of the place. Lavarone (2021, 37) refers to the cinematic pilgrimage (another term for screen tourism) when she explains:

> '[…] we could say that tourist space is *mediatized* in the sense that it is virtually explored through media (in Lefebvre's terms, *conceived space*), or that it is physically invaded by media devices (*perceived space*). Finally, that in many cases, media have assigned it a tourist use and led to the establishment of new rituals, such as those accomplished by cinematic pilgrims (*lived space*)'. (Lavarone 2021, 37)

This complex relation between place and media is described in André Jansson's work (2013) on spatial mediatisation, in which the tourist's use of an actual physical place is related to the way in which the space is represented in mass media and how smart locative technology influence the way we understand and navigate specific places. If we apply this distinction to screen tourism apps, we see three aspects of spatial mediatisation: (a) the places are presented and seen in a film, TV series, or tourism promotion (spatial representation); (b) the fictional worlds and their diegeses become conflated with the actual places and add layers of meaning as conceived space (spatial imagination); and, finally, (c) location-based smart tourism technology concretely directs and choreographs the tourist's on-site movements in the physical, lived space, including the re-enactment of stories and social interaction within the place (mediatised use of place).

The development of smartphone-based screen tourism may be understood as a progressive refinement of the convergence of imagined, physical, and mediated space. The following case studies of screen tourism apps and responsive websites trace the uses of smartphones in facilitating the convergence of various facets of a space. The case studies are then used to develop a typology of screen tourism apps, according to both the form of technology used for mediation (personal, locative, or virtual) and the way they mediatise and assign uses to a space: tourist destination, media-production site, or fictional space. The findings of the individual case studies and their synthesis into a typology inform a discussion of factors that drive and hinder 'smart' screen tourism.

Case Studies of Smartphone-Based Nordic Noir Tourism

Selection of Objects and Methods

Lord of the Rings, *Harry Potter*, and *Game of Thrones* have attracted much of the attention paid to the exploration of the economic impact of screen tourism (e.g. Olsberg SPI 2015; Li et al. 2017), its promotional use by and at the destinations in question (Çelik Rappas and Baschiera 2020; Leotta 2011; Šegota 2018), and film-tourists' practices (e.g. Lee 2012; Roesch 2009). However, the following overview of the development of smartphone-based screen tourism looks beyond those blockbusters, and takes Nordic Noir crime films and series as its central case study. There are several reasons why the 'Nordic Noir' phenomenon makes for an interesting study in the context of promoting tourism in general, and, in particular, the use of smartphone-based technology to do so. On the one hand, the term 'Nordic Noir' describes specific features of crime fiction from Scandinavia, including slow storytelling, dark colour palettes, 'broken' protagonists, and social criticism (Creeber 2015); on the other hand, Nordic Noir is a promotional label, successfully exploited, for example, by Arrow Film (Hills 2017) to sell not only DVD box sets, but also the products and experience of Scandinavia, to affluent viewers of crime drama.

A detective tour can be found in many European cities (Reijnders 2011, 33–34). The crime genre, with its emphasis on the locations where crime scenes, bodies, and eventually, perpetrators, need to be detected, prepares the ground for activities that let crime fans walk in the footsteps of their favourite characters (Reijnders 2010; van Es and Reijnders 2018). Though the crime TV programmes these tours build on cannot boast the same global fan base as the fantasy blockbusters mentioned earlier, they are a regular feature on European broadcast and video-on-demand services. Crime series also travel well within the European TV market (Bondebjerg et al. 2017, 227–39). The Nordic Noir series' international circulation has stimulated screen tourism both in the capitals and on the periphery of the Nordic region. This phenomenon has been studied in locations such as *The Bridge*'s Malmö (Askanius 2017) and *Wallander*'s Ystad (Waade 2013; Waade 2016). Among frequent viewers of European crime programmes surveyed in nine European countries,[2] one in four respondents said they would be interested in visiting locations where a crime series they watched had been shot, and eight per cent of participants claimed to have already visited places because they had previously seen them on-screen (Pagello and Schleich 2020, 55).

Nordic Noir crime narratives have been instrumental in branding wider Scandinavia as a tourism region, and for branding specific, often rural, locations in it (Hansen and Waade 2017). For example, the television adaptations of Henning Mankell's *Wallander* novels played a prominent role in rebranding the southern-Swedish city of Ystad as a tourist destination, following an oil spill in 2003 (Waade 2013, 75). Building on the trend set by *Wallander*, public institutions and tourism organisations in Scandinavia have invested in producing crime series to attract tourism and/or rebrand their image.[3] At the same time, the crime genre also exemplifies conflicts between the imagined spaces of crime-ridden cities and the actual places that seek to promote themselves as enjoyable, and of course safe, tourist destinations (Migozzi 2020).

Nordic Noir's international popularity around 2010 coincided with screen tourism's leap from printed maps and guided tours to mobile mediation. Thus, a range of smartphone-based screen tourism activities

---

[2] The data collection for the online survey was carried out between March and July 2020 in Denmark, Sweden France, Hungary, Germany, Greece, Italy, Romania, and the United Kingdom (n1321).

[3] A recent example of this is the Danish crime series, *Hvide Sande* (2021), developed with the idea of reimagining the Danish West Coast through a TV series (Waade 2021). Other examples include the Danish series, *Norskov* (2015), and the Icelandic series, *Trapped* (2015–) (Hansen 2020).

has been developed and implemented around Nordic Noir screen tourism, tapping into their place-branding potential. While the Nordic crime series are much smaller productions in terms of budget and global audience, they are more frequent than once-in-a-decade successes like *Game of Thrones*. This is why the various instances of Nordic Noir screen tourism in Scandinavia, and its promotion through smartphone apps, are easier to compare than the singular and often exceptional impact of blockbuster productions on specific destinations. Therefore, when studying and promoting screen tourism, insights into the way 'smart' screen tourism has been implemented in Scandinavia and evaluations of its promotional potential in the region may also be more easily applied to destinations elsewhere.

The following case studies of screen tourism apps and responsive websites draw on a mixed-methods approach to combine four different perspectives on smart screen tourism: the screen tourists' point of view; experiences of audiences who do not (yet) consider themselves screen tourists; the users of smartphone technologies for screen tourism; and the creators of screen tourism experiences. Participant observation and production studies of Scandinavian screen tourism experiences form the background for this research (Waade 2013; Hansen and Waade 2017). We contextualise the experiences of active screen tourists in the locations we studied through five qualitative interviews with German viewers of European crime series, who were asked about their opinions regarding screen tourism related to their favourite series. The screen tourism apps were studied through 'walkthrough' analysis (Light et al. 2018) of selected examples.[4] The core of this research is a practice-based approach, which informed the production of a pilot version of the locative screen tourism web app, DETECtAarhus.[5] This pilot version was trialled with Danish and international students, who were observed and interviewed[6] about their user experiences.

---

[4] The walkthrough method proposed by Light et al. (2018) allows for a critical analysis of an app by examining its implicit and explicit affordances through their use and context.

[5] This web app was conceived by the authors as part of the Horizon2020 research project, Detecting Transcultural Identity in European Popular Crime Narratives (DETECt) (Waade and Bengesser 2020).

[6] Eighteen individual and group interviews were conducted in November 2019 by undergraduate students, who recruited Danish and international test-users.

In *Wallander*'s Footsteps

Printed *Wallander* guides have been offered to visitors of Ystad since 2004, profiting from the stories' rising popularity (Sjöholm 2011, 49–51). After the Swedish-German television adaptations of Henning Mankell's *Wallander* (2005–2013) had already circulated successfully, bringing domestic and German tourists to Ystad, the BBC's English-language adaptation (2008–2016) brought international recognition to detective Kurt Wallander and his hometown (McCabe 2015).[7] In 2010, Ystad presented a mobile app to set tourists 'In Wallander's Footsteps' (Sjöholm 2011, 67). The app is based on Google Maps and guides tourists around the city in Swedish, English, and German, presenting information about the locations, and images and quotations in the books. The original app is now defunct, but a responsive web version of the map, which may also be used with a smartphone browser, still exists on the web.

The Wallander app directs the user to places of significance in the *Wallander* novels, and the Swedish and British TV adaptations, which might otherwise remain unmarked on tourism maps and unnoticed by visitors. Anne Marit Waade's (2016) analysis of this app argues that the quotations and stills from the Swedish TV version featured in the app bring an additional 'fictional layer' to the physical space, while scripting the tourist's experience of it. The map guides them along a specific path through Ystad, leading them to iconic staples and embodied experiences from the traditional guided *Wallander* tours, such as stepping into Kurt Wallander's Office in the Ystad Film Studios, and visiting Fridolf Konditori to sample the blue cake named after Wallander. At the same time, the app moves away from the fictional universe by using professional photographs of places and landscapes. Although not fictional, these are also mediated imaginings of place, which present the destination at its most attractive, perhaps even more attractive than what tourists may see for themselves. The aerial shots of landscapes of blue skies and blooming yellow rape fields not only evoke the Swedish flag, but also the

---

[7] In September 2020 the spin-off, *Young Wallander*, premiered on Netflix. It is not set in Ystad but urban Malmö.

aesthetic of the BBC version (which employed this colour scheme) (Waade 2011, 17). Given *Wallander*'s prominent role in rebranding Ystad for domestic and international tourists, including such appealing photographs in the app can be read as part of the city's larger effort to present itself as part of an appealing and homogenous tourism package. To accomplish this, the city's tourism stakeholders have relegated the dark, sinister, and critical sides of the crime series to the realm of fiction (Migozzi 2020), and present tourists with a pleasant version of an equally imaginary 'Wallanderland' instead (Waade 2013).

Rather than replicating its fictional representation in *Wallander*, the picturesque depiction of Ystad's sights in the app assigns 'tourist use' to the space, and addresses the need to appeal to those tourists for whom Kurt Wallander is not the primary reason to visit Ystad, such as the friends and family of avid *Wallander* viewers (Waade 2013, 78–80). The role of travel partners when choosing to become a screen tourist should not be underestimated. The belief that her husband would not be interested in *Wallander*-themed activities kept one of our German interviewees (F57) from becoming a *Wallander* tourist, and played a part in their decision to not visit Ystad (interview 15.11.2019). Her decision emphasises that smaller screen tourism destinations in particular need to be careful to not be conflated with the fictional worlds they have brought forth, by indicating that there is more to do than walk in the footsteps of famous fictional characters.[8] Here, tourism tools, such as the online Wallander map, could help to transform screen-induced interest into visits to destinations by those who do not want to engage in dedicated film location tourism. The map does not present the space as the site of a fictional world, but as a place for a variety of tourist experiences. It feeds an imagined view of southern Sweden as a place of beautiful landscapes, cosy towns, and opportunities for cultural experiences—of which screen tourism is only one.

---

[8] Careful management of the various facets of tourism prevents clashes of expectations such as those documented for Alnwick Castle, the location of *Harry Potter*'s Hogwarts. In their interviews with visitors, the British Olsberg consultancy found dedicated location tourists who actually expected more *Harry-Potter*-related information and activities, whereas other visitors criticised the 'theme-park style' atmosphere this caused, and called for a better balance between the castle as a heritage site and a film location (Olsberg SPI 2015, 39).

The online *Wallander* map is already accessible in the pre-travel phase, and identifies it as Kurt Wallander's home, but also as a place worth visiting for other reasons. With 65 points of interest inside and outside the city, the map offers far more places to visit than could actually be seen during a single visit. Though the map is called 'In Wallander's Footsteps', the user encounters the locations mainly as places that exist outside *Wallander*'s fictional world. They are presented through professional photos and with their actual names. Only when one clicks on an image is the location's role in the Wallander stories revealed. This way, the map and image gallery are also useful for the non-screen tourist who is looking for restaurants or landmarks to visit. Therefore, the *Wallander* app offers two distinct versions of Ystad, as it lets tourists switch between being a screen or literary tourist who recognises the mediatised Ystad of *Wallander* and a non-screen tourist who experiences Ystad as a destination in its own right, and is in search of the imagined Ystad marketed by the city promoters.

The Girl with the Dragon Tattoo (2009) and Movieloci

Together with Mankell's *Wallander*, Stieg Larsson's Millennium Trilogy became a founding work of Nordic Noir that achieved international prominence when *The Girl with the Dragon Tattoo* was adapted for the screen by Scandinavian producers in 2009—and by Hollywood in 2011. In contrast to the smaller and more remote Ystad, Stockholm was not as interested in developing tourism based on the popularity of Nordic Noir and the Millennium series set there (Migozzi 2020). As a capital city, it is less dependent on screen tourism, and coordinating screen tourism activities would involve more stakeholders. Guided Millennium tours are offered by private tour guides (van Es and Reijnders 2018, 509) and a printed map of Stockholm facilitates self-guided tours (Migozzi 2020), but with no official smartphone-based version. Instead, locations from *The Girl with the Dragon Tattoo* (2009) are currently featured on the Movieloci app (launched in 2012). Based on Google Maps, it provides location-specific film stills and user-generated photos. For some films, these are arranged as sliders, facilitating an easy comparison between the physical and the mediated space on screen. Movieloci may be used for a locative experience as it guides users from one film location to another, but all the information is also accessible virtually. In contrast to 'In Wallander's Footsteps', Movieloci is not dedicated to a specific audiovisual production or destination. Instead, its English-language version has entries for 5000 locations from about 900 films and series set all over the world, which have been contributed by a community of users.[9]

For the locative user, the 'pins' in the Movieloci map interface indicate that the locations they are passing have been used as sites of audiovisual production and mediated on the film or TV screen. In contrast to the dedicated *Wallander* tour, the Movieloci app does not offer a staged and centrally produced tourism experience, but has a database from which users may build their own experience. This makes the app less useful for people who are looking for locations from one specific production; a user who wanted to see the locations from *The Girl with the Dragon Tattoo* would have to assemble their tour from several locations. At the same time, the location-based functions and the interface's focus on the mapped space (location, geography, distance) make the app interesting for more casual location tourists who can gain a different perspective on the physical space in which they find themselves by using their smartphones, but who do not want to commit to specific, pre-booked location tourism activities. However, the density of pins outside Europe's capitals is low. In fact, *The Girl with the Dragon Tattoo* is the only film represented in Sweden.

Whereas the Movieloci app struggles to appeal to the screen tourist on the move, the connected website offers a different pleasure. From the perspective of the website, Movieloci presents itself as a community project of online/real-life investigations for spotting and mapping locations of popular films. It has gamification aspects, rewarding frequent contributors to the database with a score and greater online visibility. The app and website's identity as a community project and competition move it closer to the 'digital mobility' of the 'screen screen tourists' described by Schulze (2017). In our interview study, we found that digital mobility may also appeal to European crime-programme audiences. M64

---

[9] The app is also available in Czech (52000 locations) and French (200 locations).

regularly uses Google Maps to trace film locations from home and to check whether the TV representation matches the actual geography shown in series set in his hometown of Hamburg and in faraway places, for example, in the Spanish crime series, *El Hierro* (2019–) set on a Canary island. For him, the appeal of digital mobility lies in determining whether the use of locations is plausible and authentic, and in rediscovering places with which he is familiar with and/or may want to revisit in the future (interview 26.11.2019). This viewer finds pleasure in virtually comparing the locations seen on the TV screen and the physical locations as represented on the virtual maps, in a way that is reminiscent of the practices of the so-called screen screen tourists. Movieloci contributors who post pictures that let users compare film stills with location photos also facilitate such virtual visits for other users.[10]

Dicte Film Walks in Aarhus

Dicte (2013–2016) is a crime series set in Denmark's second largest city, Aarhus. It revolves around a female crime journalist who solves crimes, often in competition with the police. The series has been a landmark production for the city. Its third season was estimated to have brought 137 million Danish Kroner of turnover in location services—plus international exposure and brand/PR value for the city (Edmund Consulting 2016, 3). Building on the series' popularity in Scandinavia, *Dicte* tourism initiatives were launched. One of them was the 'Dicte Filmwalks' app (launched in 2013, now defunct). It was a locative app, which focused on the fictional Aarhus in which Dicte Svendsen carries out her investigations. Crossing the threshold between the physical and the mediated space presented on TV was facilitated by scenes from the series that the user could watch on location.

Showing scenes from films and series is often part of screen tourism tours. For example, in the *Bridge* tour in Malmö, time on the bus is used

---

[10] An example that enables such digital mobility is the Tourism Northern Ireland's *Game of Thrones* app, which not only guides on-site users to *Game of Thrones* locations, but also lets them explore them via 360° images, enabling a virtual experience of the locations.

for screenings (Hansen and Waade 2017, 279). Such focus on the fictional world appeals to dedicated location tourists who visit a place because they want to walk in the footsteps of their favourite characters. With a smartphone, the scenes from films and series become portable, but streaming clips on the go became feasible only with the expansion of mobile internet and the reduction of data costs in the latter half of the 2010s. However, producing locative screen tourism apps that include clips from films and series hinges on having the rights to re-purpose the copyrighted material. In the case of the *Dicte* app, this was possible because of a close collaboration between Filmby ('film city') Aarhus and one of the series' producers, who facilitated rights clearing (interview with Ellen Riis 16.07.2019). This difficulty may explain why movie stills are more common than clips in screen tourism apps.

The tourism-related turnover expected to be generated by *Dicte*'s last season is estimated at 95 million Danish Kroner, 70 per cent of which comes from Denmark, the remainder from Sweden and Norway (Edmund Consulting 2016, 37–40). This underscores that the series has less appeal for tourists from outside Scandinavia, who may not even know of the programme, since *Dicte* has had only limited exposure outside Scandinavia. But even in Denmark, an app about the Aarhus-based series is not automatically an attractive proposition. When interviewed about their interest in screen tourism apps, two Danish students who recently moved to Aarhus explicitly said that a *Dicte*-themed app sounded unappealing to them.[11] The case of *Dicte* shows the potential promotional impact of screen productions on smaller destinations, but also exemplifies their short half-life as tools for promoting tourism. The interviewees' sceptical reaction is a reminder that various tourist demographics—domestic versus foreign, young versus old—are attracted to different screen productions, a situation exacerbated by the abundant and fragmented video-on-demand market.

---

[11] Two Danish test-users of a pilot version of the DETECtAarhus web-app claimed that as soon as they heard that 'it was about *Dicte*', they judged it to be less interesting (Bengesser and Waade 2021, 642).

DETECtAarhus

The *Wallander* and *Dicte* apps inspired the concept of the DETECtAarhus web-app in terms of functionalities, but instead of focusing on a specific fictional world and its fans, the app addresses users predominantly as people who do not yet know that they can be screen tourists in the city. Instead of immersing users in *Dicte*'s Aarhus as imagined on the TV screen, the app presents Aarhus as a media-production site, showing them where and how crime literature, TV, and film have been produced in the city today and during the silent film era. The focus on media production is due to the limited international exposure of Aarhus-produced film and TV, but it also extends the app's appeal beyond fans of specific productions. Our interviews with international users of the DETECtAarhus pilot version indicated that the availability of general information about the place—irrespective of its role in fictional productions—provides added value for foreign visitors (Bengesser and Waade 2021, 642). Many of the international test-users actually named a café or restaurant recommendation as their favourite piece of content in the app.

As was the case with the production of the *Dicte* app, locating and obtaining rights to film material has proven difficult in the production of the DETECtAarhus web-app (Waade and Bengesser 2020, 17), because retrospective rights clearing to reuse scenes is time-consuming or even impossible. At the same time, our group discussion with international users of the DETECtAarhus pilot version suggested that they expect a screen tourism app to show them the mediatised space through scenes filmed on location (Waade and Bengesser 2020, 18). The use of promotional film trailers (e.g. *The Exception* 2020, *On the Edge* 2014), which we were able to secure rights for, did not meet the users' expectations, because their connection to the locations in which they were shown on the app was not always sufficiently clear. As one trial participant stated: 'I could have watched it at home. I could have googled movies made in Aarhus and then I could have watched the trailer' (Bengesser and Waade 2021, 644). This illustrates how users of locative screen tourism experiences look for a match between the location they see on the smartphone screen and what they perceive in the physical space.

Facilitating a convergence between the physical and fictional space through locative screen tourism apps is complicated by questions of rights ownership and the varying appeal of specific productions for the target groups of app-based screen tourism. This may be challenging for destinations such as Aarhus, which are not the homes of well-known films or series, because the fictional worlds—the imagined spaces—of their locations do not constitute sufficient attractions for tourists. At the same time, there is a promotional potential that works the other way around—promoting not the place, but the film or TV series. After taking the tour, several test-users of DETECtAarhus expressed an interest in watching some of the films produced in Aarhus, to deepen their knowledge of Danish culture. Significantly, the tour focused on silent film in the city sparked their interest in exploring Denmark's filmic heritage. This shows how a screen tourism activity has the potential to introduce tourists to various representations of the space they are visiting, and induce media consumption, thereby promoting the films and series produced there.

A Typology of Screen Tourism Apps

Based on the case studies presented above, we propose a typology of smartphone use in screen tourism that takes into account their form of mediation and their presentation of space as the site of fictional worlds, film locations, or non-screen-related tourism. The case studies have illustrated that the various uses, such as virtual and locative use, and various dimensions of space as physical, imagined, and mediated space, converge in the smartphone. Therefore, the grid below allows us to position individual apps at various intersections of mediation and dimensions of space, differentiating among places identified as tourist destinations, media-production locations, or fictional worlds. The dark grey boxes indicate where the above-mentioned Nordic Noir case studies may be positioned, whereas the white boxes include apps and offers outside the realms of screen tourism and/or technology use in screen tourism, to show how the screen tourism apps relate to other forms of tourism. The light grey boxes present further instances of smart screen tourism, to show how the grid can be used to categorise other cases (Fig. 9.1).

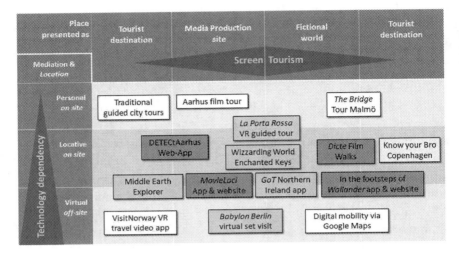

Fig. 9.1 Typology of smartphone and technology use in screen tourism. (Developed from Waade and Bengesser 2020)

There is an increasing dependency on technological mediation along the vertical axis. Personally mediated, on-site experiences may be walks through a city with a tour guide, which may or may not employ media technologies as part of the tour. On the other hand, experiences such as off-site virtual reality (VR) travel documentaries depend fully on online mediation. Situated between these two are tourist experiences facilitated by locative media, which adapt experiences to the users' geolocation (Wilken and Goggin 2015). They depend on mediation through mobile technology, GPS, and mobile data, but the tourists also interact with the locations in which they find themselves, without mediation. The horizontal dimension differentiates the screen tourism apps according to the ways in which various aspects of space are negotiated by screen tourism. Personal guided tours, locative apps, and virtual experiences may present a space primarily as a tourist destination, which only happens to have been used in film and TV. They may present it as a site in which media are produced, for example, guiding users to film studios or giving them glimpses behind the scenes. Finally, screen tourism apps and technology may focus on spaces as the sites of fictional worlds that are represented in film and TV. By presenting these mediatised imaginings, they seek to immerse users in the story-worlds of films and series while they are visiting the physical locations in which they are set. Technology use that presents a location as the site of film production or a fictional world is a screen tourism activity in a narrow sense. The apps located in the centre of the grid address users mostly as location tourists familiar with, or at least interested in, the fictional worlds, whereas the examples at the periphery present the locations outside their representation in film and TV, and therefore simply assign tourist use to the space.

In contrast to the model for technology use in tourism proposed by Neuhofer et al. (2014), our model imposes no hierarchy on the various experiences. Although Neuhofer et al. (2014) claim that ICT use in tourism experiences that employ the highest levels of technology and co-creation offer 'the most distinct and valuable experience[s]', studies of tourists who participate in screen tourism activities suggest high levels of involvement even during personally guided tours that employ no digital technology (e.g. Reijnders 2010). In fact, high levels of technologically facilitated co-creation and commitment go against the flexibility afforded by tourism apps (Waade and Bengesser 2020, 14). Because of screen tourists' diverse profiles, ranging from dedicated location tourists to visitors whose destination choice was motivated by what they saw on a screen, all the experiences in the grid may be valuable to both key target groups and destinations seeking to promote tourism.

The typology presented above may be used from different perspectives. Our case studies looked at the various ways a subgenre of crime TV is exploited by (smart) screen tourism in a specific region. The grid may also be used to map various screen tourism activities provided at a specific destination, to determine how various screen tourist target groups are addressed. Equally, it may be used to map screen tourism activities related to a specific film at multiple locations, to see how various destinations exploit the same intellectual property, and possibly differentiate themselves from one another through the types of (smart) screen tourism they offer. Another possibility is mapping how various tourism-industry stakeholders exploit a specific film or series to promote tourism, for example, differentiating between the activities offered by private enterprises and public institutions.

Conclusion: Drivers of, and Obstacles to, Smart Screen Tourism

Screen tourism has been a significant driver of visits to the locations of globally popular films and TV series such as *Harry Potter* and *Game of Thrones*. It has also inspired dedicated, site-specific tourist activities at these locations. The case studies we presented, of Nordic Noir tourism initiatives in Ystad, Stockholm, and Aarhus, exemplify how screen productions far smaller than Hollywood blockbusters can attract tourists to specific sites. Still, there are many factors at work in people's decisions to become screen tourists, which should be considered in the academic evaluation of smart screen tourism, and in its actual design. As our interviews with European crime-programme viewers and test-users of the DETECtAarhus web-app have demonstrated, it is useful to not only address users as screen tourists but also offer general information about their destinations, including food and leisure tips. In virtual use during the pre-tourism phases, this makes screen tourism apps useful for showing visitors that there are plenty of interesting sites and activities for those who accompany a dedicated location tourist.

Because screen tourism apps have a low participation threshold, they may appeal to tourists who know that something has been filmed at their holiday destination, but do not want to commit to pre-booked location tours. When users take a smartphone-guided tour, the experience is more flexible. Instead of walking through Scandinavian cities in the stereotypical rain (van Es and Reijnders 2018, 509), app users can adapt their tours to environmental circumstances. Still, locative, smartphone-based screen tourism enables the embodied experiences that are crucial to screen tourism (Leotta 2011, 168), such as stopping for a Wallander cake in Ystad. Furthermore, the smartphone makes audiovisual material from films and series portable, making it easier to cross the threshold between the experience of physical spaces and their fictional imaginings and mediations.

The COVID-19 pandemic may contribute to a rise in smartphone- and digital-technology-use in screen tourism. Physical distancing and uncertainties surrounding pre-booked activities make alternatives to guided group tours more appealing. Digital mobility that builds on-screen images of destinations helps when planning or replacing physical travel. Such 'screen screen tourism' may be co-created by active fan communities or take the form of staged virtual experiences through 360° or VR videos for audiences who lack the motivation and resources to co-create.

The flexibility of locative and virtual screen tourism experiences creates a less committed user, who may more quickly give up on a screen tourism app because of navigation problems or a lack of interest in the content. Negotiating the interests of regular visitors and dedicated screen tourists who want to immerse themselves in the imagined space of fiction productions is a challenge. It is particularly challenging for destinations outside global capitals: although their use in films and series may put them on the map, overemphasising their role as a production site and setting of fictional worlds may suggest they have nothing to offer to the regular tourist. The use of 'smart' technology in screen tourism may exacerbate this problem, since locative mobile apps increase the expectation that experiences will be personalised and customised (Gretzel et al. 2015, 181). Expectations of personalisation are fed by the many services that recommend experiences based on user location, previous activities, and one's social media circle (e.g. Facebook and Foursquare), and also by the personalised recommendations of film and TV on video-on-demand platforms such as Netflix. To be able to offer seamless adaptation to user interests, vast amounts of personal user data are required. This condition of personalised locative apps does not align well with the relatively niche status of dedicated screen tourism.

Reaching a critical mass of screen tourists is further complicated by the growing fragmentation of media audiences that has come with the rise of video-on-demand and personalised viewing suggestions. Given these factors, only a few blockbuster franchises or long-running series are likely candidates for successful, sustained screen tourism (Olsberg SPI 2015, 46–47) and rise to a level of prominence that warrants investing in dedicated smart screen tourism that goes beyond digital versions of printed maps. Yet, the high-profile franchises' intellectual property is tightly managed, making it harder for tourist destinations to access material that may be featured in an app.[12] So, even though the ubiquity of mobile data

---

[12] Northern Ireland's *Game of Thrones* app does not include footage from the series, although the Irish tourism and screen agencies and HBO have enjoyed a supportive relationship throughout their efforts to develop screen tourism in the region.

use has made it possible to stream audiovisual material on-site, aiding the convergence of fictional and physical spaces, this opportunity cannot necessarily be realised. This is particularly true if the app development rests only on stakeholders in the tourism industry. It is difficult to assemble an engaging experience for screen tourists without involving film or TV production companies that have the rights to finished material from films and TV series, access to behind-the-scenes spaces, and promotional power (Olsberg SPI 2015, 39–40). Smaller or peripheral destinations may be at a disadvantage here, because 'smart tourism' necessitates investment not only in an app but also in a broader digital infrastructure (Gretzel et al. 2015, 184).

The smartphone has facilitated an ever-smoother convergence of various phases of tourism and tourist roles, and the various aspects of place. Smartphone-based screen tourism may now occur in both physical and virtual settings at every stage of tourism. Yet, with the growing possibilities and the ubiquity of smartphone use in locative and virtual settings, expectations rise, and these are difficult to meet, particularly in location tourism outside the global capitals or homes to blockbuster productions. Therefore, the smartphone is best seen as yet another tool, but not as an inherently transformative technology for promoting film and screen tourism.

Works Cited

Askanius, Tina. 2017. "It Feels Like Home, This Is My Malmö": Place Media Location and Fan Experiences of *The Bridge*. *Participations* 14 (2): 6–31.

Beeton, Sue. 2005. *Film-Induced Tourism*. Clevedon: Channel View.

Bengesser, Cathrin, and Anne Marit Waade. 2021. Smart Crime Tourism as Multilayered Cultural Encounters: Exploring Aarhus via Locative Media and Crime Narratives. *European Review* 29 (5): 635–650. https://doi.org/10.1017/S1062798720001155

Bondebjerg, Ib, Eva Novrup Redvall, Rasmus Helles, Signe Sophus Lai, Henrik Søndergaard, and Cecilie Astrupgaard. 2017. *Transnational European Television Drama: Production, Genres and Audiences*. Basingstoke, Hampshire: Palgrave Macmillan.

Carson, Susan, and Mark Pennings. 2020. Online and on Tour: The Smartphone Effect in Transmedia Contexts. In *The Routledge Companion to Media and Tourism*, ed. Maria Månsson, Annæ Buchmann, Cecilia Cassinger, and Lena Eskilsson, 414–423. London; New York: Routledge.

Çelik Rappas, Ipek A., and Stefano Baschiera. 2020. Fabricating "Cool" Heritage for Northern Ireland: Game of Thrones Tourism. *The Journal of Popular Culture* 53 (3): 648–666. https://doi.org/10.1111/jpcu.12926 .

Creeber, Glen. 2015. Killing Us Softly: Investigating the Aesthetics, Philosophy and Influence of Nordic Noir Television. *The Journal of Popular Television* 3 (1): 21–35. https://doi.org/10.1386/jptv.3.1.21_1 .

Edmund Consulting. 2016. Samlet Værdi for Aarhus Af Tv-Serien Dicte Serien Dicte Serien Dicte Sæson III. Unpublished Manuscript. Last Modified December 8, 2016. https://filmbyaarhus.dk/wp-content/uploads/2016/08/Rapport_v%C3%A6rdien-af-Dicte3_Aarhus_F2.pdf.

van Es, Nicky, and Stijn Reijnders. 2018. Making Sense of Capital Crime Cities: Getting Underneath the Urban Facade on Crime-Detective Fiction Tours. *European Journal of Cultural Studies* 21 (4): 502–520. https://doi.org/10.1177/1367549416656855 .

Gretzel, Ulrike, Marianna Sigala, Xiang Zheng, and Chulmo Koo. 2015. Smart Tourism: Foundations and Developments. *Electronic Markets* 25 (3): 179–188. https://doi.org/10.1007/s12525-015-0196-8 .

Hansen, Kim Toft. 2020. Location Placement in Nordic Noir. In *Location Marketing and Cultural Tourism: DETECt Deliverable 4.1*, ed. Cathrin Bengesser, Kim T. Hansen, and Lynge Stegger Gemzøe, 22–27. DETECt Project.

Hansen, Kim Toft, and Anne Marit Waade. 2017. *Locating Nordic Noir: From Beck to The Bridge*. Basingstoke, Hampshire: Palgrave Macmillan.

Hills, Matt. 2017. A "Cult-like" Following: Nordic Noir, Nordicana and Arrow Films' Bridging of Subcultural/Neocultural Capital. In *Cult Media*, ed. Jonathan Wroot and Andy Willis, 49–65. Cham: Springer International Publishing.

Jansson, André. 2013. Mediatization and Social Space: Reconstructing Mediatization for the Transmedia Age. *Communication Theory* 23: 279–296. https://doi.org/10.1111/comt.12015 .

Lavarone, Giulia. 2021. Cinematic Tourism in a Time of Media Convergence. In *Routledge Companion to Media and Tourism*, ed. Maria Mansson, Annre Buchmann, Cecilia Cassinger, and Lena Eskilsson, 35–43. Oxon; New York: Routledge.

Lee, Christina. 2012. 'Have Magic, Will Travel': Tourism and Harry Potter's United (Magical) Kingdom. *Tourist Studies* 12 (1): 52–69.

Leotta, Alfio. 2011. *Touring the Screen: Tourism and New Zealand Film Geographies*. Bristol: Intellect.

———. 2016. Navigating Movie (M)apps: Film Locations, Tourism and Digital Mapping Tools. *M/C Journal* 19 (3). https://doi.org/10.5204/mcj.1084 .

Li, Shina, Hengyun Li, Haiyan Song, Christine Lundberg, and Shujie Shen. 2017. The Economic Impact of on-Screen Tourism: The Case of the Lord of the Rings and the Hobbit. *Tourism Management* 60 (C): 177–187. https://doi.org/10.1016/j.tourman.2016.11.023 .

Light, Ben, Jean Burgess, and Stefanie Duguay. 2018. The Walkthrough Method: An Approach to the Study of Apps. *New Media & Society* 20 (3): 881–900. https://doi.org/10.1177/1461444816675438 .

McCabe, Janet. 2015. Appreciating *Wallander* at the BBC: Producing Culture and Performing the Glocal in the UK and Swedish Wallanders for British Public Service Television. *Continuum* 29 (5): 755–768. https://doi.org/10.1080/10304312.2015.1068726 .

Migozzi, Jacques. 2020. Wallander and Millennium as Swedish Crime Tourism: Two Diverging Location Marketing Strategies. In *Location Marketing and Cultural Tourism: DETECt Deliverable 4.1*, ed. Cathrin Bengesser, Kim Toft Hansen, and Lynge Stegger Gemzøe, 19–23. DETECt Project.

Neuhofer, Barbara, Dimitrios Buhalis, and Adele Ladkin. 2014. A Typology of Technology-Enhanced Tourism Experiences. *International Journal of Tourism Research* 16 (4): 340–350. https://doi.org/10.1002/jtr.1958 .

Olsberg SPI. 2015. Quantifying Film and Television Tourism in England: Report for Creative England in Association with VisitEngland. Unpublished Manuscript. Last Modified January 26, 2021. https://applications.creativeengland.co.uk/assets/public/resource/140.pdf.

Pagello, Federico, and Markus Schleich, eds. 2020. *European Creative Audiences: DETECt Deliverable 5.1*.

Reijnders, Stijn. 2010. Places of the Imagination: An Ethnography of the TV Detective Tour. *Cultural Geographies* 17 (1): 37–52. https://doi.org/10.1177/1474474009349998 .

———. 2011. *Places of the Imagination: Media, Tourism, Culture*. London: Taylor & Francis.

Roesch, Stefan. 2009. *The Experiences of Film Location Tourists*. Bristol: Channel View Publications.

Schulze, Marion. 2017. Screen Screen Tourism. *Digital Culture & Society* 3 (2): 123–142. https://doi.org/10.14361/dcs-2017-0208 .

Šegota, Tina. 2018. Creating (Extra)Ordinary Heritage Through Film-Induced Tourism: The Case of Dubrovnik and Game of Thrones. In *Creating Heritage for Tourism*, ed. Catherine Palmer and Jacqueline Tivers, 115–126. London: Routledge.

Sjöholm, Carina. 2011. *Litterära resor: Turism i spåren efter böcker, filmer och författare*. Gothenburg; Stockholm: Makadam Förlag.

Waade, Anne Marit. 2011. Crime Scenes: Conceptualizing Ystad as Location in the Swedish and the British Wallander TV Crime Series. *Northern Lights: Film & Media Studies Yearbook* 9: 9–25.

———. 2013. *Wallanderland: Medieturisme og skandinavisk tv-krimi*. Aalborg: Aalborg Universitetsforlag.

———. 2016. Nordic Noir Tourism and Television Landscapes. *Scandinavica: An International Journal of Scandinavian Studies* 55 (1): 42–65.

Waade, Anne M. 2021. Screening the West Coast: Developing New Nordic Noir Tourism in Denmark and Using Actual Places as Full-Scale Visual Mood Boards for the Scriptwriting Process. In *Locating Imagination in Popular Culture: Place, Tourism and Belonging*, ed. Nicky van Es, Stijn Reijnders, Leonieke Bolderman, and Abby Waysdorf, 99–117. London: Routledge.

Waade, Anne Marit, and Cathrin Bengesser. 2020. Locative Media in Screen Tourism: The Production of the DETECt Aarhus App. In *Location Marketing and Cultural Tourism: DETECt Deliverable 4.1*, ed. Cathrin Bengesser, Kim Toft Hansen, and Lynge Stegger Gemzøe, 13–18. DETECt Project.

Wilken, Rowan, and Gerard Goggin. 2015. Locative Media: Definitions, Histories, Theories. In *Locative Media*, ed. Rowan Wilken and Gerard Goggin, 1–19. London: Routledge.

Part III

Tourist Gaze, Identity, and Race

10

Wonderland of the South Pacific: Romantic and Realist Tendencies in Amateur Tourist Films

Rosina Hickman

A Māori woman in a *korowai* (tasselled cloak) and *piupiu* (flax skirt) extends a raised arm in a welcoming gesture. Behind her in the distance, a well-dressed tourist couple marvel at the impressive water jet and steam clouds of a geyser. Below the image are printed the words 'NEW ZEALAND: South Pacific Wonderland'. Proudly displayed on a Tourist Department poster of the 1950s designed by Marcus King, the image encapsulates what was by the mid-twentieth century an archetypal representation of New Zealand: a picturesque playground inhabited by a traditional Indigenous population and leisured white tourists. This basic iconographic division—Māori as traditional or historical and Pākehā (New Zealanders of European descent) as sophisticated, modern travellers enjoying the country's scenic offerings—was reiterated across a plethora of tourist media including cinema (Fig. 10.1).

The geothermal region of the central North Island was frequently depicted in promotional images of New Zealand such as the one above.

R. Hickman (✉)
Victoria University of Wellington, Wellington, New Zealand
e-mail: rosina.hickman@vuw.ac.nz

© The Author(s), under exclusive license to Springer Nature Singapore Pte Ltd. 2021
D. Bonelli, A. Leotta (eds.), *Audiovisual Tourism Promotion*,
https://doi.org/10.1007/978-981-16-6410-6_10

Fig. 10.1 Publicity poster designed by Marcus King, c.1955. Reproduced courtesy of Tourism New Zealand

Originally settled by the *iwi* (tribe) Te Arawa, the area became a popular destination with European tourists, both local and international, especially following the establishment of the Auckland-Rotorua railway line in 1894. Rotorua was promoted as a European-style spa town, with the nearby Māori village of Whakarewarewa adding the appeal of unique local heritage.[1] From a marketing perspective, it was an almost perfect

---

[1] For those interested in the development of Rotorua as a tourist destination, Margaret McClure offers a detailed history (2004, 29–63).

mix. Spectacular topography (such as Pohutu Geyser seen in King's poster), Indigenous culture, and modern recreational facilities coalesced, conjuring the impression of a country simultaneously exotic and civilised, a picturesque wonderland perfect for the adventurous traveller. The ubiquity of such imagery in travel guides, postcards, advertising posters, and publicity films ensured visitors were likely to arrive at Rotorua 'well informed' about what they could expect to find there and how to go about documenting it. By the mid-twentieth century, many sightseers came armed with movie cameras to record their encounter with Rotorua's landscape and people. Did the films taken home by these enthusiastic amateurs differ greatly from those made by their professional counterparts? Not restricted by the ideological and economic imperatives of commercial tourist media, amateurs were, in theory, free to record whatever they liked. Nonetheless, as Pākehā or European visitors, they were the intended audience for tourist images. Moreover, they were the beneficiaries of colonial rule that had marginalised Indigenous peoples, an integral step in the commodification of cultural other as tourist attraction. Did this influence the kinds of images tourist-filmmakers recorded? This chapter examines three amateur travel films—two by local Pākehā filmmakers and one by an American visitor to our shores—that feature Rotorua. It considers the extent to which private individuals replicated public media representations, or whether they created a more personal view of the popular tourist location.

Romantic Maoriland

Before exploring some amateur recordings, it is worth looking at the depiction of Rotorua and its environs in professionally made tourist publicity films in a little more detail. The area was strikingly cinematic. A landscape of geysers, bubbling mud, boiling hot pools, and steam rising from cracks in the earth's surface, along with the colourful display of *Māoritanga* (cultural traditions and way of life), offered plenty of scope for visual drama. Tourist films often featured images of amenities such as Rotorua's public baths, landscaped gardens, sports grounds, and tea rooms as well, just to reassure potential visitors that their stay would be comfortable, awe-inspiring nature and congenial modernity finding an agreeable onscreen coexistence.

With its combination of natural and cultural attributes, Rotorua, or more specifically Whakarewarewa, became the most filmed location in New Zealand (Blythe 1994, 51). The government's tourist and publicity departments were the main producers of early scenics or travelogues, although a number of independent production companies were also operating within the country. Despite some reorganisation of government production in the years prior to World War II, the general ethos of filmmaking remained much the same, focused on tourist promotion and the consolidation of a distinctive national identity. While the local landscape conveniently supplied what a 1925 feature, *Glorious New Zealand*, described as a 'never ending panorama of scenic gems', the nation's colonial history complicated the representation of its inhabitants. European settlement in the nineteenth century had left the Māori population marginalised and impoverished. The uniqueness of Māori culture was one of the biggest drawcards the country had to offer tourists, however. Faced with the need to present a positive image of the nation, the government's publicity section and other promoters of tourism sought to capitalise on the country's 'exotic' Māori heritage whilst downplaying anything likely to be deemed unfavourable in the eyes of tourists. The solution proved to be a parallel vision of essentially timeless, ancient Māoridom nestled alongside the modern Pākehā world, effectively eliding contemporary inequities between the populations. Rotorua, with its picturesque qualities, took centre stage in this tourist narrative.[2]

An independent film dating from 1905, *Sights in New Zealand*, displays a selection of images that would become standard visualisations of the location, repeated with alacrity in subsequent productions. In the surviving scenes of the film,[3] steam is seen rising from nearby Lake

---

[2] The history of government tourist promotion through cinema, photography, and other media, including the respective representations of Māori and Pākehā, has been widely discussed elsewhere. For a more in-depth analysis than space permits here, see McClure (2004), Blythe (1994), Leotta (2011), and Taylor (1998). Alsop et al. (2012) offer both a number of short essays and an extensive collection of illustrations.

[3] All films discussed in this chapter may be viewed online via the websites of their respective custodial institutions. *Sights in New Zealand,* shot by T.J. West and his cameramen, originally included 16 scenes recorded around the country (Ngā Taonga Sound and Vision catalogue notes, 2009).

Rotomahana. Māori women demonstrate the local method of cooking, lowering *kete* (flax baskets) into a steam vent, and washing clothes in hot pools. A large group of women perform an action dance. An assembly of men on a beach initiates a *haka*-style performance waving *taiaha* (spears). The 'Māoriland'[4] iconography is yet to be fully established on film, however. The separation of the Māori world from Pākehā modernity is not complete. Māori are seen sporting a mixture of traditional and contemporary European garments, even in the dance sequence. Furthermore, the *haka* quickly digresses into leaping about and gesticulating wildly in front of the camera, the participants undermining the presumably serious intent on the part of the filmmakers to record an authentic cultural performance rather than a parody thereof or exaggerated display of 'acting primitive' for European spectators.

Such idiosyncrasies in the cinematic representation of Maoriland had been ironed out by the 1930s. The feature-length publicity film, *Romantic New Zealand: The Land of the Long White Cloud* (1934), opens with a *haka* dramatically performed amidst a backdrop of rising steam. Māori are seen in traditional clothing engaged in activities such as *kapa haka* (performing arts), carving, weaving, paddling *waka* (canoe), washing in hot pools, steam cooking, and even feeding trout at nearby Fairy Springs. Many scenes noticeably transpire at the model *pā* (fortified village) at Whakarewarewa, which was built specifically for touristic purposes.[5] The opening narration locates Māori existence within a mythical terrain of noble savages referred to in the past tense. Switching focus to the present day, the narrator declares that the country's 'wonderful transformation from savagery to civilisation' occurred within a century of the arrival of European settlers. Rooted in colonialist ways of seeing space and time, the tourist narrative drew upon romantic conventions about the representation of landscape and exotic cultures, along with Eurocentric notions

---

[4] According to Martin Blythe, 'Maoriland' was used from the late nineteenth century mainly as 'an exotic and utopian synonym for New Zealand', appearing in the titles of numerous literary publications and periodicals, and even the cable address of the Department of Tourist and Health Resorts. Subsequently, Maoriland came to refer more exclusively to a fictionalised world of noble savages and (semi-)historical Māori figures (1994, 16–7). Rotorua was the location most commonly identified with the Maoriland image onscreen.

[5] Built in the first decade of the twentieth century, the model *pā* was criticised by Māori for its inauthentic representation of pre-colonial life (Weckbecker 2015, 150).

Fig. 10.2 *Romantic New Zealand: The Land of the Long White Cloud* (1934). Public Domain

of progress and modernity. The epitome of this contrived mythology is perhaps the inclusion of a still image of what appears to be a diorama with a painted backdrop featuring a Māori hunter beside the extinct moa, frozen as it were together in history. Trapped in a primordial timespace, Māori inhabit a discrete sphere seemingly detached from contemporary New Zealand, a scenic people relegated to a scenic past. By comparison, Pākehā—when they appear at all in the film—are, for the most part, pleasure-seeking tourists blessed with modern mobility (Fig. 10.2).[6]

---

[6] Government filmmaking of the interwar years largely adhered to a policy of excluding people from images with the object of preventing films from being 'dated by changes in fashion' (Dennis 1994, 118). Vehicles or other forms of technology do not appear to have been subject to the same consideration, nor the style or technology of filmmaking itself. Leotta discusses the ideological implications of this iconography in more detail (2011, 21).

This separation is largely maintained in *Magic Playgrounds in New Zealand's Geyserland* (1935). Pākehā are seen playing tennis and golf, swimming, water-skiing, fishing, sightseeing on Lake Rotomahana, and visiting hot pools, while Māori are associated with the 'old-time' arts of carving, *kapa haka*, and weaving (although the influence of cultural contact is acknowledged in this instance). In *Railways of the Pacific Wonderland* (1939), a film in which Pākehā travellers are again associated with modern transport and recreational pursuits, Rotorua's attractions are condensed into less than a minute. Tennis and swimming, *kapa haka*, and a Māori guide showing tourists steaming mud pools form a convenient shorthand for Pākehā leisure, Māori tradition, and untamed nature.

The representation of Māori culture as essentially static and picturesque, belonging to pre-European days of yore, had an economic and political rationale. Film and tourism developed alongside colonial expansion in the nineteenth and early twentieth centuries. Technology made faraway places more accessible, both physically through modern transport and virtually through photographic images. Tourists could comfortably journey to distant locations, while armchair travellers whet their appetite for the exotic through an array of visual representations of supposedly primitive cultures. Postcards, tourist posters, stereoscope cards, and scenic films all created 'knowledge' of distant places and societies. Photography extended the legacy of earlier means of visualising faraway lands, historical events, or other cultures, which included landscape painting, magic lantern slides, the panorama, and diorama. Regardless of medium, the identity of non-European peoples was typically circumscribed within the confines of primitivist imagery. Photography therefore helped to distinguish European civilisation from those subjugated through colonial rule, 'the leisured tourist from the commodified Other, the spectator from the object of the sight-seeing gaze'. As Ellen Strain suggests, tourism 'brought spectators not necessarily closer to the experience of the Other but more aligned with the conquering spirit of European explorers and soldiers' (1996, 95–96).

The colonialist overtones and voyeuristic dimensions of tourist encounters were not intended to induce any sense of guilt in European visitors. Far from it. Situating Māori culture within a time-space distinct from a contemporary Pākehā milieu had a particular expediency in this respect.

The trope of the 'dying native' (soon to be) extinct in the modern world conveniently relegated Māori (or other Indigenous people elsewhere) to a bygone era, thereby justifying European possession of (assumed to be vacant) tribal lands.[7] Yet one significant role was reserved for Indigenous populations within this specious rationalisation. Preserved in a supposedly authentic historical state, isolated pockets of Maoriland (and its overseas equivalents) catered to the curious gaze of tourists and their cameras. Cultural performances, demonstrations of traditional crafts, or even everyday activities that appeared unusual to outsiders (such as washing in hot pools) were safely contained and commodified within recognised tourist spots for the benefit of European sightseers. Prior to arrival, tourist media primed the expectations of visitors through codified representations that transformed social, cultural, and geographical differences into a picturesque exotic, as seen in the marketing of New Zealand as the 'South Pacific Wonderland'.

For local Pākehā visitors, Māori were of course not exotic in the sense of originating from a distant or less developed part of the world. This presented no great impediment, however. As in the films above, proximity was easily overcome by promoting Māori culture through a guise of romantic primitivism that rendered a satisfyingly stark contrast with modern Pākehā lifestyles. Looking at such imagery today, it might be wondered why the Maoriland iconography was considered sufficiently plausible or authentic to be propagated so persistently. In the realm of tourism however, apparent signifiers of an exotic culture's origins in a frequently ill-defined, distant past conveniently predating written records are often perceived authentic. Derived from a murky historicity, the presumed authenticity of sites, objects, people, or practices may be difficult to refute (Taylor 1998, 33–34). In the absence of alternative representations, simplistic or derogatory stereotypes had ample opportunity to flourish. Moreover, most Māori and Pākehā resided in largely separate

---

[7] Far from being a dying race, the Māori population was in fact recovering by the early twentieth century from the initial impact of European settlement the previous century, which included significant loss of land and the arrival of infectious diseases such as measles and influenza (Pool and Kukutai 2018). The trope of the 'dying native' (or more specifically, the 'vanishing Indian') was also a feature of early American travelogues. See Jennifer Peterson (2006, 92–96) for further discussion of this aspect of tourist films.

communities prior to World War II, often having relatively little contact with each other (King 1983, 3; 21). Given this, there was plenty of scope for ignorance amongst Pākehā who were exposed to neither accurate representations, nor first-hand experiences of actual Māori ways of life. For many, the artificiality of the tourist encounter was likely to be the extent of intercultural exchange.

A kind of 'corrective' to the mythical Maoriland image appeared in the early post-war years. Following a highly critical appraisal by renowned documentary-maker John Grierson, government filmmaking was reorganised with the establishment of the National Film Unit in 1941. Although not enacted in detail, Grierson's report emphasised the importance of documenting 'the real things' people do. Unimpressed by New Zealand's 'very pleasant scenic pictures', the British filmmaker noted, with the exception of Māori 'who staged shows for rich tourists', he was left with little idea of what people actually did in the country (1981, 21–22). Films made primarily for local audiences now addressed social issues such as housing, education, and health. Māori at last gained an onscreen foothold in the contemporary world. Yet Māori-focused content was largely prescriptive; that is to say, films had a tendency to expound how Māori should live (according to Pākehā filmmakers representing the government) rather than depict how they actually lived. Nor were Māori perspectives on Māori issues considered important to document (Weckbecker 2015, 154). Tourist films, especially those for overseas markets, largely ignored social issues altogether, continuing to promote cultural difference in much the same vein since the advent of tourism in the late nineteenth century (ibid., 149). According to Lars Weckbecker, in films of the post-war years 'Māori were to live an idealized presence that is constantly torn between an authentic past and a better, more desirable, future' (ibid., 144).

Rotorua remained the prime tourist destination, combining exotic landscape and commercialised *Māoritanga*. A subtle romanticism enters into *Maori Village* (1945), an early National Film Unit production featuring scenes of a concert party rehearsing at Whakarewarewa. The film opens with shots of steam rising from the landscape, bubbling geysers, and the silhouetted figures of tourists being guided around hot pools. The concert party appears in artfully arranged ensemble echoing *tableaux vivants* and countless postcard images of reclining Māori maidens in traditional dress.[8] Rangitīaria Dennan (better known as Guide Rangi) tempers this picture, however, by providing a brief introduction to the history and meaning of the songs, dances, and games. The shift is subtle but distinct. By framing the practice of *kapa haka* as a way of keeping heritage alive, such activities become a link between past and present, neither the sum of Māori existence at the time nor simply markers of otherness unfolding in an essentially lost ancient world. Children go to European-style schools, for example, even if they are depicted playing traditional games at lunchtime.

Some of this footage reappears in *Meet New Zealand: The People* (1949), a film that opens with an assurance that any impression tourists take home that the Māori population is 'just a picturesque remnant living in the midst of thermal wonders' is far from the truth. Yet in its attempt to dispel such notions, the film paints an overly rosy image of Māori and Pākehā equality. Children are seen attending school together and are alleged to have the same opportunities upon leaving, although the more observant viewer will notice that the New Zealanders inhabiting modern dwellings or attending chamber concerts, for example—that is to say, enjoying the fruits of a sophisticated modernity—all appear to be of European extraction. Despite the greater acknowledgement of contemporary life, the portrayal of Māori onscreen continued to be highly strategic, offering slender insight into anything beyond the orchestrated cultural displays of Whakarewarewa (Weckbecker 2015, 154). The documenting of a Māori world on film would remain problematic until cameras were grasped by Māori hands (Fig. 10.3).

Tourist images made the unfamiliar accessible and enticing. They did not encourage viewers to question the veracity of what they saw, nor the limitations of the tourist experience. Bearing this in mind, what did tourist-filmmakers see when they stepped onto the geyserlands of Rotorua? Did they replicate professional images to the best of their ability, or record an intrinsically personal view? The answer to this question

---

[8] Postcards were a popular form of commercial photography in the early twentieth century. For an overview of the representation of Māori women in postcards and the 'pseudo-knowledge' such images constructed, see Jacqui Beets (1997).

Fig. 10.3 *Maori Village: A Concert Rehearsal Near Rotorua* (1945) and *Meet New Zealand: The People* (1949). Collection of Archives New Zealand (CC BY 3.0)

perhaps lies somewhere between professional expediency and personal idiosyncrasy, public presentation and private intimacy.

Personal Film Souvenirs

It is particularly noticeable looking at personal travel films that the common term denoting an amateur recording, 'home movie', is something of a misnomer. While home movies were usually watched at home, they were frequently recorded elsewhere, most often in outdoor spaces, which were likely to be at least semi-public, in order to make use of natural light. Holidays, travel, and outings were popular subjects, instances when filmmakers and families had leisure time to pursue their hobby and something that was not quite an ordinary, everyday occurrence to record. There is nothing unusual in fact about a home movie collection featuring only special events in the life of the family. The familiar routines of daily tasks, housework, or dirty chores were seldom recorded by amateurs.

A vacation recording by Charles R. Faulkner is a fairly typical example of an amateur travel film dating from the middle years of the twentieth century. Filmed in 1941 when possession of a camera and film stock were a luxury few could afford, the black-and-white 8 mm home movie highlights the mobility of affluent Pākehā with a series of travelling shots filmed through the windscreen of a moving vehicle. The opening shot of the reel, which shows a map of Lake Rotorua and the surrounding district, sets the scene of the road trip. The selection of images that follow would, by and large, not be out of place in a professional tourist film, the occasional shot of a family group—presumably the filmmaker's own—replacing those of generic tourists. The family are seen at Fairy Springs, for example, looking at trout before the film cuts to Whakarewarewa, where local Māori are glimpsed sitting in hot pools. The greater part of the Rotorua footage is, however, devoted to the drama of the landscape itself. A series of wide shots and close-ups show steam rising from the geothermal terrain, spluttering geysers, trickling springs, and different permutations of bubbling mud. Three women walk towards the camera through a carved gateway. Māori children are seen diving for pennies, which they then display for the camera. The Rotorua sequence is bookended with further travelling shots recorded from the car, which happens to encounter yet another iconic New Zealand scene on the road: a flock of sheep. Although the images are generally well focused with good exposure, the recording nonetheless demonstrates stylistic 'flaws' such as excessively fast panning to and fro across the landscape that does not follow any particular movement within it. A relatively common quirk of amateur filmmaking, the technique of scanning across the field of vision seems to approximate a human beholder's way of looking at physical space, particularly that of the sightseer who has simply come to gaze at whatever is in view.

Silent like most home movies, Faulkner's recording contains no specific narrative beyond the documenting of a road journey, making it more difficult to interpret in many ways than a professional scenic or travelogue. While some home movies do feature intertitles, Faulkner opted instead for the common amateur practice of including signage, either to record place names—in this instance, a sign points to Fairy Springs—or some other point of interest. At Whakarewarewa the camera captures signs indicating the area is 'dangerous' and that visitors should 'keep off terrace formation'. Close-up shots of these warnings inject a sense of adventurousness into the vacation, which finds a parallel in publicity films that draw attention to the untamed nature of the landscape and the supposedly primal people who inhabit it. Although Faulkner did not record any displays of *kapa haka*, the presence of traditional Māori culture is evident in the carved gateway. More notably, the Māori population of Whakarewarewa are living very much in the present day, wearing European clothes and diving for coins presumably thrown by tourists.

Children are also seen diving at Rotorua in another amateur travel film recorded around the same time by Dr W.R. Lawrence. Here the Pākehā family are much more prominent than in the scenes of Rotorua Faulkner chose to record. Initially seen posing beside a sign indicating the way to Rotorua and consuming a snack on the roadside, the family (consisting of a woman, two girls, and a boy) then appear mingling with local Māori children on a bridge from which the latter jump into the river below. This is followed by an image of Māori children crowded into a small outdoor bath. The scene shifts to the geothermal area, alternating between shots of the family with a Māori guide and the geysers and mud pools they are viewing. There is a brief shot of carvings taken at the model *pā*. Lastly, the family are seen enjoying the geothermal waters of Rotorua's Blue Baths. Part of 16 minutes of black-and-white vacation footage shot during a tour of the North Island by car, the Rotorua sequence is again fairly typical in its mixture of family documentation and familiar tourist sights. The camera is at times unnecessarily mobile or unsteady, and there is no attempt to develop narrative continuity between sequences filmed at different locations.

As with Faulkner's recording, while aspects of the *mise-en-scène* are unmistakably amateur, the aesthetic of Dr Lawrence's movie also reveals the influence of professional filmmaking and other tourist media. What Heather Norris Nicholson describes as the 'borrowed visual vocabulary' of amateur filmmaking was nevertheless adapted to suit the individual filmmaker's own purposes (1997, 208). The shared shot of tourist and tourist attraction, for example, enabled travellers to insert themselves into images that replicated postcards and other tourist media depicting renowned sights and locations.[9] Roadside stops aside, Dr Lawrence was seemingly content to capture his family largely on the fly rather than deliberately posing them beside a specific feature as if for a snapshot. The camera repeatedly cuts back and forth between the geothermal activity at

---

[9] Alexandra Schneider describes the 'shared shot' of tourist and tourist attraction as the 'dominant composition' of amateur travel films (2006, 162).

Whakarewarewa and the people looking at it, registering the family's presence within the unusual landscape. They are also seen ascending the steps of the Blue Baths, the children pausing hesitantly for a moment as if to ascertain that the camera is indeed rolling to document the occasion. Similarly, the filmmaker may have instructed the family to walk towards the camera in one shot across a bridge. Tom Gunning suggests the combination of cinema, travel, and fantasy has the ability to 'render every distant thing somehow available to us' via a virtual voyage (2006, 28). By contrast, the amateur lens bears witness to the traveller's actual experience in a specific place. Of course when filmmakers and families returned home, travel films enabled physical journeys to be re-lived in virtual form. As personalised holiday souvenirs, vacation recordings seemed to hold out the promise that distant things would remain available, not simply fade into distant memory.[10]

Although Lawrence likely edited his films in-camera only, as did most amateurs, he appears nonetheless to demonstrate some knowledge of professional filmmaking. This is most evident when the footage cuts between wide shots of the family's guide pointing to features of the landscape and close-ups of bubbling mud pools. Whether or not these close-ups represent the actual features in question can only be surmised. However, the editing creates the impression this is certainly so.[11] These shots are also interesting in terms of what they might suggest about Māori-Pākehā relations at Rotorua. While there is little to indicate how the travellers felt about what they saw or the people they met there (beyond the significance one might attach to the act of recording in itself), the attentive demeanour of the family whilst listening to their guide implies a courteous interaction. Guides acted as knowledgeable intermediaries between Māori and Pākehā worlds and were generally well respected amongst both communities. Given the tendency of professional cinema to separate Māori

---

[10] Vivian Sobchack uses the term 'film-souvenir' to describe a home movie, arguing both souvenirs and personal recordings fulfil a similar mnemonic function (1999, 248). Home movies are not necessarily successful in this sense, however. Nico de Klerk observes that decades later 'original participants tend to become spectators' like any other, unable to recollect events associated with specific images in their own films (2008, 148–9).

[11] A similar effect is seen in Faulkner's sequence at Fairy Springs, which cuts between shots of trout and those viewing them.

and Pākehā into disparate time-spaces, amateur filmmakers were seemingly better placed to capture more informal moments of intercultural encounters such as those glimpsed in Dr Lawrence's film.

A more colourful vision of Rotorua is observed in a holiday recording made 15 years later by American visitor, Bernadine Bailey. Unlike the wartime home movies, Bailey's film was recorded in lush Kodachrome and features a generous 27-minutes of footage shot around New Zealand. The Rotorua segment opens with some rather dark images of trout swimming at Fairy Springs, which contrast with the vivid scenes of Whakarewarewa that follow. Two Māori women in traditional dress appear with several children. A tableau shot captures women demonstrating the use of *poi* (ball on a string) in front of a meeting house, while another woman accompanies the performance on a ukulele. The sequence shifts to geothermal activity, the camera panning restlessly from one bubbling mud pool to another. The filmmaker's interest appears to lie more in the realm of human habitation, however. A guide is seen speaking at the model *pā*, an area glimpsed only briefly in Faulkner's and Lawrence's films. Here, however, the camera scans most of the buildings on display. More informal activity at Whakarewarewa is also documented. Wide shots of the European-style houses of local residents nestled amongst the irregular terrain with its crevices and clouds of rising steam, along with women going about their daily business of childminding and washing, capture the coexistence of the mundane and the unusual (unusual, that is, for the outsider in this landscape).

It would be rather easy to assume those features of Whakarewarewa most readily identifiable with the wonderland image presented the greater point of appeal to the eye of the American tourist desiring the exotic. Certainly, more footage is devoted to traditional Māori culture in Bailey's films than in the two previous recordings made by local tourists. The staged performances depicted in rich colours accord with those seen in the images of tourist media. Yet this was clearly not the limit of Bailey's interest. The vibrant spectacle of *kapa haka* is juxtaposed against images of the ordinary daily activities of women and their surroundings. Again, it is tempting to reach a potentially simplistic conclusion that Bailey's choice of subjects merely reflects her position as a female filmmaker and tourist who would likely be more attentive to the trappings of domestic routines than a male visitor. Bailey, who was a journalist and travel writer for children, used her camera as a means of documenting the places she visited for later reference in her work (Wolf-Astrauskas 2015). Moreover, the reduced cost of filmstock in the post-war years permitted amateurs to be more expansive in their recording habits. Consequently, while Bailey's footage appears in turns more romantic and realist in its aesthetic and subject matter than Faulkner's and Lawrence's home movies, her intentions were also presumably somewhat different to the majority of tourist-filmmakers simply concerned with creating a souvenir of their travels.

Ordinary Within the Extraordinary

Our understanding of amateur travel films is, like their moment of creation, necessarily referential. Original meanings and memories that images once evoked for makers and participants are lost when films are transferred from family home to public archive. Yet this does not render such films meaningless. Home movies made by tourists exist within a wider field of media production, social norms, and cultural values, which governed ways of looking at people and places. Tourists blended elements of quasi-professional and distinctly amateur technique within their films. They situated themselves, their families, or travel companions within a pre-existing iconography of tourist attractions, both replicating and personalising the visual regime of promotional media. There is considerable overlap in the selection of subjects seen in professional and amateur films of Rotorua, the latter distinguished most readily by their less polished aesthetic and the absence of narration. What often appears haphazard in form was nonetheless the result of deliberate selection on the part of filmmakers desirous of a more personalised account of their vacation than the mere purchase of a commercial postcard, for example, could satisfy.

Looking at the recordings above, we can only speculate what prompted each filmmaker's individual choices with regard to subject and framing. The correspondences with widely circulated publicity images are conspicuous, however. Whether or not filmmakers consciously imitated other media, the wonderland image seemingly infiltrated the tourist gaze. This is most apparent in recordings such as Bailey's that feature the official performances of *kapa haka*, which catered specifically to tourists' desire to look upon the spectacle of cultural difference. A fascination with unusual topography is also prevalent in both amateur and professional tourist films, panoramic shots of the steaming landscape transforming physical space into a framed view of exotic dimensions. The modern romance of the road is another seemingly universal dimension of the tourist experience. Whether the train journeys of *Railways of the Pacific Wonderland* or Faulkner's footage taken from a moving vehicle, the mobility of European travellers was foregrounded in tourist films.

It would be reductive, however, to think of the cinematic efforts of tourists as merely clumsy reproductions of professionally made films. While amateur and professional tourist films share a comparably cheerful vision of time away from everyday concerns (or at least one's own), they diverge ideologically in significant respects. As John Urry notes, the touristic gaze is premised upon a binary division between the ordinary and the extraordinary (1990, 12–23), yet this divide lies simply in the eye of the beholder. This is perhaps most evident in the images of women cooking in steam vents or washing clothes in hot pools that feature in both professional and amateur recordings of Whakarewarewa. By dint of geological anomaly filtered through an outsider's gaze, the women's everyday is transfigured into the visitor's exotic (Fig. 10.4).

In Bernadine Bailey's film this division is not so straightforward, however. One shot depicts a woman sitting down to wash some garments in

Fig. 10.4 Women at Whakarewarewa recorded by Bernadine Bailey, 1956. Reproduced courtesy of Indiana University Libraries Moving Image Archive

a pool. She glances over her shoulder towards the camera, presumably aware she is being filmed, or at least has an audience. As the woman is wearing traditional attire rather than European clothes, this scene may be a demonstration for an assembly of tourists. In any event, the shot is similar to those of publicity films. When Bailey's camera strays beyond what appear to be official displays of *Māoritanga*, the effect is very different. Rather than seeing what was intended to be seen by outsiders, we are thrust into the everyday lives of the inhabitants of Whakarewarewa. The roving camera takes in not just the houses dotted amongst the hills but, somewhat disconcertingly, a backyard view of laundry drying on washing lines, untidy piles of ruins from demolished or decayed buildings, and children playing in the street. This rather voyeuristic view of the village is quite unlike the carefully arranged images of promotional media. It is also a distinctly powerful one, the apparent realism of which creates an impression that the camera simply found whatever happened to be there. The filmmaker nevertheless chose to record these divergent visions of Whakarewarewa: the public performances and the (not exactly) private daily goings on. The contrast is stark. Even in the midst of the extraordinary steaming landscape, there is nothing very exotic or romantic about the appearance of everyday life.

Although tourists are largely absent onscreen in Bailey's film, visible only in the background at the model *pā*, the social divide between the filmmaker and her Māori subjects may nonetheless be inferred. As in other tourist films—amateur or professional—to be white, mobile, and affluent is the norm against which difference is measured. Whereas economic and class divisions are largely side-stepped in publicity films through Māori occupying a historical rather than a contemporary timespace, amateur recordings inadvertently or otherwise draw attention to social realities not seen in professional cinema of the time. The residents of Whakarewarewa are visibly impoverished in comparison with their visitors who could afford cameras, travel, and leisure time. Nothing highlights this distinction better perhaps than the image of a group of Māori children crammed into a tiny pool in Dr Lawrence's film followed moments later by that of Pākehā tourists enjoying the spacious waters of Rotorua's Blue Baths, their swimsuits and bathing caps setting them apart as people who can afford specialised leisurewear (as well as presumably an entry fee). Rather than just taking a dip in whatever one happens to be wearing (or nothing at all), Pākehā travellers dress purposefully for the occasion. Moreover, amateur tourist films, like their professional equivalents, underline the unequal relations of power that existed between image-makers and those filmed. Pākehā or overseas visitors to Rotorua determined how local Māori were represented onscreen. Māori had the opportunity to record neither their own lives nor how they viewed their visitors.

Due to the additional expense and limited audio fidelity, few amateurs recorded either synchronised sound or voiceover narrations to accompany their films, preferring instead to rely upon the spontaneous live discussion typical of family screenings. While a small minority added intertitles or recut their films subsequently, most home movies preserve the ad hoc sequence of images created at the moment of filming. Consequently, amateur tourist films are characterised by the ambiguities inherent in their fortuitous configuration and silent form. As such, they are not easy archival documents to read, but may nonetheless be understood within a broader historical trajectory, including tourism and tourist promotion. While travel recordings made by sightseers do not contain explicit master narratives of nation-building or progress from savagery to civilisation, courtesy of European modernity, these could be interpreted as implicit in ways of looking at Indigenous people as tourist attractions. The perceptions or attitudes of tourist-filmmakers always remain somewhat elusive, however.

When accounting for why home movies look the way they do, there is a certain amount of guesswork involved. It is impossible to know whether tourists who recorded their own films had watched those made by the New Zealand Government or other local production houses. Their apparent familiarity with the picturesque-exotic tourist iconography could have derived as much, if not more, from other sources. Print media, such as the publicity poster described in the opening passage, may have reached a much wider audience than locally made scenic films. It is also noteworthy that home movies recorded by tourists elsewhere in the world, particularly in former European settler societies, bear a great deal of aesthetic similarity to those filmed at Rotorua. In this sense, we might speak of an 'international style', local specificity being more a feature of the home movie subject than the way it was filmed. The aesthetic was also remarkably resilient, the basic form of home movies changing little over time, seemingly unhindered by developments in professional cinema. Such considerations paint a complex picture when attempting to trace the origins of the tourist gaze witnessed in home movies. What is evident, however, looking at home movies and professional tourist media side by side is a shared ideological terrain broadly concerned with the spectacular and the exotic from a Eurocentric point of view. Yet the amateur camera could also afford to meander according to the whim of the individual, taking in whatever the tourist-filmmaker saw fit to record at a given moment. In this way, home movies can offer a behind-the-scenes glimpse of tourist locations that did not feature in glossy promotional images. In so doing, they document economic disparities and allude to imbalances of power that existed between tourists and Indigenous communities, realities the promoters of tourism usually seek to obscure.

Popular tourist locations such as Rotorua commodified the alterity of Indigenous peoples and unusual landscapes for the gaze of European visitors and their cameras. Preserved in the images of the countless thousands of amateur travel films that remain in public and private collections worldwide, the tourist gaze of the twentieth century has itself become an object of scrutiny as we examine the legacy of colonialism and past intercultural encounters. As material documents of tourist activity, amateur films form a significant record of how private individuals reconstituted popular visions of the exotic for their own ends, as well as how they looked upon more mundane aspects of social and cultural difference.

Works Cited

'1956 New Zealand, 1955 Bali-Djiharta, Malay Wedding, Angkor Wat.' Directed by Bailey, Bernadine. Indiana University Libraries. https://media.dlib.indiana.edu/media_objects/5425kh91t.

Alsop, Peter, Gary Stewart, and Dave Bamford, eds. 2012. *Selling the Dream: The Art of Early New Zealand Tourism*. Nelson: Craig Potton Publishing.

Archives New Zealand YouTube Channel. "Maori Village: A Concert Rehearsal Near Rotorua". 1945. Produced by National Film Unit. https://youtu.be/1tpT6YUOESc.

Archives New Zealand YouTube Channel. "Meet New Zealand: The People". 1949. Produced by National Film Unit. https://youtu.be/0J3_j-t66AY.

Beets, Jacqui Sutton. 1997. Images of Maori Women in New Zealand Postcards After 1900. *Women's Studies Journal* 13 (2): 7–24.

Bernadine Bailey Collection. Indiana University Libraries. https://libraries.indiana.edu/bernadine-bailey-collection. Accessed 24 August 2020.

Blythe, Martin. 1994. *Naming the Other: Images of the Maori in New Zealand Film and Television*. Metuchen: Scarecrow Press.

de Klerk, Nico. 2008. Home Away from Home: Private Films from the Dutch East Indies. In *Mining the Home Movie: Excavations in Histories and Memories*, ed. Patricia Zimmermann and Karen Ishizuka, 148–162. Berkeley: University of California Press.

Dennis, Jonathan. 1994. Restoring History. *Film History* 6 (1): 116–127.

Faulkner, Charles R. Personal Record [Rotorua]. 1941. Ngā Taonga Sound and Vision. https://www.ngataonga.org.nz/collections/catalogue/catalogue-item?record_id=91359.

"Glorious New Zealand". 1925. Produced by New Zealand Government Publicity Office. Ngā Taonga Sound and Vision. https://www.ngataonga.org.nz/collections/catalogue/catalogue-item?record_id=66890.

Grierson, John. 1981. The Face of a New Zealander. In *The Tin Shed: Origins of the National Film Unit*, ed. Jonathan Dennis, 21–22. Wellington: New Zealand Film Archive.

Gunning, Tom. 2006. The Whole World Within Reach: Travel Images Without Borders. In *Virtual Voyages: Cinema and Travel*, ed. Jeffrey Ruoff, 25–41. Durham: Duke University Press.

King, Michael. 1983. *Māori: A Photographic and Social History*. Auckland: Heinemann Publishers.

Lawrence, Dr W.R. Personal Record [Exhibition Trip]. 1940. Ngā Taonga Sound and Vision. https://www.ngataonga.org.nz/collections/catalogue/catalogue-item?record_id=76489.

Leotta, Alfio. 2011. *Touring the Screen: Tourism and New Zealand Film Geographies*. Chicago: Intellect.

"Magic Playgrounds in New Zealand's Geyserland". 1935. Produced by New Zealand Government Tourist Office. Ngā Taonga Sound and Vision. https://www.ngataonga.org.nz/collections/catalogue/catalogue-item?record_id=65551.

McClure, Margaret. 2004. *The Wonder Country: Making New Zealand Tourism*. Auckland: Auckland University Press.

Norris Nicholson, Heather. 1997. In Amateur Hands: Framing Time and Space in Home Movies. *History Workshop Journal* 43 (1): 198–213.

Peterson, Jennifer Lynn. 2006. "The Nation's First Playground": Travel Films and the American West, 1895–1920. In *Virtual Voyages: Cinema and Travel*, ed. Jeffrey Ruoff, 79–98. Durham: Duke University Press.

Pool, Ian, and Tahu Kukutai. 2018. Taupori Māori – Māori Population Change – Population Recuperation, 1900–1945. Te Ara: The Encyclopedia of New Zealand. http://www.teara.govt.nz/en/taupori-maori-maori-population-change/page-3. Accessed 25 August 2020.

"Railways of the Pacific Wonderland". 1939. Produced by New Zealand Government Film Studio. Ngā Taonga Sound and Vision. https://www.ngataonga.org.nz/collections/catalogue/catalogue-item?record_id=64152.

"Romantic New Zealand". 1934. Produced by Filmcraft and New Zealand Government Tourist Office. Ngā Taonga Sound and Vision. https://www.ngataonga.org.nz/collections/catalogue/catalogue-item?record_id=64279.

Schneider, Alexandra. 2006. Homemade Travelogues: Autosonntag – A Film Safari in the Swiss Alps. In *Virtual Voyages: Cinema and Travel*, ed. Jeffrey Ruoff, 157–173. Durham: Duke University Press.

"Sights in New Zealand". 1905. Produced by West's Pictures. Ngā Taonga Sound and Vision. https://www.ngataonga.org.nz/collections/catalogue/catalogue-item?record_id=64500.

Sobchack, Vivian. 1999. Towards a Phenomenology of Nonfictional Film Experience. In *Collecting Visible Evidence*, ed. Jane Gaines and Michael Renov, 241–254. Minneapolis: University of Minnesota Press.

Strain, Ellen. 1996. Exotic Bodies, Distant Landscapes: Touristic Viewing and Popularized Anthropology in the Nineteenth Century. *Wide Angle* 18 (2): 70–100.

Taylor, John Patrick. 1998. *Consuming Identity: Modernity and Tourism in New Zealand*. Auckland: University of Auckland.

Urry, John. 1990. *The Tourist Gaze*. London: Sage Publications.

Weckbecker, Lars. 2015. *Governing Visions of the Real: The National Film Unit and Griersonian Documentary Film in Aotearoa/New Zealand*. Bristol and Chicago: Intellect Books.

Wolf-Astrauskas, Marianne. 2015. Her World Travels Inspired Stories for Children. Illinois Women's Press Association. https://www.iwpa.org/her-world-travels-inspired-stories-for-children/. Accessed 24 August 2020.

11

A 'White' Country for 'White' People: Poland in Tourism Promotional Videos of Regions and Metropolitan Cities

Piotr Dzik and Anna Adamus-Matuszyńska

Introduction

Poland participates in global tourism as a large reception market, but as a state, it has not yet conducted systematic, international promotional campaigns. Between 2007 and 2016, a number of promotions commissioned by regional (*voivodesip*) and large cities' authorities were carried out. Promotional videos addressed to the international markets were prepared as part of regional and city advertising campaigns. Therefore, the present chapter asks the following research question: how are Poland and Polish society presented in regional and cities' promotional campaigns?

P. Dzik (✉)
Academy of Fine Arts in Katowice, Katowice, Poland
e-mail: piotr.dzik@asp.katowice.pl

A. Adamus-Matuszyńska
University of Economics in Katowice, Katowice, Poland
e-mail: adamus@ue.katowice.pl

The authors decided to examine the period from 2007 to 2016 because during that time, countries, regions, and cities were able to take advantage of the European Union (EU) funds dedicated to tourism promotion. The promotion was financed by the so-called Regional Operational Programmes run by regional self-government units. Since 2016, the EU has no longer financed tourism promotion. The subjects of this study were promotional activities organized by *voivodeship* and metropolis self-governments. Overall, 16 regions (*voivodesips*) and 12 large cities (members of the Union of Polish Metropolises) were selected for the study. To answer the research questions, the authors used content analysis as a qualitative method (Echtner 1999) and examined every official tourism and universal (i.e., addressed to a large unspecified audience) promotional film (tourism commercials and tourism promotional videos) of regions and large cities in Poland available online during the period in question (2007–2016).

The authors initially found that the analysed videos focus on 'white' hosts and 'white' guests in their stereotypical social roles. Poland is portrayed in these videos as a 'white' country awaiting 'white' guests, and such a portrait of the country is firmly established in its history. Norman Davies, an authority on Polish history, writes that Polish national consciousness was built on four fundamental sources of inspiration: the Catholic Church, language, history, and race (Davies 2005, 14). He also stresses that in the twentieth century, the "noble culture" became the culture of the whole nation (Davies 1997, 586). Beginning in the sixteenth century, Sarmatianism as an ethno-cultural concept—which used to be an ideology of nobility in Poland—has been a typical feature of Polish culture. It became an ideology, perhaps not fully developed in every aspect, which emphasizes the national values among the nobility (Ulewicz 2006). One of the features of Sarmatianism is ethno-separatism (Niewiara 2009, 75–78). Historically, people of colour in Poland have been statistically imperceptible and/or traditionally absent from public spaces. This cultural invisibility is also visually noticeable in Polish strategic documents on tourism (Walas 2011), despite the fact that many contemporary visitors represent various religions and world views (Zamoyski 1998; Szacki 1995, 45–50).

Poland is a large reception market,[1] readily visited by foreign tourists and, at the same time, is nationally and ethnically homogeneous. Thus, the next question that arises is: what aspects of itself should Poland promote to develop tourism and how can Poland promote itself as an attractive destination for a wide range of foreign tourists in the time of globalization?

In terms of tourist attractions, a document by the Polish Tourist Organization (POT), entitled "Marketing Strategy of Poland in the Tourism Sector for 2012–2020" (Walas 2011), explains what attractions Poland offers and how they should be presented to foreign tourists. According to the document, Poland's key visual features are urban and cultural tourism, represented in the report as the 5As: attractions, amenities, accommodation, access, and atmosphere. Supplementary products are urban tourism (city break), active and specialized tourism, tourism in rural areas, and business tourism (i.e., meetings, incentives, conventions, and exhibitions—the so-called MICE [Walas 2011, 54–55]). Considering the recommendations of the POT and other strategic documents regarding the country's marketing communication, the following questions should be asked:

1. Who should be a referential character (Bal 2017, 109–110) in promotional videos?
2. How should government bodies present the specificity of Polish tourist attractions in the media?

Within the context of this chapter's objective, two research questions are important: (1) what was the formal content of the promotional messages (i.e., what content was used, what was the style and form of texts) and (2) what media were used to disseminate them?

---

[1] In the Polish literature on brand destination, 'reception market' means a product, place, or event that attracts tourists. The 'emission market' is the country (region) that tourists come from (Kruczek and Walas 2010, 133). These terms correspond to the destination and target market in English literature (Pike 2008). Detailed and up-to-date information and reports on as well as analyses of tourist traffic can be found on the websites of the Polish Tourist Organization (POT) (pot.gov.pl), Regional Tourist Organizations (ROT), Local Tourist Organizations (LOT), and in the statistics of the Central Statistical Office. According to these sources, around 20 million tourists from abroad visited Poland in 2019.

As a starting point for the analysis, all promotional videos of 16 regions (*voivodesips*) and 12 metropolises produced between 2007 and 2016 (broadcast and available on the Internet) were examined. In total, the authors watched over 13,000 videos prepared for the above-mentioned territorial units. To analyse the content of the promotional messages included in those videos, it was necessary to identify them, adopt the criteria for their selection, and indicate why the selected material was relevant for more detailed study.

For our research, we made the following assumptions:

1. The subjects of the study were promotional films funded by the European Union Structural Funds between 2007 and 2013 (some activities financed by this fund continued until 2016, that is why the period examined is longer than the tourism promotion financing period). This decision was justified by the following premises: (a) at that time, a number of analytical and planning documents concerning the tourism promotion of Poland were being developed; (b) during that period Poland as a country did not carry out any promotional campaigns in foreign markets (Zaborowski 2018); and (c) tourism promotional offers were carried out mainly by local government units, including regions (*voivodesips*) and by the Regional Operational Programmes (Panasiuk 2016, 279–281). In the current EU Multinational Financial Framework (financial perspective) for 2014–2020, there are no separate funds for the development and promotion of the tourism sector in Poland (Portal Funduszy Europejskich 2014). In recent years, many videos promoting cities and regions have been produced, but the size of the production depended on the strategic plans and budget of the individual territorial units. There is therefore a large variety of stylistic approaches that make it difficult to compare cities and regions in this respect.

2. According to the literature on the subject, the National Tourism Organization should be responsible for the tourism promotion of the country (Pike 2008). In Poland, this role is played by the Polish Tourist Organization. However, the promotional activities of the Polish Tourist Organization were, in the researched period, very limited and did not involve video promotion (Zaborowski 2018). This means that in Poland, organizations such as the Regional Tourist Organizations (ROT) were

responsible for the overall promotion of Poland's identity and heritage. As Rojek writes:

> A country's brand, sometimes defined as a country's market identity, is not a specific product or service that can be identified by means of national marketing measures in content and form, but it is the image of the country and its nation in the opinion of recipients, who can be both citizens of the country as well as other communities. (Rojek 2007, 62)

Poland's national brand was built from the ground up, as the overall image of the country was created through ROT promotional activities. Therefore, it is possible to reconstruct the "projected image" (Moingeon and Soenen 2002, 17) of the country by researching and analysing the marketing communication of the regions. The image of a brand is described as "perceptions about the place as reflected by the associations held in tourist memory" (Cai 2002, 723). Thus, in accordance with the availability heuristic (Kahneman 2012), the visitor may build an image of the country based on the images available in his/her consciousness that he/she can easily recall.

3. In the twenty-first century, arguments about the fundamental importance of the Internet—including official websites—for the promotion of destinations and for the activities of Destination Marketing Organizations (DMOs') had already been demonstrated (Swarbrooke and Horner 2007, 169; Pike 2008, 271–275; Morrison 2013, 369–372; Camilleri 2018, 25, 78, 87; Fernández-Cavia and Castro 2015; Kruczek and Walas 2010, 118–130; Kaczmarek et al. 2010, 263–264). However, while the virtualization of tourism promotion gained importance in the late 1990s and the beginning of the New Millennium (Morrison 2013, 369–374)—and guidebooks on promotion in digital media began to appear around the year 2000 (Carter and Bédard 2001, 14–33)—the history of research on social media is much shorter, due to the relative novelty of this phenomenon and the methodological difficulties. It can be argued that there is a consensus among researchers that social media sites are important in tourism marketing and should at least be linked with official websites (Kiráľová and Pavlíček 2015; Mukherjee and Nagabhushanam 2016; Molinillo et al. 2017). It can be also noted that these media facilitate promotion when serious budget

constraints exist (Hays et al. 2013). A similar position is presented in Polish (Pawlicz 2015; Hereźniak 2016) and East European literature (Labanauskaite et al. 2020).

4. While both television promotion and the impact of spot advertising are well recognized and described (Sutherland and Sylwester 2003, 165), the role of time-based visual data[2] in the promotion of destinations is a new research problem—especially when it concerns embedding videos on websites and using videos on social media (e.g., videos on Facebook, specialized video channels on YouTube). The following claims seem to be confirmed in the literature: (1) video influences the decisions of potential tourists, especially in the context of social media (Kiráľová and Pavlíček 2015; Lange-Faria and Elliot 2012; Leung et al. 2013; Gretzel 2017), but (2) there are differences in the impact on audiences between user-generated material/content (UGC) (cf. Stankov et al. 2010) and marketer-produced videos—the so-called Marketer Generated Video (MGV) (Lim et al. 2012; Kavoura et al. 2019).

Summarizing the above considerations, it can be argued that between 2007 and 2016 the promotion of Poland's image was carried out in a bottom-up fashion, mainly by regions and large cities, while public institutions were responsible for the promotion and development of *voivodesips* and metropolises. During that time, a number of initiatives were implemented that presented Poland as an attractive and tourist-friendly country. Yet there was no film-based advertising campaign used as a promotional tool that would show Poland and its inhabitants as a defined and coherent social whole.

Research Problem

The literature on destination branding highlights both how tourism promotion has a political significance (Buhalis 2000; Pike 2008; Salazar 2012) and how it reflects the dominant ideology within a given socio-cultural context (Ateljevic and Doorne 2002). One of the forms of

---

[2] On the Internet, the visual data can be divided into "space-based", such as photos, maps, tables, and so on, and "time-based", that is, video, animated GIFs, interactive infographics, and so on.

destination branding is nation branding, the process through which countries tell their stories or present themselves and influence how potential visitors may think about a particular country (Sevin and White 2011; Yalkin 2018). This is why a destination's promotional content and form in time-based media are grounded in a specific socio-cultural and political context (Crilly et al. 2008, 430). Therefore, the main research problem may be formulated as four questions:

1. How do the images and verbal messages contained in videos promoting tourism present the projected image of Poland and its inhabitants?
2. What characters represent Poland, who are they, and how do they act?
3. Who are the 'default' tourists imagined by the creators and principals of promotional videos?
4. What interactions are there between visitors and hosts?

According to Scollon and Scollon (2003, 91), visual images convey cultural values and stereotypes. Furthermore, colours used in marketing communication—which are one of the basic determinants of brand identity and image (Mollerup 2013, 246–276)—may have political, social, or even commercial implications. Colours are nonverbal signs that carry significant meaning and can support existing stereotypes and prejudices (Kress and van Leeuwen 2006, 229). That is why the presented research focused on heroes and heroines of promotional videos who might symbolize various cultures and ethnic groups in a stereotypical fashion. The connotations expressed by producers of the examined videos have social implications impacting the perception of the promoted destination. In general, advertisements reproduce stereotypes (Owsianowska 2014, 106). However, it should also be noted that in particular commercials, the text does not convey stereotypes while the visual content encodes stereotypes (Kress and van Leeuwen 2006, 20). Many destinations still suffer from negative stereotypes, prejudices, and perceptions of being "underdeveloped", "unsafe", "boring", or "backward" (Avraham and Ketter 2016, 2). Every destination has its own identity, its own spirit, genius loci, but place branding is not capable of telling the whole story about the given place. Rather, it presents one version of the reality, and therefore establishes the place in a stereotypical manner (Liu 2017, 329).

Research Method and Data Analysis

We used a qualitative approach because, in the case of tourism promotion, structured (quantitative) approaches are not beneficial for the analysis of unique and holistic components of the image (Govers and Go 2003, 26; Echtner and Ritchie 2003, 41–43). The examination of these unique and holistic features of Poland's projected images in promotional videos is the aim of the research presented here. Defining unambiguously the tourism commercial is a complex task (Leotta 2020). Therefore, the authors decided to adopt the definition of 'visual data' (Grady 2008), assuming that these data have two dimensions: a physical one and a time-based one. According to standard definitions, a video/film is a time-based, visually perceptible artefact that records human actions of one kind or another.

The research problem outlined required searching for videos in the following platforms:

* on the websites of the marshal and municipal offices, as well as official websites promoting tourism (such as 'slaskie.travel', www.poznan.travel/en/),
* on official channels on YouTube (official, ROT, and LOT),
* on fan pages on Facebook (section 'films') of relevant offices and DMOs.

The following keywords were used to search for videos: (1) 'promotional film' + '*voivodesip*/name/city/name'; (2) 'promotional spot' + '*voivodeship*/name/city/name'; (3) 'TV/television advertisement' + '*voivodeship*/name/city/name'; (4) 'video advertisement' + '*voivodeship*/name/city/name'.

This procedure was necessary because of the withdrawal of promotional videos from official websites after the end of a campaign—or the so-called durability period (e.g., only videos made after 2018 appear on the official website of the city of Łódź). The authors also used their own sources obtained during the consulting practice (e.g., promotional videos of the Małopolskie *Voivodeship* were obtained while the authors were working for the Marshal's Office of the Małopolska *Voivodeship*).

After reviewing the sources, official videos, and promotional spots, the Marketer Generated Video criteria were selected. Taking into account the research problem and the formulated analytical assumptions, the following videos were eliminated from further analysis:

- TV and internet reports (e.g., documentation of events, speeches, openings, etc.),
- TV programmes containing product placement (e.g., culinary programmes featuring local cuisine), for the above-mentioned reasons,
- Reporting "Snapshots",
- Documentation of events such as films commemorating the city's festivals, anniversaries, or opening cultural facilities, sports events, and so on,
- Private videos posted on official websites. (Lim et al. 2012)

The authors were guided by two criteria in the final selection of videos for analysis. First, the videos had to meet the requirements of a 'tourism film'—understood as a media form that features one or more geographical locations and whose main purpose is tourism promotion (Bonelli 2018, 49). Second, they had to match the definition of the advertising spot, which in marketing practice is defined as a short commercial movie with a clear promotional purpose[3] (Belch et al. 2004; Landa 2016).

One might notice that a large number of videos have been produced, but few of them met the research criteria. The data shown in Tables 11.1 and 11.2 require additional explanations.

1. The term "around" in column 2 is justified as the videos often use the same shots in different configurations, with differences in duration (e.g., a 30-second spot or its shorter, 15-second version) and 'local' variants. The 'local' variant should be understood as one in which an identical construction of the film is used to show different places or products in a given geographical location. This was the case, for

---

[3] It is difficult to find a scientific definition of an advertising spot in the literature on the subject. If one can find any, it is usually a description not embedded in science (theory), but rather in marketing and consulting practice, and—importantly—in law. For example, in the Polish legal regulation there is a limit of 12 minutes of advertising per clock hour in television programmes (Act on Radio and Television, Journal of Laws 1993, No. 7, item 34).

Table 11.1 Number of promotional videos analysed—*voivodesips*

voivodesip (region)	Number of videos found	Videos chosen for further examination
1. Dolnośląskie	Around 80	4
2. Kujawsko-Pomorskie	Around 200	3
3. Lubelskie	Around 30	3
4. Lubuskie	Around 500	9
5. Łódzkie	Around 500	3 (one of the videos has 12 versions)
6. Małopolskie	Around 380	29
7. Mazowieckie	Around 400	1
8. Opolskie	Around 550	13
9. Podkarpackie	Around 1200	7
10. Podlaskie	Around 200	7
11. Pomorskie	Around 400	4
12. Śląskie	Around 200	5
13. Świętokrzyskie	Around 200	5
14. Warmińsko-Mazurskie	Around 1200	4
15. Wielkopolskie	Around 50	2
16. Zachodniopomorskie	Around 200	4
Total	Around 6290	100 (112)

Table 11.2 Number of promotional videos analysed—cities, capitals of the regions

City	Number of videos found	Videos chosen for further examination
Białystok	Around 200	1
Bydgoszcz	Around 50	1
Gdańsk	112	3
Katowice	Around 30	1
Kraków	Around 4300	3
Lublin	Around 385	4
Łódź	Around 40	1
Poznań	34	1
Rzeszów	Around 30	1
Szczecin	Around 100	1
Warszawa	Around 1000	0
Wrocław	Around 800	1
Total	Around 7000	19

example, in the Łódzkie *voivodesip* ("Dumni z Łódzkiego" series), and therefore two figures were provided in this case. There are also instances where videos with minor modifications (e.g., differing in length by a few seconds) are repeated and can be found on the official website, Facebook (FB) and YouTube (YT). There are also different language versions of the same video (e.g., the video itself is the same, but the promotional slogans are different, depending on the language used). There are also situations in which it can be presumed that ready-made shots available in photo banks were used.

2. In the Podkarpackie *voivodeship*, the vast majority of materials are reports of TV Podkarpackie. There were around 20 videos identified as related to tourist promotion, out of which 7 were selected for this research.
3. In the Warmian-Masurian *voivodeship*, more than 1000 videos document the region's participation in the "Seven Wonders of Nature" competition in 2011. Internet users voted for the region by making a short film and sending it to the organizer. These videos could therefore be defined as User-Generated Content (UGC).
4. In Bydgoszcz, in the 2009 film "Guests from other cities and countries" 'non-white' people appear, but these are only professional athletes employed by the clubs operating in the city.
5. In Kraków, a large number of videos are so-called event videos (promotion of festivals, events, etc.—over 700 such videos were broadcast), while over 200 videos in Wrocław documented the efforts to become the European Capital of Culture in 2016.
6. Poznań is a significant exception. At least a few spots promoting multiculturalism and tolerance were created there, but because they were created after 2016, they were not included in the examination.
7. Warsaw has never featured in any videos promoting the city as the capital of Poland. All the videos promoting this city are related to events (e.g., European Football Championship, Euro 2012) or institutions such as museums.

In the second phase of the investigation, videos belonging to the following formal categories were selected:

- spots or longer promotional videos,
- official videos (identified through the region's logo, the city's logo or coat of arms, the so-called packshot, i.e., the final shot showing, for instance, financing from European funds, as well as by description or metadata),
- videos conceived between 2007 and 2014 (2016),[4]
- videos conceived for tourism promotion.

In the next phase, it was necessary to decide how to classify the so-called universal videos, which presented the region or city as attractive for both tourists and investors, as well as an attractive place to live. Such videos were identified, for example, in the Lubelskie *voivodesip* (campaign "For a moment or longer" from 2014). It was decided that if the function of tourism promotion was clearly articulated in the video, then such videos were subject to further analysis.

The last stage of the research involved the analysis of the content of the selected videos in relation to the main research questions. Taking into account assumptions about the stereotypical personal features of the characters presented in promotional videos, the focus was on representations of ethnic or national culture (Ewa Nowicka-Rusek 2003, 198). Therefore, the following cultural symbols were searched for in the promotional videos' content:

- ethnic/racial identification of the characters appearing in a video expressed through visual signs such as clothing,
- interaction between film characters (physical and visual contact, interaction between characters in physical and social space),
- verbal communication (is there dialogue between the characters, are there subtitles, etc.)
- elements of nonverbal communication (symbols, gestures, clothes, age, or physical condition).

---

[4] The time limits are set in accordance with the N+2 rule. It means that projects in the EU's long-term financial perspective may be continued up to two years after its completion.

It was also possible to formulate more detailed assumptions that allowed the authors to research promotional messages in terms of their 'racial' nature. In the literature on urban space, for example, the concept of 'racialisation of space' refers to the fact that the physical space itself (shapes and forms of objects, graffiti, signs, shop displays, merchandising) communicates to viewers which racial groups will belong or will feel alien in that particular environment (Sibley 1998; Lacy Michael and Ono 2011). This concept allows for the initial formulation of the indicators of virtual space racialization developed in its promotional aspect (Dyer-Witheford and de Peuter 2009, 157). We referred to research on measuring sexism in promotional photos (Morgan and Pritchard 1998; Goffman 1976) and, inspired by those analytical schemes, we proposed one that would allow us to measure the levels of racialization in promotional messages:

Level 0—undefined situation. Videos without human participation. Only objects and/or nature are shown, digital or analogue animation is used;

Level 1—there are characters in the film, but none that could be identified as a racial 'other';[5]

Level 2—a racial 'other' is a visitor. He/she does not interact with the people presented as hosts, only watches cultural or natural objects. At this level, the visitor is a person, shown as a tourist taking pictures, consuming, sightseeing, watching stage performances, and so on;

Level 3—a racial 'other' is a guest, and there is a commercial relationship with local people (who act as guides, waiters, receptionists, etc.). The video shows an interaction: one person does something, and his/her action activates a (visual and/or verbal) reaction from the others;

Level 4—a racial 'other' is a guest who interacts personally with the landlord (having fun together, participating in a non-commercial event; there is a suggestion of personal contact in the image and/or dialogue).

---

[5] The authors have adopted the following definition of 'race' for analytical purposes (Delgado and Stefancic 2001, 153): "Race: Notion of a distinct biological type of human being, usually based on skin colour or other physical characteristics".

The levels of racialization in promotional messages listed above were used for further analysis, as shown in Table 11.3.

Findings

Over 13,000 videos were collected for the present research, 119 of which met the criteria described in the methodology. Non-white characters were identified in four videos, but only in one video a person presented by name and surname appears. This character talks about his origins, the circumstances of his arrival to Poland, and his activities in the country. Non-white tourists do not appear in any other tourism promotional videos.

In all the videos analysed, the hosts are racially white, and they appear in service roles. If there is a 'host-guest' interaction, it is not shown as a social interaction. Tourists experience local attractions only through professional interactions such as waiter—guest, masseur—customer, ticket seller—paying customer, stall owner—guest. The guests are also typically 'white'. Only in one case (Opolskie *Voivodeship*) is it clear that the protagonist of the story is a genuine foreigner. However, that foreigner is assimilated, resides permanently in Poland, owns his own business, and speaks Polish.

The research confirmed that there is a commonly shared image of the nation in promotional videos of Poland's cities and regions. When analysing their content (images and spoken or written words), one can notice the existence of a touristic standard: tourism in Poland is associated with kayaks, horses, bicycles, greenery, hang gliders, manors, and traditional Polish cuisine. When a city is shown, one can see monuments or their remains, and, sometimes, watch particular events happening in the city. People in this landscape appear as 'pictures' or as elements of the pictures, not as protagonists of the story filmed. They are presented as colourful moving points that animate static planes. One gets the impression of the ubiquitous loneliness of people. Interactions between visitors or visitors and locals are very rare. The standard scenario seems to feature the following elements: a historic palace or manor house, horses running in the meadow, someone in a canoe or on a bicycle, muzak-type background

11 A 'White' Country for 'White' People: Poland in Tourism… 235

Table 11.3 'Others' in Polish promotional videos

	Screenshot documenting the conclusions	Remarks
1. https://www.youtube.com/watch?v=7KzvUGVYA4g&t=0s&list=PLS8e3ZpN5xxIomOx4kyPqWHDqY2y5EUxq&index=25		Lubuskie, a video made in 2012 promoting tourism, business, and life in the region. The characters do not speak; there is music and voice-over narration. Level 4
2. https://www.youtube.com/watch?v=00z54xYLk9Y		Kujawsko-Pomorskie. The video was produced in 2015. There is no dialogue; characters are shown visiting Bydgoszcz, the capital of the region. In the background one can hear music. The guests have no interaction with local people. Level 2
3.		Śląskie, 2016. The characters do not talk. There are hints of a commercial interaction. In the background, music and titles identify attractions. Level 3

(continued)

Table 11.3 (continued)

Screenshot documenting the conclusions	Remarks
4. https://www.youtube.com/watch?v=r_-HYkon4Rg	Opolskie. A series of videos presenting the attractions of the *voivodeship*. The Marshal of the region acts as the guide (on the left, in a suit). In each film of the series, the Marshal talks with a person associated with the attraction presented. Here, Mr Piyush Mittal is presented as the owner of a building, talking to the Marshal in Polish. Level 4
https://www.youtube.com/watch?v=-c2YYfxtcGo&list=PLeeYc66chO-p-fgWGN9BXTbD_NX14fKc_&index=5	

music, no dialogue. If we see people in a full shot or an American shot, it is usually a heteronormative, 'white' family with one or two children. This pattern seems permanently present in Polish tourism videos of the destinations in question. It is also important to notice that no characters with visible intellectual and/or physical disabilities (e.g., a person in a wheelchair) appear in any of the videos analysed.

Additionally, three conclusions could be made after the examination of the promotional videos: (1) there is an evident heteronormativity of both hosts and guests (not a single video aimed at the so-called pink market has been identified, nor have LGBTQ+ people been shown in any situation), (2) there are videos in which actors appear to approach the retirement age, which means that their age group is not excluded, and (3) there is a visible gender balance (see Morgan and Pritchard 1998, 194–195).

Referring to the content of the analysed videos, it can be stated that the projected destination image of Poland is:

1. 'White'
2. for White people
3. for heteronormative people
4. for healthy people (although there are some spa offers)
5. for those who are not interested in modern cities or post-industrial heritage (an important exception is the Śląskie *Voivodeship* and its "Industrial Monuments Route")
6. for people of various ages

These results contradict the stereotype of Poland as an open and hospitable country. The recipient of the commercials promoting a particular Polish tourist attraction is clearly shown, as is who is welcome in Poland and who is not.

Discussion

Here, it is worth starting a discussion about the extent to which the absence of people of colour is evidence of Polish society's aversion to cultural diversity. The prevalence of images of nature over people and their activities requires further sociological and anthropological research. Based on the content of the commercials, it can also be hypothesized that Poland is not a country free from racism, because the mere avoidance of images of people from different cultures and different cultural behaviours (both as guests and hosts) may be regarded as a 'reflexive' belief in the natural superiority of the white race (Pędziwiatr 2015; Pielużek 2017; Bobako 2018, 278). Right-wing Polish social media suggest that Poland's success in the tourism market is due to the fact that there are no 'coloured' or non-heteronormative people here (Pielużek 2017; Wężyk 2020).

The authors are aware that the research sample is not exhaustive (this is due to the difficulties of internet searches) and the conclusions may be revised after an analysis of additional (and more diverse) sources. Furthermore, a study of the content of promotional videos could also have included:

- videos intended for screening events, such as tourism fairs or exhibitions;
- commercials of events (e.g., as part of Wrocław's efforts to organize the EXPO 2012 exhibition, promotional videos were created that emphasize multiculturalism [Dudziak 2008]);
- promotional videos of other cities and communes (e.g., in the promotional film of the Krośnice commune, there are African ('black') children dancing and playing the drums).

Such a large sample could allow for broader quantitative and qualitative analyses, as could comparative research involving other countries.

Since we assumed that Poland is ethnically a relatively homogeneous country, the 'host-guest' relationship was examined only in terms of the ethnic diversity of guests. In more ethnically diverse countries, such analysis would need to be more detailed and the research model would likely need to be matrix-based (e.g., 'white' host in-service function and 'black' guest, and vice versa).

It should also be mentioned that the media texts signal the significance of Ukrainian workers in the Polish tourism sector. It is even argued that hotels and restaurants constitute an industry based on the employment of Ukrainian citizens. However, none of the researched commercials showed their presence in service roles (there are no speakers with an Eastern accent and no references to the origin of the employees in the dialogues).

Poland is no longer a 'white country', but in promotional videos it is presented as such. It seems that the presented research could confirm the Borgerson and Schroeder thesis about a link between visual representation and ontological attribution. Poland in the twenty-first century is no longer a 'white country', however, it is exposed in promotional videos as such. So, one can conclude that the analysis done in this chapter can be an example of tacit representational convention and its role in sustaining social stereotypes (Borgerson and Schroeder 2005, 270–271).

Final Remarks

While writing this text, we realized that we were walking through a minefield. We tried to capture the issue of *sine ira et studio*, but we were also aware of the inevitable emotions associated with the topic. Our research findings partially confirmed the thesis of Anne Cronin regarding tourism promotion (Cronin 2000, 3–4). In her opinion, advertisements of destinations are aimed mainly at "white men from the West" who are heterosexual and able-bodied. In the case of Poland, the only exceptions are messages addressed to people who are ill or feel the need to improve their health. The country has developed a spa sector and medical tourism is therefore a significant element of tourist promotions (Walas 2011). Historically, Poland has always been an ethnically and racially homogeneous country, which has an impact on the content that is communicated by authorities and through promotional messages. Since 1989, right-wing ideas have permeated discourse in the Polish public space (Pielużek 2017). Such an intellectual atmosphere also influences tourism promotion. Between 2007 and 2016, various political forces were in power in Poland, making it possible to formulate a conclusion that the presentation of Polish cities and regions was not politically motivated, but strongly anchored in national history and culture. This may sound very controversial, but the promotional message of the videos is based on the exclusion of people coming from different cultures and ethnic groups. Tradition, culture, and the ideology of Sarmatism have become so strongly embedded in Polish culture that they render invisible global changes and acknowledgements that today's Poland is inhabited by people from many regions of the world.[6]

Concrete institutions, in our case local government units, are responsible for influencing the local socio-cultural and political context, including tourism promotion. Therefore, to conclude, it is worth quoting Sara Ahmed, professor of race and cultural studies: "After all, institutions provide collective or public spaces. When we describe an institution as 'being' white, we are pointing to how institutional spaces are shaped by the proximity of some bodies and not others: white bodies gather and cohere to form the edges of such spaces" (Ahmed 2006, 132).

Works Cited

Ahmed, Sarah. 2006. *Queer Phenomenology. Orientations, Objects, Others*. London: Duke University Press.

Ateljevic, Irena, and Stephen Doorne. 2002. Representing New Zealand. Tourism Imagery and Ideology. *Annals of Tourism Research* 29 (3): 648–667. https://doi.org/10.1016/S0160-7383(01)00077-9.

Avraham, Eli, and Eran Ketter. 2016. *Tourism Marketing for Developing Countries Battling Stereotypes and Crises in Asia, Africa and the Middle East*. Basingstoke: Palgrave Macmillan.

Bal, Miek. 2017. *Narratology. Introduction to the Theory of Narrative*. Toronto: University of Toronto Press.

---

[6] The data of the Office show that among the foreigners who had valid residence permits on January 1, 2020, there are 12.1 thousand Vietnamese, 9.9 thousand Hindu, and 8.5 thousand Chinese.

https://www.prawo.pl/prawo/cudzeniem-w-polsce-na-poczatku-2020-r-423-tys-osob-przebywalo-497222.html.

Belch, George E., and Michael A. Belch. 2004. *Advertising & Promotion: An Integrated Marketing Communications Perspective.* New York: Tata McGraw Hill.

Bobako, Monika. 2018. Posłowie. In *Dlaczego nie rozmawiam już z białymi o kolorze skóry*, ed. Reni Eddo-Lodge, 263–283. Kraków: Karakter. (Afterword ('Posłowie') is included in the Polish edition only of the book *Why I'm No Longer Talking to White People About Race* (2017)).

Bonelli, Diego. 2018. *This Is Wellington. The Representation of Wellington in New Zealand Tourism Film from 1912 to 2017.* Doctorate thesis, Victoria University of Wellington. https://researcharchive.vuw.ac.nz/xmlui/bitstream/handle/10063/7045/thesis_access.pdf?sequence=4. Accessed 1 June 2020.

Borgerson, Janet L., and Jonathan E. Schroeder. 2005. *Identity in Marketing Communications: An Ethics of Visual Representation.* In *Marketing Communication: New Approaches, Technologies, and Styles*, ed. Allan J. Kimmel, 256–277. Oxford: Oxford University Press.

Buhalis, Dimitors. 2000. Marketing the Competitive Destination of the Future. *Tourism Management* 21: 97–116. https://doi.org/10.1016/S0261-5177(99)00095-3.

Cai, Liping. 2002. Cooperative Branding for Rural Destinations. *Annals of Tourism Research* 29 (3): 720–742. https://doi.org/10.1016/S0160-7383(01)00080-9

Camilleri, Mark A. 2018. *Travel Marketing, Tourism Economics and the Airline Product. An Introduction to Theory and Practice.* Cham: Springer.

Carter, Roger, and Francois Bédard. 2001. *E-Business for Tourism. Practical Guidelines for Tourism Destinations and Businesses.* www.e-unwto.org. Accessed 15 June 2008.

Crilly, Nathan, David Good, Derek Matravers, and John P. Clarkson. 2008. Design as Communication: Exploring the Validity and Utility of Relating Intention to Interpretation. *Design Studies* 29: 425–457. https://doi.org/10.1016/j.destud.2008.05.002.

Cronin, Anne. 2000. *Advertising and Consumer Citizenship. Gender, Images and Rights.* London: Routledge.

Davies, Norman. 1997. *Europe. A History.* London: Pimlico.

———. 2005. *God's Playground. A History of Poland in Two Volumes. Volume II 1795 to the Present.* New York: Columbia University Press.

Delgado, Richard, and Jean Stefancic. 2001. *Critical Race Theory. An Introduction.* New York: New York University Press.

Dudziak, Arkadiusz. 2008. *Kultura czasu wolnego jako element kreowania wizerunku medialnego. Studium przypadku: internetowa kampania promocyjno-*

reklamowa Wrocławia na EXPO 2012. In *Homo creator czy homo ludens? Nowe formy aktywności i spędzania wolnego czasu*, ed. Wojciech Muszyński and Marek Sokołowski, 357–363. Toruń: Wydawnictwo Adam Marszałek.

Dyer-Witheford, Nick and de Peuter G. 2009. *Games of Empire. Global Capitalism and Video Games*. Minneapolis: University of Minnesota Press.

Echtner Charlotte M. 1999. The Semiotic Paradigm: Implications for Tourism Research. *Tourism Management* 20: 47–57. https://doi.org/10.1016/S0261-5177(98)00105-8

Echtner, Charlotte M., and J.R. Brent Ritchie. 2003. The Meaning and Measurement of Destination Image. *The Journal of Tourism Studies* 14 (1): 37–48.

Fernández-Cavia, Jose, and Daniela Castro. 2015. Communication and Branding on National Tourism Websites. *Cuadernos.info* 37: 167–185. https://doi.org/10.7764/cdi.37.682. Accessed 30 July 2018.

Goffman, Erving. 1976. *Gender Advertisements*. New York: Harper Torchbooks.

Govers, Robert, and Frank M. Go. 2003. Deconstructing Destination Image in the Information Age. *Information Technology & Tourism* 6: 13–29. https://doi.org/10.3727/109830503108751199.

Grady, John. 2008. Visual Research at the Crossroads. *Forum: Qualitative Social Research* 9 (3): art. 38. http://nbn-resolving.de/urn:nbn:de:0114-fqs0803384.

Gretzel, Ulrike. 2017. The Visual Turn in Social Media Marketing. *Turismos. An International Interdisciplinary Journal of Tourism* 12 (3): 1–18.

Hays, Stephanie, Stephen J. Page, and Dimitors Buhalis. 2013. Social Media as a Destination Marketing Tool: Its Use by National Tourism Organisations. *Current Issues in Tourism* 16 (3): 211–239. https://doi.org/10.1080/13683500.2012.662215.

Hereźniak, Marta. 2016. Komunikacja cyfrowa marek miejsc: doświadczenie, partycypacja, współtworzenie. *Zeszyty Naukowe Wyższej Szkoły Bankowej w Poznaniu* 67 (2): 109–123.

Kaczmarek, Jacek, Andrzej Stasiak, and Bogdan Włodarczyk. 2010. *Produkt turystyczny. Pomysł, organizacja, zarządzanie*. Warszawa: Polskie Wydawnictwo Ekonomiczne.

Kahneman, Daniel. 2012. *Thinking Fast and Slow*. London: Penguin Books Ltd.

Kavoura, Andriniki, Efstathios Keffalonitis, and Prokopios Theodoridis, eds. 2019. *Strategic Innovative Marketing and Tourism. 8th ICSIMAT, Northern Aegean, Greece, 2019*. Cham: Springer.

Kiráľová, Alžbieta, and Antonin Pavlíček. 2015. Development of Social Media Strategies in Tourism Destination. *Procedia – Social and Behavioral Sciences* 175: 358–366. https://doi.org/10.1016/j.sbspro.2015.01.1211.

Kress, Gunther, and Theo van Leeuwen. 2006. *Reading Images. The Grammar of Visual Design.* 2nd ed. London: Routledge.

Kruczek, Zygmunt, and Bartłomiej Walas. 2010. *Promocja i informacja w turystyce.* Kraków: Proksenia.

Labanauskaite, Daiva, Mariantonietta Fiore, and Rimantas Stasys. 2020. Use of E-Marketing Tools as Communication Management in Tourism. *Tourism Management Perspectives* 34 (100652): 1–8. https://doi.org/10.1016/j.tmp.2020.100652.

Lacy Michael, G., and Kent A. Ono, eds. 2011. *Critical Rhetorics of Race.* New York: New York University Press.

Landa, Robin. 2016. *Advertising by Design: Generating and Designing Creative Ideas Across Media.* 3rd ed. Hoboken, NJ: Wiley.

Lange-Faria, Wendy, and Statia Elliot. 2012. Understanding the Role of Social Media in Destination Marketing. *Tourismos: An International Multidisciplinary Journal of Tourism* 7 (1): 193–211.

Leotta, Alfio. 2020. 'This Isn't a Movie … It's a Tourism Ad for Australia': The Dundee Campaign and the Semiotics of Audiovisual Tourism Promotion. *Tourist Studies Vol.* 20 (2): 203–221. https://doi.org/10.1177/1468797619894462.

Leung, Daniel, Rob Law, Hubert van Hoof, and Dimitrios Buhalis. 2013. Social Media in Tourism and Hospitality: A Literature Review. *Journal of Travel & Tourism Marketing* 30 (1–2): 3–22. https://doi.org/10.1080/10548408.2013.750919.

Lim, Yumi, Yeasun Chung, and Pamela A. Weaver. 2012. The Impact of Social Media on Destination Branding: Consumer-Generated Videos Versus Destination Marketer-Generated Videos. *Journal of Vacation Marketing* 18 (3): 197–206. https://doi.org/10.1177/1356766712449366.

Liu, Erica. 2017. Branding Ideas for the Tokyo Olympics 2020. In *Advertising and Branding: Concepts, Methodology, Tools and Application*, ed. Mehdi Khosrow-Pour, 326–345. Hershey, PA: IGI Global.

Moingeon, Bertrand and Soenen G. 2002. The Five Facets of Collective Identities: Integrating Corporate and Organizational Identity. In Corporate and Organizational Identities. Integrating Strategy, Marketing, Communication and Organizational Perspectives, eds. Bertrand Moingeon and Guillaume Soenen, 13–34. London: Routledge.

Molinillo, Sebastian, Francisco Liébana-Cabanillas, and Rafael Anaya-Sánchez. 2017. Destination Image on the DMO's Platforms: Official Website and Social Media. *Tourism & Management Studies* 13 (3): 5–14. https://doi.org/10.18089/tms.2017.13301.

Mollerup, Per. 2013. *Marks of Excellence*. London: Phaidon Press.

Morgan, Nigel, and Annette Pritchard. 1998. *Tourism, Promotion and Power. Creating Images, Creating Identities*. Chichester: Wiley.

Morrison, Alastair M. 2013. *Marketing and Managing Tourism Destinations*. London: Routledge.

Mukherjee, Anwesha, and Manasa Nagabhushanam. 2016. Role of Social Media in Tourism Marketing. *International Journal of Science and Research (IJSR)* 5 (6): 2026–2033.

Niewiara, Aleksandra. 2009. *Kształty polskiej tożsamości. Potoczny dyskurs narodowy w perspektywie etnolingwistycznej (XVI–XX w.)*. Katowice: Wydawnictwo Uniwersytetu Śląskiego.

Nowicka-Rusek, Ewa. 2003. Etniczność w świecie współczesnym – antropolog w działaniu. *Lud* 87: 193–203.

Owsianowska, Sabina. 2014. Stereotypes in Tourist Narrative. *Turystyka kulturowa* 3: 103–116.

Panasiuk, Aleksander. 2016. Finansowanie regionalnej gospodarki turystycznej ze środków Unii Europejskiej w perspektywach finansowych 2007–2013 i 2014–2020. *Ekonomiczne Problemy Usług* 125: 275–288. https://doi.org/10.18276/epu.2016.125-22.

———. 2015. Wykorzystanie mediów społecznościowych jako narzędzia marketingu turystycznego przez gminy leżące na terenach parków narodowych w Polsce. *Ekonomia i Środowisko* 4 (55): 176–187.

Pędziwiatr, Konrad. 2015. *Islamophobia in Poland. National Report 2015*. Istanbul: SETA. Foundation for Political, Economic and Social Research.

Pielużek, Marcin. 2017. *Obrazy świata w komunikacji polskiej skrajnej prawicy*. Wrocław: Wydawnictwo Libron.

Pike, Steven. 2008. *Destination Marketing. An Integrated Marketing Communication Approach*. Oxford: Butterworth-Heinemann.

Portal Funduszy Europejskich. 2014. Online Database, Description of Priorities. https://www.funduszeeuropejskie.gov.pl/strony/o-funduszach/dokumenty/#/domyslne=1. Accessed 01.03.2019.

Rojek, Roman. 2007. *Marka narodowa. Relikt czy fenomen na globalizującym się rynku*. Gdańsk: GWP.

Salazar, Noel B. 2012. Tourism Imaginaries: A Conceptual Approach. *Annals of Tourism Research* 39 (2): 863–882. https://doi.org/10.1016/j.annals.2011.10.004.

Scollon, Ron, and Suzies W. Scollon. 2003. *Discourse in Place: Language in the Material World*. London/New York: Routledge. https://doi.org/10.4324/9780203422724.

Sevin, Efe, and Gizem S. White. 2011. Turkayfe Org: Share your Turksperience. *Journal of Place Management and Development* 4: 80–92. https://doi.org/10.1108/17538331111117188.

Sibley, David. 1998. The Racialisation of Space in British Cities. *Soundings* 10: 118–127.

Stankov, Uglješa, Lazar Lazic, and Vanja Dragićević. 2010. The Extent of Use of Basic Facebook User-Generated Content by the National Tourism Organizations in Europe. *European Journal of Travel Research* 2 (3): 105–113.

Sutherland, Max, and Alice Sylwester. 2000. *Advertising and the Mind of Consumer*. London: Allen and Unwin. Polish edition: Sutherland, M., and A. Sylvester. 2003. *Reklama a umysł konsumenta*. Trans. G. Kranas. Warszawa: Wydawnictwo PWN.

Swarbrooke, John, and Susuan Horner. 2007. *Consumer Behavior in Tourism*. 2nd ed. Oxford: Butterworth-Heinemann.

Szacki, Jerzy. 1995. *Liberalism After Communism*. Budapest: Central European University Press.

Ulewicz, Tadeusz. 2006. *Sarmacja. Studium z problematyki słowiańskiej XV i XVI wieku. Zagadnienie sarmatyzmu w kulturze i literaturze polskiej. Problematyka ogólna i zarys historyczny*. Kraków: Collegium Columbinum. (The book contains the comprehensive summary in English).

Walas, Bartłomiej. 2011. *Marketingowa Strategia Polski w sektorze turystyki na lata 2012–2020*. Warszawa: Polska Organizacja Turystyczna.

Wężyk, Katarzyna. 2020. Bunt szympansów. An Interview with Stephen Holmes. *Gazeta Wyborcza*, October 11–12, pp. 14–17.

Yalkin, Cagri. 2018. A Brand Culture Approach to Managing Nation-Brands. *European Management Review* 15: 137–149. https://doi.org/10.1111/emre.12129.

Zaborowski, Adam. 2018. *Promując Polskę. Dyplomacja, gospodarka, turystyka, sport, kultura*. Toruń: Wydawnictwo Adam Marszałek.

Zamoyski, Adam. 1998. *The Polish Way: A Thousand-Year of the Poles and Their Culture*. New York: Hippocrene Books.

12

Colourful Scenery, Colourful Language: Representing White Australia in the 'Where the Bloody Hell are you?' Australian Tourism Campaign

Panizza Allmark

One of the most provocative and memorable Australian tourist campaigns was marketed as the country's invitation to the world. In 2006, the $180 million television advertisement presented key features of the nation. It showcased iconic sites of Australia in which individuals introduced each scene with their efforts of hospitality, stating 'We've poured you a beer; we've saved you a spot on the beach; we've got the sharks out of the pool; your taxi is waiting; and dinner is about to be served ….' In the campaign, the vast Australian landscape is presented with extraordinary views by 'ordinary' people. It is presented in a colloquial style. The presenters are not experienced, professional actors, but everyday Australians. This aims to provide an impression of authenticity to the campaign (Campaign Brief 2006). Each scene presents a picturesque landscape that further welcomes and entices the tourist gaze. The 'tourist gaze,' it should be remembered, represents an idealized view that is not

P. Allmark (✉)
Edith Cowan University, Mount Lawley, WA, Australia
e-mail: p.allmark@ecu.edu.au

© The Author(s), under exclusive license to Springer Nature Singapore Pte Ltd. 2021
D. Bonelli, A. Leotta (eds.), *Audiovisual Tourism Promotion*,
https://doi.org/10.1007/978-981-16-6410-6_12

part of the everyday experience (Urry and Larsen 2011, 15). In around a minute, a montage of spectacular Australian iconography such as the Outback, kangaroos, the Great Barrier Reef, Indigenous dancers, Uluru, and the Sydney Harbour Bridge is revealed. The final scene is of a white sand beach with a white, young, petite, blonde, bikini-clad woman addressing the camera. She asks "Where the bloody hell are you?." Her query is unlike the welcoming remarks made earlier. It is a phrase that is a cheeky part of Australian vernacular. However, what was considered ordinary to Australians was understood as an extraordinary and provocative remark internationally. As such, the use of the phrase was bold and distinctive in the global tourism market, and the 'Australian Invitation' campaign became commonly referred to as the 'Where the Bloody Hell are you?' ad.

The Australian catchphrase did not translate as an invitation, as intended, but rather as an offensive term. Seen as impolite or vulgar, it was censored in various target markets such as the UK, Canada, Singapore, Korea, Thailand, and Japan. The advertising campaign had garnered widespread media attention, including commentary from national leaders. It was deemed as successful in gaining international attention, but unsuccessful in attracting international tourists to Australia. This chapter will examine the discourse and semiotics surrounding the controversy, the cultural impact of the original campaign, and the satirical parodies of the 'Where the Bloody Hell Are You' advertisement. In particular, it focuses on how the audio and the visual aspects of Australian national identity in the advertisement convey white settler, colonial sentiments in relation to the landscape, gender relations, and Indigenous people.

The Australian invitation advertisement, developed by the Sydney branch of M&C Saatchi, aimed to reflect a young, radiant nation and include a memorable tagline. The advertisement presents as a celebration (even with fireworks over the Sydney Harbour Bridge). It includes colourful scenery, but even more colourful language, the meaning of which is somewhat lost in translation. According to Christopher, "the advertisement was enormously popular in Australia where it was considered very funny. Australians on the whole are very polite to strangers but rude to their friends as a form of shared humour" (2018, 457). However, the welcome strategy was misinterpreted elsewhere. Its recycling of an old

12 Colourful Scenery, Colourful Language: Representing White... 249

formula of ockerism (e.g., its irreverent masculinity and use of Australian slang) proved unsuccessful in increasing tourism; following the launch of the campaign, tourism numbers dramatically reduced from the three countries that had the most exposure from the campaign: Japan, Germany, and Britain (The Daily Telegraph 2008). The controversy surrounding the advertisement and the important point that it did not result in a major increase in tourists to Australia suggest that the communication across cultures was fraught. The advertisement was memorable but not in a positive way.

The phrase 'Where the bloody hell are you' was seen as provocative. It received a lot of publicity because of the use of the words 'bloody' and 'hell.' The then-Australian Prime Minister John Howard defended it: "I think the style of the advertisement is anything but offensive. It is in the [right] context and I think it's a very effective ad" (AAP 2006). Some of the media comments suggested that the 'bloody hell' phrase "indicated a backward step and a return to an unsophisticated 'Ocker' image which reflected poorly on contemporary Australians" (Winter and Gallon 2008, 310). The ad was censored in a number of international markets. It did not translate well in Japan where swear words are not acceptable in everyday conversation. In Japan, "Where the bloody hell are you?" would be used in anger, never for fun (Cameron 2006). So the ad was changed to "So, why don't you come?." Notably, the number of Japanese tourists to Australia dropped by 12% following the campaign, which suggests the lack-lustre appeal of the ad (Rebranding Australia 2008). The ban of the word 'bloody' from the television campaign in Britain, by the Broadcast Advertising Clearance Centre, provoked a delegation from Australian Tourism (including the featured young model in the ad, Lara Bingle) to go to Britain to lobby the censors and demand that the ad be re-released in full. After the argument was presented—the argument that the word bloody was not regarded as offensive and had previously been used in UK advertisements—the ban was lifted (AAP 2006).

Although the phrase was one of the most controversial elements, the content of the ad was also considered problematic. It reinforces what John Urry (1990) refers to as a tourist 'romantic gaze,' which invites the onlooker to 'take in the view' of spectacular sites. However, the romantic gaze presented is an old romance with an outdated version of Australia.

The 'Australian Invitation' campaign was intended to reach "a more sophisticated global traveller who not only has high levels of income and education, but is open-minded and well-travelled" (Winter and Gallon 2008, 302). But, it is not a cosmopolitan image or sophisticated invite that prevails in the ad. Instead, what is offered is a formulaic parade of iconic images of the Australian landscape (beach, bush, and desert—and occasionally Aboriginals) and Australian masculinity (and ockerism) which have proved successful for previous Australian tourism campaigns. An example of this approach was the highly successful "Come and Say G'day" campaign (1984) featuring Paul Hogan, who has been praised for presenting to the world an image of Australians as laid back and irreverent. But "the twist of this old formula did not work. ... Its image of Australia was pilloried at home and abroad, and it was unceremoniously dumped in 2008" (Crawford 2010, 43).

The 'Real' Australia

At the time of the ad's release, creative director Tom McFarlane stated that the ad presents "the real Australia and who we really are—an easygoing, welcoming nation. And people like us for that" (cited in Stanley 2006). But in the invitation campaign, the 'real' Australia depicted is of white Australia. Jon Stratton claims whiteness is still "a key category in the construction of the nation" and is used in political practice (1999, 180). He argues "the ideology that underlies the White Australia policy [which was built on The Immigration Restriction Act of 1901] still haunts us" (1999, 183). In the 2006 Australian tourism campaign, there is no reference to Australia's cultural diversity or multiculturalism. The individual men and women providing the 'invitations' were marketed as real, everyday Australians (Campaign Brief 2006). However, the Anglo-Australian look did not reflect the actual ethnic make-up of real contemporary Australia. At the time of the campaign, the majority of Australians born overseas were from Asia (and still are). Moreover, around 30% of Australians have parents born overseas and their ancestry is from over forty countries (ABS 2006). The chairman of Aegis Media responded to the campaign, stating that "Sometimes I wonder if our media and marketing people understand this rapidly diversifying country" (cited in Burrowes 2013). It seems that tourism marketing looks backwards to the past rather than the present.

The campaign reflects the national myth of white Australia. Writing in the *Australian Quarterly*, Australia's longest-running political journal, in 1953, Carlotta Kellaway refers to the myth of White Australia as "one of those grand-scale national fairy-tales that weave together and fuse a people, drawing a magic cloak across disunity and disaffection" (1953, 17). In 2004, two years prior to the 'Invitation' ad being released, similar commentary was being made highlighting that

> the myth of White Australia [has] denied Aborigines citizenship and national inclusion. It is linked to the dominant power structure of Australian society and has the economic resources, media influence, and institutional power to perpetuate the idea that Australia *has* a national identity and does not require a new one. (Allegritti 2004)

Gordon Waitt in his analysis of early 1990s Australian tourist campaigns asserts that the Australian Tourism Commission are "marketing particular regimes of fantasy and desire that contribute to the maintenance of a national mythology which defines Australianness as Anglo-Celtic, masculine, and rural" (2008, 48). Notably, the rural may include references to Indigenous Australia as part of the scenery of the natural landscape. This is an aspect of the colonial, romantic view of the land. Waitt further states that the "government's understanding of national identity not only relies upon unsophisticated conceptualisations but also employs a national-type reminiscent of the 1950s" (Waitt 2008, 50). He adds that it does not acknowledge the shift in demographics and culture, in particular the multiculturalism agenda of political leaders such as Whitlam, Fraser, and Hawke (2008, 50). Notably, over a decade after Waitt's analysis, the 2006 Australian tourism campaign was still relying on the formulaic strategy of past tourist campaigns, which presented a colonial perspective of Australia.

Despite the increasing racial diversity of the Australian population, the only people of colour presented in the tourism campaign are Indigenous Australians performing traditional dance in the outback landscape. As Pomering suggests:

> While the ad's copy acknowledged Indigenous Australians' lengthy presence in the country, the suggestion that their ancient culture had been practice for the arrival of international tourists in the 21st century might be seen to have trivialised their cultural heritage as mere commercial entertainment for touristic consumption. (Pomering 2010, 7)

The soundtrack of the ad resonates with the Indigenous sounds of a dijeridoo and clapsticks, before transforming into an up-tempo electronic rhythm with non-lexible vocals of da, da, da, da, found in Western musical styles such as doo wop and in a capella. The latter dilutes the resonance of cross-cultural 'otherness.' This usage is similar to early twentieth-century recordings of indigenous music and hybrid compositions in the 1980s and 1990s labelled as 'world music,' which were created by the commercial music industry. The soundtrack presents a sonic bridge between cultures. It attempts a harmony between the ancient and modern. In this way the references to traditional Indigenous music and dance are presented as cultural artefacts for the tourist.

The tourist gaze is directed to pre-European/pre-colonial contact aspects of Aboriginal culture. The scene in the tourism campaign that presents the Indigenous dancers is set in a desert terrain, with large rock formations in the background, to suggest an isolated, ancient culture. This is reinforced with a female Indigenous dancer stating, "we have been rehearsing for over 40,000 years." Whilst it may acknowledge that white Australia has a long black history, the use of the word 'rehearsing' as part of the national narrative suggests that the Indigenous Australians are simply there for aesthetic consumption. The use of a smiling young female addressing the camera also contributes to the notion of a welcoming feminine invite. The gendered approach presents a non-threatening feminized, exotic Other. According to Gregory, "The exotic is a spectacle that generates curiosity" (2017, 89). The woman is surrounded by around ten Indigenous dancers presenting a traditional-style performance. Their faces are obscured with face paint and their shadowy semi-naked bodies are offered as a spiritual link with the desert landscape. This view is reinforced by the wide-angle landscape perspective and the extreme aerial gaze, known as the 'God's eye view.' With the camera placed directly above the subjects, it provides an omniscient and commanding perspective: "Throughout its history the top-down angle has played a key role in conducting panoptic surveillance, exercising air supremacy, defending territory, trapping subjects in sight, and in some cases, facilitating 'the more efficient annihilation of humans'" (Mangold and Goehring 2019, 25). A darker, sinister reading of this scene may relate to the history of genocide and governmental surveillance of Australia's Indigenous people. The statement "We've been rehearsing for over 40,000 years," as Stratton aptly states, "rewrites Aboriginal genocide in the benign terms of a present-day cultural welcome for the consumption of visitors" (2011, 129).

The Indigenous content is aestheticized for the tourist gaze. This situates the onlooker in a powerful viewing position with mastery over the landscape and the Indigenous people. Notably, the visual encounter with Indigenous Australians in the advertisement only takes place in the remote outback landscape, not in any urban settings. The Indigenous people are presented as the exotic 'Other' and are literally situated away from 'civilization' in a romanticized view of Aboriginality. While acknowledging that tourism advertising can only provide snapshots of a nation to convey it as an enticing holiday destination, this romanticized view nevertheless presents, and indeed repeats, colonial power relations. The scene of dancers is presented as oppositional to the myriad of ways white Australians are presented in the tourist campaign. Moreover, in the other ten scenes in the advertisement, the white Australians are engaged in leisure spaces, such as the pub, the golf greens, the pool, and the beach. Unlike the remote desert landscape, these are spaces of leisure, pleasure, and settler occupation of the land. The Indigenous people are relegated to the fringes of society and portrayed in terms of entertainment. As Waitt aptly asserts:

> Aboriginality is socially constructed to serve a particular political context and a deliberate economic strategy, that of selling Australia as an escape from civilization to a primordial, timeless world, and/or a return to Nature where Aborigines as the original conversations live in perfect harmony with the environment. (2008, 50)

The Indigenous identity presented in the tourism ad and in similar Australian tourism ads to follow, such as 'Come Walkabout' (2008), demonstrates that Indigenous elements are an integral component of Australian tourism and helps showcase Australia as unique. It provides an opportunity to celebrate Indigenous cultural traditions. It is important to highlight that the identity of Indigenous Australians in tourism advertising does not reflect the reality of everyday life for the colonized (Pomering 2010; Craik 2001). It is a museumized version that is presented in the tourism campaign. It is museumized in the "way art and artefacts from non-Indo-European cultures have traditionally been represented as ethnological or anthropological curiosities" (Brazier 2018, 72). Jennifer Craik notes, "it is important that Indigenous communities, governments, the tourism industry, and the Australian public tackle the place of Indigenous culture in Australian life and redress problems and contradictions" (2001, 109). The Indigenous performance in the tourism advertisement is very much a "staged authenticity" (MacCannell 1979). The performance may contain aspects of the original tradition, but it is staged to create an appealing promotion of an 'authentic' cultural product for tourists. Craik aptly adds that Australia faces a problem with "packaging and managing simultaneously the unique qualities, exotic elements and everyday life for the tourist gaze, a challenge that is more difficult in a culture that is the object of colonial and postcolonial exploitation" (Craik 2001, 109). As previously highlighted, in the colonial perspective Indigenous people have been seen as a picturesque part of the landscape, rather than inhabitants of the land. For example, this is reinforced in the myth that Indigenous Australians were classified as flora and fauna until the 1967 referendum (in which "Australians voted overwhelmingly to amend the Constitution to allow the Commonwealth to make laws for Aboriginal people and include them in the census" [Thomas 2017]). The persistence of the myth is related to the colonial history of Australia being termed as 'terra nullius'—no one's land.

Australia's settler-colonial history is evident in the very form of the nation-state. Its national day is celebrated on the anniversary of European invasion. Anthony Moran has highlighted how Australia nationalism has shaped government policies, with a past quest for a 'white Australia' that first emerged in the nineteenth century (Moran 2005). This discourse is also evident in the promotion of a White Australia in the 'Where the bloody hell are you ad'?, which presents an Arcadian Australia. The opening sequence conveys a remote country pub, and then later, an isolated colonial homestead, both signs of British colonization within the stark Australian landscape. The advertisement delivers the frontiers of 'civilization,' a nostalgic reminder of the survival and triumph of the white settlers over the rugged environment and the Indigenous people. They are also sites of inclusion and exclusion; as highlighted earlier, the visual absence of Indigenous people from most of the scenes of Australia in the ad has historical underpinnings in which "white rural settlers, in the main, wanted Aborigines out of sight: not in their schools, their neighborhoods, their public spaces, not even in their towns, except where they could be used as a cheap and, in some cases, essential labour supply" (Moran 2005, 173). The pub and the homestead, like the beach, are deemed iconic Australian spaces, but they are also zones of exclusion, and very much constructed around White identity and nationalism (Fiske et al. 1987, Stratton 2011). Otherness is diluted, and the depictions of Aboriginal culture are presented as exotic and safe, far away from symbols of white communities.

In the ad the depictions of a large-scale country homestead and of the pub, which presents the comfort of a home away from home, represent an establishment of family and community signalling the ambitions of settler-colonial Australia. This desire includes the controlling and taming of the natural environment, which includes the presentation of Aboriginal culture in a way that it merges with the natural landscape. The advertisement has white Australians making statements such as "we've had the camels shampooed," "we've got the sharks out of the pool," and "we got the roos off the green." The latter statement, the clearing of kangaroos, as Stratton highlights could "work as substitution for the genocide of Aborigines" (Stratton 2011, 128). The possible dangers of the natural environment are cleared to present Australia as a safe and welcoming place.

The choice of the iconic Australian pub as the opening image also sets the scene in regards to gendered relations. In the pub, the only female visible is a young, blonde, white woman behind the bar serving the drinks with a smile. Clare Wright (2014) has presented a feminist history of colonial pubs which documents the high prevalence of female publicans in Australia. It was a place where women lived, "worked and took their pleasure." At the same time the country pub is still considered an archetypal male social institution (2014, 9). Certainly in the tourism advertisement the all-male clientele in the pub does not present it as a welcoming place for a woman. Rather, it alludes to how the "male-dominated culture of the pub has worked to isolate, segregate and intimidate women" (Wright 2003, 8). It is a space that represents unequal gender relations, and the scene seems scripted for a male audience. It is important to note that unequal gendered messages are also expressed throughout the entire ad, which has only three female voices in comparison to six male voices. The dominant voice in Australia is male and this inequality of voices conveys a masculine and patriarchal positioning of Australia. This harks back to tourism ads of the 1980s and 1990s that privileged the masculine position, "in which women and indigenous people exist, but only at a lower status" (Waitt 2008, 58). It seems this inequity was still occurring in the 2000s. Throughout the ad the male voices exert masculine authority, such as the "we got the roos off the green" and "we've got the sharks out of the pool." By contrast, the young women are there to be looked at, smiling behind the bar, in the Outback, in the city, or at the beach. The male statements suggest activity and mastery over nature, whereas the female statements and behaviour suggest a nurturing and accommodating demeanour. This is demonstrated in the lines, "We've saved you a spot on the beach" and "We've turned the lights on." The opening scene in the pub sets the tone for the unequal power relationships. The first voice we hear is male and his voice is speaking for the woman who is pictured. The scene reveals a young blonde woman behind the bar at the pub, and then an extreme close up of her hand pouring a beer. Then the related statement "We've poured you a beer" is announced by the male sitting and holding a filled beer glass. The camera then pans to a close up of the young woman's smile and her look at him. This presents a superficial and romanticized view of male-female relations in Australian culture. However, this may also be read as a surprise outrage that he spoke on her behalf. He used the term 'we,' when it was clearly her effort to pour the beer. Her look, perhaps, reflects, it was 'me' not 'we' that poured the drink. It is evident that patriarchal power relations are reinforced in the ad.

The 'Where the Bloody Hell are you?' ad is no different to "various campaigns since the early 1980s. Australia's tourism agencies have marketed an image of Australians as mostly white, blonde, and either on a beach or in a pub" (Khamis 2012, 60). This image of Australia is clearly reinforced in the 2006 ad. As mentioned earlier, the pub is featured in the opening scene, which also has a white, blonde woman. The final scene also features another white blonde woman on the beach. This is the eighteen-year-old Lara Bingle who became the face of the tourist campaign, and subsequently became a media celebrity by delivering the payoff final line in the ad 'So where the bloody hell are you?.' With the media focus on the teenager, the ad has also been referred to as the Bingle campaign (Khamis 2012). Bingle can be considered as the ad's main selling point. She is presented as the tourist spectacle and she is there to privilege the male, heterosexual gaze. This is confirmed in that final scene in which Bingle is situated on an idyllic, secluded beach. The purity of the white sand and the lone young woman pictured in the landscape is a tourism postcard cliché and is the "most commonly occurring representation in the pages of Western travelogues and brochures" (Morgan and Pritchard 2000, 896). The woman is there to be encountered. She is available, and she is awaiting the arrival of the male. Marketed in the tourism landscape, she is presented as a sexualized subject, as the camera lingers over her and the beach "as an exoticized commodity which is there to be experienced" (Pritchard and Morgan 2000, 891). In the final scene, after Bingle delivers her infamous line, the camera then pans out to present a wide-angle view of Bingle on the beach. She represents the quintessential Australian beach girl, cheeky and appealing to the cliché of the four S's of mass tourism: sun, sea, sand, and sex. Presented on a deserted beach, the barely-of-legal-age Lara Bingle is there to lure the tourists.

In Tourism Australia's advertisements, the beach is the site where the exotic is eroticized. Unlike the pub or the bush, the Australian beach is often represented as a place for young, athletic, white people. It is far from the Australian myth of an egalitarian space, with the concept that the Australian beach is open to all to enjoy (Fiske et al. 1987; Dutton 1985; Ellison 2013). For example, tourism images typically represented the beach as deserted except for a few affable figures that match this stereotype. The isolation hints at salacious activities permitted (or at least possible) in this space but, crucially, this sexualized Australia is sold as belonging only to white bodies (Gregory 2017, 92). I discussed earlier the Indigenous bodies presented as exotic. Tim Gregory asserts "the exotic exists as a rehearsal, as an incomplete space until it is contrasted by white heteronormativity—the body of colonizer, the tourist, the porn star" (2017, 92). Notably, Gregory is referring to porn narratives, but in the tourism ad this pattern is replicated. Even the word 'rehearsal' is used by the Indigenous women, which marks the way for the white Australian girl to play the leading role in the ad. As we see in the ad, the body of Lara Bingle is celebrated with the longest screen time, in which she is the object of the gaze. The sexualization of Bingle became further evident in the subsequent media attention she received after her role in the campaign, in which Bingle's unclothed body became the subject of tabloid scrutiny and as paparazzi target.[1] Her bikini-clad body in the national campaign became a prelude to her naked exposure across Australian mainstream national media, in magazine reportage and television current affairs coverage.

Bingle's final statement in the tourist campaign sparked media interest that, indeed, further increased her visibility as a sexualized and exoticized white body. She used the term 'bloody hell,' which as Winter and Gallon argue, "had been used extensively in prior advertising campaigns within Australia. [But] its use by a young female actor was subject to extensive criticism, and we can only speculate whether this would have occurred had the actor been a male" (Winter and Gallon 2008, 312). The use of the words "bloody hell" references her association with an ocker image, which has a history in the working-class, brash, somewhat crude Australian masculine figure. The ocker image has been cultivated and celebrated in Australian media since the 1970s and is particularly dominant in advertising (Crawford 2010, 48). Ockerism is distinctly Australian. As highlighted earlier, since the 1980s the 'ocker' image,

---

[1] An example of tabloid scrutiny is the publication of an image of Bingle in the shower, taken by Australian footballer, Brendon Fevola. Presented as personal porn, and without her consent, the sexually explicit photograph was published in a national magazine, *Woman's Day*. Two years later, her privacy was again violated when the television program *A Current Affair* broadcast heavily pixelated photographs of a naked Lara Bingle taken from her bedroom window.

represented by Paul Hogan as the face of the "Come and Say G'day" campaign (1984–1987)—better known as "throw another shrimp on the barbie" ad—focused on 'friendly residents,' and Hogan's earnest and amicable ocker image proved highly successful: "His persona sold such a seemingly authentic image of Australia as laid-back, warm, and welcoming, that tourism chiefs have yet to supplant this image with an equally successful alternative" (Khamis 2012, 53). The advertising company Saatchi "had assumed that Hogan's success could be replicated by updating the old formula" in the 'Where the bloody hell are you?' ad (Crawford 2010, 44). However, even with the lure of a young woman as the key spokesperson, it failed in its objective of increasing international tourist numbers to Australia.

Significantly, Australian tourism advertisements have not previously featured women. Bingle delivering the punchline 'Where the bloody hell are you?' with a cheeky, girlish smile may have softened the ocker image, but it also classed her as unsophisticated and made her the target for media scrutiny. Stratton argues that "one way of understanding the rise to prominence of ockerism is as an Anglo-Australian backlash against the breakdown of the drive of assimilation of the Mediterranean migrants and the putting into place of the policy of multiculturalism" (2011, 114). As such, the use of ockerism as the final message in the ad reflects a yearning for the myth of white Australia. There has been media interest in Bingle's home background. She has been labelled with terms such as 'Lara from Cronulla' and the 'Shire girl as the face of the nation' (The Daily Telegraph 2015, n.p). Bingle originates from the Shire (Sutherland Shire, Sydney), which has a status as a "white sanctuary," a space of racial exclusion (Perera 2007, 4). It was also the scene of the Cronulla Race Riots of 2005, in which over 5000 white men at Cronulla beach attacked people of 'Middle-Eastern' appearance. It is poignant to note that the "Shire is also the originary scene of Aboriginal dispossession" (Perera, 2007, 4). Furthermore, "the media's construction of place has ascribed stereotypes of privilege, whiteness and racism to the Sutherland Shire and its residents" (Norquay and Drozdzewski 2017, 104). The media highlighting Bingle's association with this area links her to the discourse of white Australian nationalism.

Final Remarks, Getting in the Last Word

As highlighted earlier, there has been much commentary about what was considered a controversial final statement in the 2006 Australian tourism ad. The ad also presented a myopic view of the nation. The veracity of the ad was questioned by Australians "through satire, parody and ridicule" (Khamis 2012, 58). The approximately sixty-second ad has had a long-lasting impact on popular culture. There have been numerous parodies of the 'Where the bloody hell are you?' ad. For example, the Nine Network produced an ad to promote the television coverage of cricket's 2006–2007 Ashes series. The cricketing theme presented the preparations for the events, with statements such as 'We've rolled the ground,' 'we've put in the stumps.' There is then a reference to the English predilection for warm beer. The final phrase is the benign 'And we've been waiting all year,' instead of the notorious tagline of the original ad. This presents it without controversy and ockerism, a much more polite welcome invitation. In other parodies the notorious line is used for dramatic or comedic effect. For example, in 2015, media celebrity Sophie Monk, who was also a presenter for the TV travel show *Get Away* promoted the video game *The Elder Scrolls Online: Tamriel Unlimited*'s PS4 and Xbox One release. The images shown are of the mythical land presented in the games and Monk delivers the punchline of 'Where the bloody hell are you?.' In 2019 Lara (nee Bingle) Worthington also resurrected her final line, directed it at then current Prime Minister Scott Morrison (who not so ironically was the Director of Tourism Australia who supported the original ad) to ask about his absence at the time of the national bushfire crisis. On Twitter, Worthington posted "'Scott Morrison: Where the bloody hell are you???' … to her 106.6 thousand followers, including the 'AustraliaBurns' and 'AustraliaFires' hashtags in her pointed attack" (Rogers, 2019). The infamous question used for political purpose positions Lara as more than just a bikini model. She is no longer a passive object of the gaze, but as a political subject with agency.

In 2016, almost ten years after the original tourist campaign aired, Lee Lee Chin, a SBS TV veteran (of almost forty years), featured in a parody of the tourism ad in a Facebook promotional video for a special edition of SBS TV series The Feed on Sydney's "lock out" laws. The laws were introduced in February 2014 to ban patrons from entering a venue for the first time after 1.30 a.m., and to stop pubs and clubs serving alcohol to patrons after 3 a.m. in the entertainment precinct of Kings Cross. In the parody, Lee Lee Chin stands alone in a dark, empty, iconic Kings Cross Street. She delivers the final line that made Lara Bingle famous "So where the bloody hell are you?." Of a mature age, Lee Lee Chin, born in Indonesia to Chinese parents, delivering the infamous line presents a stark contrast to the young white Lara Bingle. Lee Lee Chin's physical presence distances the line from its ocker past of white Australia and the beach, instead offering a vision of contemporary urban Australia, far removed from the Australian national tourist images.

Dean MacCannell refers to a second tourist gaze: "that in every seeing there is an unseen; a backside, a dark side" (MacCannell 2001, 23). Dan Ilic, from Downwind Media, produced a video that went viral. It presented a political satire of the 'Where the bloody hell are you' tourism campaign with an alternative visual montage of Australia, a second gaze that is much closer to reality for Australian people of colour. It shows the darker side, the horrific human rights issues that pervade contemporary Australia. It was a strong critique of the facets of Australia that were not represented in the original tourism ad. It critiqued the marketing of Australia as described earlier, as mostly white, blonde and either at a beach or pub while utilizing the same structure of the original Tourism Australia ad:

> It referred to the death of Azaria Chamberlain, the mandatory detention of refugees, Aboriginal deaths in custody and the race-based Cronulla riot of 2005. As a young man of Middle Eastern appearance says in a "Leb-speak" accent, seconds before he is beaten up on a beach: "where the fucken hell are yous." (Khamis 2012, 58)

As highlighted earlier, the beach plays a fantastical role within Australian mythology as a white space. This parody is acerbic from the opening line ("We've got the Ethnics off the Beach") to the final line, including the scene of a young brown man being attacked on the beach, referencing the race riots in Cronulla. Ilic's biting commentary on contemporary cultural issues was moving because it highlighted police brutality towards Indigenous Australians and racial intolerance. The parody went viral but Ilic was forced to take the video down because it breached copyright laws. This ruling was instigated by Tourism Australian lawyers on the grounds that the music was infringing copyright. Tourism Australia further described the parody as "mean spirited and humourless" (Braithwaite 2006); however "Parody is often given greater leeway in copyright law than other forms of copying. The reasoning for this privileged position rests upon the acknowledgement that critical and expressive speech is necessary and desirable in a healthy society" (Suzor 2008, 220). Nevertheless, Ilic had to alter the tune and tempo before he could re-release the video to avoid prosecution. Ilic's parody video offers what the tourist gaze does not see. It does not present the idyllic images that Tourism Australia wants to present to the rest of the world. Rather, it shows the extraordinary sights of exclusionary violence and xenophobia which underlie present-day Australia.

The 'Where the bloody hell are you?' campaign fulfils the fantasy of a white Australia. It gives a nostalgic colonial, patriarchal perspective in which women are there to host and indigenous people are safely part of the landscape to be viewed from a distance. Significantly, both are there to service the Western male gaze. In 2006, when the campaign launched, it already seemed outdated as it relied on an old formula from twenty years earlier: an amicable, laid-back ocker image of white Australia. As Khamis has argued, the 'Where the bloody hell are you?' campaign "was not too far removed from the Hogan series, with blondes on a beach, outback pubs and Aborigines at Uluru" (2012, 54). Khamis highlights that subsequent campaigns have attempted to present a politically progressive and cosmopolitan view of Australia. However, the success of this is somewhat questionable. *Come Wallkabout* (2009), by celebrated cinematic director Baz Lurmann, the first tourist campaign since the controversial campaign discussed in this chapter, was also problematic. Whilst it did not convey the Australian landscape as one of colonial-settler society (e.g., country pubs and homesteads), the advertisements resurrect the myth of the noble savage, and the focus of indigeneity that is linked to a mythical past untouched by Western civilization.

The advertisements feature twelve-year-old Brandon Walter, playing the character of Nullah, a young mixed-race Aboriginal boy from Baz Lurmann's epic film *Australia* (2008) (it was an attempt at cross-promotion from the film). The advertisements suggested going to Australia as a transformative experience, and was heavily reliant on Aboriginal spirituality and the land. Young Nullah, barefoot and scantily clothed, is depicted bewitching people who are unhappy with their hectic, stressful urban lives. Presented as an Indigenous Peter Pan character, he magically transports them from cities, such as New York and Shanghai, to a dream holiday where they can experience the natural wonders of Australia. The destination is not Pan's Neverland, but the equally mythical Never Never, a remote uninhabited Australian region and "an indigenizing space that can be entered imaginatively" through cultural texts and cultural practices including touristic experiences (Stadler and Mitchell 2010, 173). The tourism advertisements emphasize the positive links between Indigenous people and harmony with the natural world. The advertisements were at odds with much of the lived experience of Indigenous people at the time of its release and of the present. Alan Pomering and Leane White remark that "at the same time that Black Deaths in custody were making headlines in Australia and around the world, the new TA advertising campaign reached into the archives to take a page from the report, *Australia's Travel and Tourism Industry 1965* (Harris, Kerr, Forster and Company 1966), to appropriate Indigenous Australians' spiritual link with the land" (2011, 171). Whereas the 'Where the bloody hell are you?' campaign looked back twenty years for its inspiration, the Walkabout tourist advertisements went even further back and resurrected notions of Indigeneity from at least forty years past. The next tourist campaign, the 'There's nothing like Australia' in 2010, presented another opportunity to readdress the problems of Australian tourism campaigns and provide a more contemporary perspective of the nation:

> With the strap-line 'There's nothing like Australia', Tourism Australia invited up to 15,000 Australians to submit personal snapshots and twenty-five-word descriptions of their favourite Australian experience. The "best" of these (as judged by Tourism Australia) formed an interactive online map, and were linked to a television campaign. (Khamis 2012, 56)

It had the potential to provide a cosmopolitan representation of Australia, and to represent Indigenous Australians in non-stereotypical ways. However, the television campaign presented conventional iconic representations of Australia and white Australians dominated the screen spaces, in a similar fashion to the previous tourism advertisements.

It is evident that there is a limited range of images used to present the national narrative. Tourism destination images create and sell fantasies of idyllic sites. At the same time they are responsible for promoting gendered and raced perceptions of a place. Urry argues that "tourism has the capacity to illuminate what would otherwise remain opaque" (1990, 1). The tourism ad 'Where the bloody hell are you?' exposes outdated patriarchal and parochial versions of Australia. It did not reflect contemporary Australia and the invitation to the world was generally declined. It was not worth seeing. When Lara Bingle asked Where the bloody hell are you? "the world did not answer" and stayed where they were (Razer 2018). The world was waiting for a better offer.

Works Cited

AAP. 2006. PM defends that 'bloody' ad. *The Sydney Morning Herald*, February 24. https://www.smh.com.au/national/pm-defends-that-bloody-ad-20060224-gdn12i.html. Accessed 24 October 2021.

ABS. 2006. 2016. Census. Australian Bureau of Statistics Quick Stats. https://www.abs.gov.au/websitedbs/D3310114.nsf/Home/2016%20QuickStats. Accessed 30 October 2020.

Allegritti, Inta. 2004. The Republic, Citizenship and the Politics of Culture. *Australian Review of Public Affairs*, November 29. http://www.australianreview.net/digest/2004/11/allegritti.html. Accessed 8 August 2020.

Braithwaite, David. 2006. Tourism Spoof Not Bloody Funny. *The Sydney Morning Herald*, March 28. https://www.smh.com.au/national/tourism-spoof-not-bloody-funny-20060328-gdn92s.html. Accessed 9 September 2020.

Brazier, Danielle. 2018. White Australia, Black Bodies: The Use of Aboriginal bodies and Artefacts in Australian Public Discourses. *New: Emerging Scholars in Australian Indigenous Studies* 4: 70–75. https://doi.org/10.5130/nesais.v4i1.1515. Accessed 8 August 2020.

Burrowes, Tim. 2013. Harold Mitchell: I Wonder If Adland's Anglo-Australian Force Understands This Country's Diversity. Mumbrella, February 16. https://mumbrella.com.au/harold-mitchell-i-wonder-if-adlands-anglo-australian-force-understands-this-countrys-diversity-140256. Accessed 8 August 2020.

Cameron, Deborah. 2006. Too Bloody Hard to Teach Japan to Swear. *Sydney Morning Herald*, March 28. https://www.smh.com.au/national/too-bloody-hard-to-teach-japan-to-swear-20060328-gdn96r.html. Accessed 8 August 2020.

Campaign Brief. 2006. Australia to the World. So Where the Bloody Hell are You? *Campaign Brief*, February 23. https://campaignbrief.com/australia-to-the-world-so-wher/. Accessed 8 August 2020.

Christopher, Elizabeth. 2018. Communication across Cultures. *World Englishes* 37 (3): 455–460.

Craik, Jennifer. 2001. Tourism, Culture and National Identity. In *Culture in Australia: Policies, Publics and Programs*, ed. Toni Bennet and David Carter. Cambridge: Cambridge University Press.

Crawford, Robert. 2010. Learning to Say G'day to the World: The Development of Australia's Marketable Image in the 1980s. *Consumption, Markets and Culture* 13 (1): 43–59.

Dutton, Geoffrey. 1985. *Sun, Sea, Surf and Sand: The Myth of the Beach*. Melbourne: Oxford University Press.

Ellison, Elizabeth. 2013. The Australian Beachspace: Flagging the Spaces of Australian Beach Texts. PhD. Queensland University of Technology. https://core.ac.uk/download/pdf/18312113.pdf. Accessed 20 February 2021.

Fiske, John, Hodge Bob, and Graeme Turner. 1987. *Myths of Oz: Reading Australian Popular Culture*. Abingdon-on-Thames: Taylor and Francis.

Gregory, Tim. 2017. The Maintenance of White Heteronormativity in Porn Films That Use Australia As an Exotic Location. *Porn Studies* 4 (1): 88–104. https://doi.org/10.1080/07256868.2017.1268573.

Kellaway, Carlotta. 1953. White Australia - How Political Reality became National myth. *The Australian Quarterly* 25 (2): 7–11.

Khamis, Susie. 2012. Brand Australia: Half-Truths For a Hard Sell. *Journal of Australian Studies* 36 (1): 49–63. https://doi.org/10.1080/14443058.2011.646284.

MacCannell, Dean. 1979. Staged Authenticity: Arrangements of Social Space in Visitor Settings. *American Journal of Sociology* 79 (3): 589–603.

———. 2001. Tourist Agency. *Tourist Studies* 1 (1): 23–37.

Mangold, Eli B., and Charles Goehring. 2019. The Visual Rhetoric of the Aerial View: From Surveillance to Resistance. *Quarterly Journal of Speech* 105 (1): 25–41. https://doi.org/10.1080/00335630.2018.1553305.

Moran, Anthony. 2005. White Australia, Settler Nationalism and Aboriginal Assimilation. *Australian Journal of Politics and History* 51 (2): 168–193.

Norquay, Melinda, and Danielle Drozdzewski. 2017. Stereotyping the Shire: Assigning White Privilege to Place and Identity. *Journal of Intercultural Studies* 38 (1): 88–107. https://doi.org/10.1080/07256868.2017.1268573.

Perera, Suvendrini. 2007. Aussie Luck: The Border Politics of Citizenship Post Cronulla Beach. *ACRAWSA e-journal* 3(1). https://acrawsa.org.au/wp-content/uploads/2017/09/64SuvendriniPerera.pdf. Accessed 10 September 2020.

Pomering, Alan. 2010. The Portrayal of Aboriginal Spiritual Identity in Tourism Advertising: Creating an Image of Extraordinary Reality or Mere Confusion? 1–15. https://ro.uow.edu.au/commpapers/1172.

Pomering, Alan, and Leanne White. 2011. The Portrayal of Indigenous Identity in Australian Tourism Brand Advertising: Engendering an Image of Extraordinary Reality Or Staged Authenticity? *Place Branding and Public Diplomacy* 7 (3): 165–174.

Pritchard, Annette, and Nigel Morgan. 2000. Privileging the Male Gaze: Gendered Tourism Landscapes. *Annals of Tourism Research* 27 (4): 884–905.

Razer, Helen. 2018. Where the Bloody Hell Is the Diversity in the Latest Tourism Australia Ad? SBS. January 31. https://www.sbs.com.au/topics/voices/culture/article/2018/01/31/where-bloody-hell-diversity-latest-tourism-australia-ad. Accessed 10 September 2020.

Rebranding Australia. 2008. How should Australia sell itself. *The Economist*, May 10. https://www.economist.com/business/2008/05/08/rebranding-australia. Accessed 9 August 2020.

Rogers, Samantha. 2019. Lara Worthington to PM Scott Morrison: 'Where the bloody hell are you?' Perth Now Dec 18. https://www.perthnow.com.au/news/australia/lara-worthington-to-pm-scott-morrison-where-the-bloody-hell-are-you-ng-b881415536z. Accessed 30 October 2020.

Stadler, Jane, and Peta Mitchell. 2010. Never-Never Land: Affective Landscapes, the Touristic Gaze and Hetero-topic Space in Australia. *Studies in Australasian Cinema* 4 (2): 173–187.

Stanley, Bruce. 2006. Australian Tourism ministry swears by its new ad. *The Wall Street Journal*, March 14. https://www.post-gazette.com/life/travel/2006/03/14/Australian-tourism-ministry-swears-by-its-newad/stories/200603140155. Accessed 24 October 2021.

Stratton, Jon. 1999. Multiculturalism and the Whitening Machine, Or How Australians Become White. In *The Future of Australian Multiculturalism: Reflections on the Twentieth Anniversary of Jean Martin's The Migrant Presence*, ed. Ghassan Hage and Rowanne Couch, 163–188. Sydney: University of Sydney.

———. 2011. *Uncertain Lives: Culture, Race and Neoliberalism in Australia*. Newcastle: Cambridge Scholars Press.

Suzor, Nicolas. 2008. Where the Bloody Hell Does Parody Fit in Australian Copyright Law? *Media and Arts Law Review* 13 (2): 218–248.

The Daily Telegraph. 2008. Kevin Rudd Slams Lara Bingle's 'Where the Bloody Hell' Ads. June 25. https://www.dailytelegraph.com.au/news/national/kevin-rudd-slams-lara-bingles-where-the-bloody-hell-ads/news-story/c539130304fd89b2c52acac4bb258e94?sv=7ed8d8c994fd4d3fcc25968fdfd90fbb. Accessed 10 September 2020.

———. 2015. From Lara Bingle to Lara Worthington: How a Fresh-faced Shire Girl Grew Up. October 16. https://www.dailytelegraph.com.au/entertainment/sydney-confidential/from-lara-bingle-to-lara-worthington-freshfaced-shire-girl-is-all-grown-up/news-story/39baae7dd59456bd56d96c160850e5d1. Accessed 10 September 2020.

Thomas, Mathew. 2017. The 1967 Referendum. Parliament of Australia. May 25. https://www.aph.gov.au/About_Parliament/Parliamentary_Departments/Parliamentary_Library/FlagPost/2017/May/The_1967_Referendum. Accessed 20 February 2021.

Urry, John. 1990. *The Tourist Gaze*. London: Sage.

Urry, John, and Jonas Larsen. 2011. *The Tourist Gaze 3.0 Third ed. Theory, Culture & Society*. Los Angeles: Sage.

Waitt, Gordon. 2008. Selling Paradise and Adventure: Representations of Landscape in the Tourist Advertising of Australia. *Australian Geographical Studies* 35 (1): 47–60.

Winter, Caroline, and Sharon Gallon. 2008. Exploring Attitudes Toward Tourism Australia's 'Where the Bloody Hell Are You' Campaign. *Current Issues in Tourism* 11: 301–314.

Wright, Claire. 2003. 'Doing the Beans': Women, Drinking and Community in the Ladies' Lounge. *Journal of Australian Studies* 27 (76): 5–16. https://doi.org/10.1080/14443050309387819.

———. 2014. *Beyond the Ladies Lounge: Australia's Female Publicans*. Melbourne: Text Publishing.

Index[1]

A

Air New Zealand, 39, 40, 50–59
Amateur filmmaking, 210, 211
Australia, 13–30, 247–264

C

Commonwealth Film Unit (CFU), 14, 15, 18, 20, 23, 24, 26, 29
COVID-19, 87–101, 107–121

D

Digital marketing, 89

F

Faroe Islands, 107–121

G

Gender, 248, 256
Grierson, 14, 15

I

In-flight safety videos, 37–40, 50–52, 58
The Invisible Boy, 141, 144, 145, 147, 148
Ireland, 87–101
Italy, 129–148
I Will Return, 87–101

---

[1] Note: Page numbers followed by 'n' refer to notes.

M

Maoriland, 201–209, 203n4
Media-induced tourism, 156, 158, 164, 165

N

New Zealand, 199, 200, 202, 204, 206, 207, 210, 213
Nordic Noir, 177–187, 190
Nostalgia, 154, 160–163

P

Poland, 221–240
Portugal, 65, 70, 73, 80, 81
Presence, 154, 159–164
Promotional videos, 221–240

R

Race, 222, 238, 240, 261
Radio programming, 64, 72–75, 78, 80

S

Scandinavian tourism, 107–121
Screen tourism, 131, 136, 173–192
Smartphone, 173–192
South Pacific Wonderland, 199, 206

T

Tale of Tales, 141–143, 147
Tourism film, 13–30
Tourism marketing, 50, 51, 54, 57

V

Video games, 153–165
Virtual tourism, 107–121

W

Where the Bloody Hell are you?, 247–264

Printed in the United States
by Baker & Taylor Publisher Services